Keyboard Music

Keyboard Music

EDITED BY
DENIS MATTHEWS

PRAEGER PUBLISHERS
New York · Washington

BOOKS THAT MATTER

Published in the United States of America in 1972
by Praeger Publishers, Inc., 111 Fourth Avenue,
New York, N.Y. 10003

© Penguin Books 1972

Library of Congress Catalog Card Number: 77-185335

Printed in Great Britain

CONTENTS

INTRODUCTION

THIS symposium offers an account of the development of
solo keyboard music from the earliest known examples to
the present day. By 'keyboard' we imply the piano and its
predecessors, excluding organ music (which has its own
niche) and duets for one or two keyboards (though these
may be mentioned in passing when they have some bearing
on the solo works). The solo repertoire, even the familiar
repertoire, is vast enough to raise severe editorial problems,
and against any apology for omissions (intentional or
accidental) may be mentioned the danger of reducing discussion to a mere catalogue. Nevertheless it is hoped to
provide a useful listener's guide, parallel to the Penguin
volumes on chamber music, choral music, the symphony
and the concerto.

In a larger book Beethoven and Chopin, to take only two
examples, would have merited a chapter apiece. But more
specialized works are available which deal with individual
composers. By relating them to a wider context it is easier to
see them in historical perspective, adherent to or divergent
from a main stream. As in other art forms, the main stream
of keyboard music does not run a steady course. Important
works as well as lesser ones resist classification; where
exactly does romanticism supplant classicism, and who is,
or was, entirely a 'virtuoso', a nationalist, or an avant-
garde? Hard and fast divisions seldom exist in history, yet
we are often obliged to speak of 'chapters of history' for the
sake of convenience. Our own later chapters were bound to
converge in places – or to complement one another – and
in the long run the editor allowed ease of argument, rather
than chronology or geography, to prevail in his contributors' battle for composers. Rachmaninov, Ravel and
Schoenberg were born within two years, and in any case 'the

highways and byways of the repertoire can be viewed from many angles'.

Howard Ferguson's opening chapter, with its valuable bibliography, reminds us of the wealth of pre-piano music. Opinions conflict over the rightness or not of playing this inherited repertoire on a modern piano, but only an extreme purist will ban the pianist from exploring the beauties of Couperin or Scarlatti for his own pleasure. Circumstances of performance have changed too, and we can guess that many pre-piano composers would have accepted the later 'clavier' for the sake of keeping their music alive. Conversely, modern taste (helped by radio and records) has rediscovered the delights of the harpsichord and the clavichord. With Bach the situation is different again, for, as Charles Rosen points out, he often wrote with no specific instrument in mind. 'Clavier' was a generic term, and Mr Rosen rightly insists on *The Well-Tempered Keyboard*. As to purism, Eva Badura-Skoda hints that artistic perception will far outweigh historical 'correctness' in the performance of Haydn's earlier sonatas, even though they were written when the piano was still in its infancy.

And the piano itself? For many music-lovers it is the most familiar and accessible of all instruments. It is also the most versatile: on the one hand a general practitioner of music, on the other a supreme soloist whose popularity is undimmed. Few of the smallest music-clubs survive a season without a piano recital, and the largest halls are packed to hear Rubinstein or Richter. The piano's advantage over its rivals was its ability to play soft and loud, *piano e forte*, at the will of the performer as expressed through his fingers. Having grown up during the eighteenth century it even threatened, by the middle of the nineteenth, to become an end rather than a means. Pure virtuosity still has its appeal, but many of the most serious composers have accepted the piano as an intimate and almost instinctive medium. In structure the instrument has scarcely changed in a century, and despite modern science and the demands of the avant-garde it will retain its old character for the sake of its legacy.

Masters of the keyboard – whether Beethoven, Chopin, or Debussy – were inspired by its limitations as well as its assets. In fact limitations became assets: the inherent diminuendo of each note was turned to the most subtle artistic purposes. The answer lies in the repertoire, which has long been the envy of every other instrument.

Since the great romantics are still a mainstay of so many recital programmes John Ogdon's task was to follow this tradition through, dealing in detail with the familiar works of Chopin, Schumann, and Liszt, while tracing their forbears and successors. It was not simply to ease his burden that Brahms was placed in the previous chapter, as will be explained. James Gibb, like Howard Ferguson, inevitably made geographical subdivisions, with French music taking a lion's share, ranging as it does from César Franck to 'Les Six' and encompassing Debussy and Ravel. (There are fascinating cross-currents with the Spanish school.) Susan Bradshaw's difficult final chapter readily accepts that in the complex modern scene new developments may arise even between writing and printing, printing and reading! The editor thanks all his colleagues, most of them practising performers, for the time and labour they have devoted to making this symposium as far-ranging as possible.

Finally a word to the general reader. It is hard to discuss musical works without recourse to certain basic technicalities. These need not daunt the untrained listener who has ears to hear. No one complains of a description of a moon flight in terms of launching-pads and gravitational fields. The editor has found, in lecturing, that most laymen will grasp the meaning of musical jargon as soon as it is backed up by audible illustration. Those who do not read music or play, however modestly, can nowadays get to know almost the entire range of keyboard music through radio and records, if not in the concert hall. Some critics have objected to 'descriptive' analyses of works on the ground that the listener 'can hear it for himself', but it is surely helpful, especially with unfamiliar music, to know what to listen *for*. Though this book may prove of value to musicians, professional or amateur, it is also, in the main, addressed to the wider public of music-lovers.

DENIS MATTHEWS

I

Early Keyboard Music

HOWARD FERGUSON

*

AT first sight it seems surprising that our knowledge of solo keyboard music goes back no further than the early fourteenth century – that is, to much the same period as the far more highly developed vocal music of the French composer-poet Guillaume de Machaut (1300–1377) and the Italian Francesco Landini (1325–97). There can be little doubt, however, that this is due not so much to any lack of keyboard composers as to the loss of manuscript sources, and to the fact that the music must often have been extemporized rather than written down; for both instruments and players are known to have existed long before.

THE INSTRUMENTS

The early composers made little distinction between one keyboard instrument and another. They wrote in a 'generalized' style that was more or less equally suited to organ, harpsichord or clavichord. For this reason, certain works intended primarily if not exclusively for organ are discussed in the present chapter, though organ music as such lies outside the scope of the book.

The organs used were of three principal types: the small *portative* and slightly larger *positive*, both suitable for either the court or the home, and the much larger *church-organ*, which sometimes had more than one manual and occasionally even a pedal-board. The stringed keyboard instruments can be divided into two families: those in which the strings were struck, i.e. the clavichord, and those in which the strings were plucked, i.e. the harpsichord, spinet and virginals. All have been revived in recent years and can now be heard frequently; nevertheless, a short description of their mechanical and musical characteristics may help to show how they differ, not only from one another but also from their descendant the modern piano.

The *Clavichord* (French: *clavichorde*; German: *Klavichord*; Italian: *clavicordo, manicordo*). This is the simplest and perhaps the most perfect of all keyboard instruments. It is oblong, with the keyboard set in one of the long sides, and the wire strings running from the player's left to his right. At the far end of each key is a small upright brass blade, or tangent. When the key is depressed the tangent rises and strikes the string, at the same time stopping it like the finger of a violinist's left hand. The section of string to the right of the tangent vibrates to produce the note required, while the section to the left is damped by a piece of felt wound round the end of the string. When the key is released the tangent falls back, the whole length of string is damped by the felt, and the note ceases to sound. There is no sustaining pedal.

Simple though this action is, it can produce wonderfully subtle results; for the clavichordist, unlike the player of any other keyboard instrument, remains in direct (though diminishing) control of the string as long as the key is depressed. Against this sensitivity must be set the instrument's lack of power, for its tone is so delicate that it would scarcely be heard in most concert halls. Thus it was essentially a solo, practice instrument for the home.

The *Harpsichord*, including the Spinet and Virginals (French: *clavecin, épinette*; German: *Klavicimbel, Clavicembalo, Cembalo, Spinett*; Italian: *clavicembalo, gravicembalo, spinetta*). In appearance, the harpsichord resembles a narrow grand piano, the spinet is a wing-shaped polygon, and the virginals are oblong. The wire strings of the harpsichord stretch away from the player, as on a grand piano, while those of the spinet and virginals run from left to right, as on the clavichord. Though the harpsichord generally includes a number of more or less complicated refinements that are not found in the other two instruments, the basic mechanism of all three is the same.

On the far end of each key rests a slim upright piece of wood, called a 'jack', the top of which is level with the strings. Projecting from the side of the jack, and normally resting below the strings, is a plectrum of quill or leather. When the key is depressed the jack and plectrum rise, the latter plucks the string in passing, and the whole string-length vibrates to produce the note required. When the key is released the jack falls back to its original position (an ingenious device allowing the plectrum to pass the strings silently), the string is damped by a small piece of felt attached to the upper part of the jack, and the note ceases to sound. Again there is no sustaining pedal.

The harpsichord (but not the spinet or virginals) often has two, or occasionally even three, keyboards. It generally also has more than one set of strings, together with the extra jacks and plectra needed to operate them. Hand-stops or pedals enable the player to use whichever set of strings, or combinations of sets, that he may require.

The plucking action of all three instruments produces a much louder and more brilliant sound than that of the clavichord. They are also comparatively insensitive to variations in the player's touch, and so cannot match the clavichord's tonal and dynamic variety. The spinet and virginals have only a single set of strings and jacks, and are therefore limited to a single tone colour. On the other hand a harpsichord with, say, two keyboards, three sets of strings (two of eight-foot pitch and one of four-foot) and four stops or pedals can produce a considerable variety of dynamics and tone colour – though not a gradual crescendo or diminuendo, since the changes must always be made in clearly defined steps.

Because of their tonal limitations the spinet and virginals were essentially instruments for the home. The harpsichord, with its greater variety and power, fulfilled much the same function in public and private music-making as the grand piano of today.

Both harpsichords and clavichords were occasionally fitted with pedal-boards, like an organ. These were primarily to enable organists to practise at home, without the services of an organ-blower.

FORMS

The music written for these instruments can be divided into two main categories: works that are derived in some way from vocal music, and works that are purely instrumental. The first group includes (1) pieces based on liturgical plainsong; (2) pieces based on chorales (i.e. metrical hymn tunes); (3) transcriptions or imitations of motet-type works; and (4) arrangements of popular songs. To the second group belong (5) preludes and toccatas; (6) dances; (7) illustrative, or character, pieces; (8) variations; and (9) sonatas. Though these types are not mutually exclusive, it will nevertheless be convenient to consider them separately.

(1) In plainsong settings one contrapuntal strand of a keyboard composition is supplied by a liturgical plainsong melody (see example 4). This is generally set out in long, equal notes, and confined to a single 'voice' or part; but it may also be decorated rhythmically and/or melodically, and may move from one voice to another. This borrowed part is called a *cantus firmus* (literally 'fixed song'). The remaining voices weave contrapuntal figuration around it, either freely or in imitation. At times only the alternate verses of the plainsong are set, in which case the work is performed *alternatim* during the liturgy, with the missing verses sung in unison by the unaccompanied choir.

(2) In Protestant Germany *canti firmi* were often derived from Lutheran chorales. The result was naturally somewhat different, for the chorale is a metrical setting of square-cut verse (see example 15), whereas most plainsong is an unmetrical setting of prose.

(3) Forms descended from motet-type works are some of

the most important in early keyboard music. Their ancestor was the sixteenth-century unaccompanied vocal motet, in which successive portions of a text were set in imitative counterpoint. Each section might be built on a different musical subject, known in England as a 'point of imitation', or simply a 'point'; or alternatively the same subject, or some variation of it, might appear in different sections, in a sequence such as AAB, ABA, AABA, etc. Instrumental descendants of the motet include the *ricercar* (from the Italian *ricercare*, 'to search' or 'to seek out'), which tended to be recondite and serious; the *canzon*, lighter in mood since it was derived from the secular French *chanson* (see example 7); the *fantasia* or *fancy*, not to be confused with the pseudo-improvisation of the eighteenth and nineteenth centuries; the *capriccio*, similar to the canzon and fantasia, but often freer in treatment; and, at a further remove, the *fuga*, which is the forerunner of the eighteenth-century fugue, though the name originally implied a canon.

(4) Arrangements of popular songs may be more or less straightforward keyboard versions (see example 13), or they may include variations of one kind or another (see (8), below).

(5) Of the purely instrumental forms, preludes and toccatas are closely related. The *prelude* was originally a short improvisation, such as might be played by a lutenist to test the tuning of his instrument, or by an organist to give his choir the pitch and mode of the work they were about to sing. At a later stage such preludes were written down for instructional purposes or for the benefit of those who could not improvise them. They often include a brilliant flourish of some sort; and this led by extension to the longer *toccata* (from the Italian *toccare*, 'to touch'), which was primarily a keyboard work in several contrasted sections designed to display the varied capabilities of a player and his instrument (see example 8).

(6) Though dances were originally no more than an accompaniment to dancing, they came to be written and enjoyed for their own sake. At first they were often grouped

in slow-quick pairs (see example 13), such as a pavan and galliard, a passamezzo and saltarello, or an alman and corant. Later contrasting dances were added, and the resulting group, generally in a single key, became known as a *suite*. The basic movements were most often an allemand, courante, saraband and gigue.

Certain harmonic patterns appeared so frequently in dances that they became known throughout Europe. The most popular was the *passamezzo antico*, known in England as the passameasures. (In Shakespeare's *Twelfth Night*, V, i, 205, Sir Toby Belch complains, 'Then he's a Rogue and a passy measures Pavyn: I hate a drunken rogue.') In essence it is a common-chord progression on the following bass, or some variation of it:

Ex.1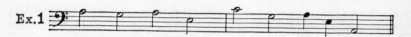

The well-known tune 'Greensleeves' is founded on a version in which each bar of the above example is played twice. Other common patterns were the *romanesca* and *folia*, which only differed from example 1 in having, respectively, a C major chord instead of an A minor one at the beginning, and the two halves of bar 1 interchanged. A fourth formula was the *passamezzo moderno*:

Ex.2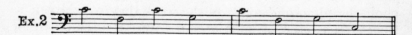

This was known in England as the quadran, and is found in pieces such as John Bull's *Quadren Paven and Galiard* (*Fitzwilliam Virginal Book*, Nos. 31–3).

(7) Illustrative or character pieces attempt to present in terms of music some mood, state, event, object or person. Examples can be found from every country; but such works were particularly popular in France (see examples 11 and 12) and to a lesser extent in England.

(8) Variations are of great importance, for one of the most

natural ways of extending any piece of music is to vary it. With dances and popular songs the principle can work in either or both of two ways: firstly, the repeat of each strain of a tune may be varied instead of being played unaltered (e.g. AA¹BB¹, instead of AABB); and secondly, the complete tune, with either varied or unvaried repeats, may serve as a theme for a set of variations.

Another type of variation, the *Ut, re, mi*, is closely related to the plainsong settings described above. Here, however, the *cantus firmus* is supplied by repetitions of the ascending and descending notes of part of the diatonic scale – often the section known as the hexachord, which contains six notes with a semitone interval in the middle, e.g. G,A,B:C,D,E. Like the plainsong *cantus firmus*, the series is generally set out in long, equal notes; and though it usually remains at one pitch, it may also modulate, as in John Bull's remarkable 'Ut, re, me, fa, sol, la' (*Fitzwilliam Virginal Book*, No. 51), where the hexachord begins successively on each of the twelve degrees of the chromatic scale.

Yet another type is the *ground-bass* or *ground*, in which a short, continuously repeated bass line provides the foundation for an ever-changing superstructure (see example 5). Allied to this are the *chaconne* and *passacaglia*; though here the recurring element is a series of harmonies rather than a bass line. (In France a *chaconne* or *passacaille* is frequently a rondeau (see example 10) rather than a set of variations.) In both Italy and Germany a *partita* was also originally a set of variations; but in Germany the title was sometimes applied to a combination of variations and suite, and hence, confusingly, to a normal suite with no trace of variations.

(9) Finally, the title *sonata* originally signified no more than a 'sound piece' as opposed to a *cantata*, or 'sung piece'. Up to the time of Domenico Scarlatti (see example 9), it was given both to single movements, and to groups of two or more movements embodying the familiar contrasts of tempo and mood. The classical type of sonata form was not developed until the mid eighteenth century.

With the foregoing sketch of the instrumental and formal

background in mind, we may pass on to a brief survey of sources, composers and works. They will be grouped under the four main headings, England, Italy, France and Germany, with a short section on Iberia and the Netherlands interpolated between the first and the second.

ENGLAND

The earliest of all keyboard music, by fully a century, is found in the Robertsbridge Fragment of *c.* 1320 (British Museum, Add. MS. 28550). This incomplete two-leaf manuscript from the former Priory of Robertsbridge in Sussex is a curious hybrid, for though it may have been copied in England, the music itself is probably French or Italian in origin, and it is written in Old German Keyboard Tablature, in which the top part appears as notes and the lower parts as letters of the alphabet. The two main categories of keyboard music are represented: the 'instrumental' by two and a half estampies – an estampie was a dance-like form popular in the thirteenth and fourteenth centuries – and the 'vocal' by two and a half arrangements of three-part motets, two of which occur with Latin words in the fourteenth-century *Roman de Fauvel*. In the motets the top part is 'coloured' (that is, embellished melodically), while the remaining parts are left almost unaltered. The strongly rhythmical dances are mainly in two parts, No. 3 making almost continuous use of parallel fifths in a way reminiscent of the vocal music of a century earlier. Similar in treatment to these motets are the dozen arrangements of fifteenth-century English vocal works in the *Buxheim Organ Book* of *c.* 1460–70 (see below, under Germany). They too are mostly in three parts, the vocal originals being by John Bedyngham, John Dunstable (d. 1453), Walter Frye and Robert Morton (d. 1475).

The first significant source of indisputably English virginals music is British Museum MS. Royal Appendix 58, usually dated *c.* 1520. Among its varied contents are ten keyboard pieces, of which three make use of the type of left-hand broken-chord figuration that is so characteristic of the virginals. They are a *Hornpype* by Hugh Aston, the only composer named in the book, and an anonymous pair, *My Lady Careys Dompe* and *The Short Mesure off my Lady Wynkfylds Rownde*. Aston's dates are usually given as *c*. 1480–1522, but his assured style of keyboard writing suggests that a quarter of a century later might be nearer the mark.

A larger and more varied manuscript is the so-called *Mulliner Book*, copied about 1545–70 by Thomas Mulliner, who was probably connected with St Paul's in London. It contains 120 pieces and names sixteen composers, among whom are John Redford (d. 1545), also of St Paul's; Thomas Tallis (*c*. 1505–1585), one of the greatest mid-Tudor composers of church music; and William Blitheman (d. 1591), an organist of the Chapel Royal. Almost half the pieces are plainsong settings, including several on the *Gloria Tibi Trinitas*, better known in England under the title *In Nomine*. These were probably intended mainly though not exclusively for the organ; but other pieces, such as the anonymous and untitled galliard (C.E., No. 2)* and Newman's *Pavan* (C.E., No. 116), are well suited to the virginals.

The first printed volume of virginals music was the exquisitely engraved *Parthenia*, 1612/13, dedicated to Frederick V, Elector Palatine of the Rhine, and his bride Princess Elizabeth, the only daughter of King James I. It contains twenty-one pieces by the 'three famous Masters, William Byrd, Dr John Bull and Orlando Gibbons, Gentlemen of his Majesty's most Illustrious Chappell', who fittingly represent three successive generations of composers. Byrd's short but striking *Pavana: The Earle of Salisbury* (C.E., No. 6) gives a good idea of their assured grasp of a virginals idiom:

---

* Here and elsewhere C.E. refers to the collected edition concerned, as shown in the list at the end of the present chapter.

Ex.3

* This is one of the two ornament-signs used by the virginalists, the other being a single sloping line. Their interpretation remains uncertain; but the first probably stands
for a shake, short or long, with upper or lower auxiliary, or for an upper or lower
appoggiatura, depending on the context; the second, for an upward slide of a third
or a lower appoggiatura.

This is a typical pavan, except that it contains only two
strains instead of the usual three. Characteristic features of
the keyboard style are the quasi-contrapuntal texture (bars
1–2, tenor part), the use of short snatches of imitation (bars
5–7), the broken-chord basses (bar 8), and the continually
changing number of voices employed. The many ornaments

are also typical, though they remain something of a puzzle in two respects: for no contemporary explanation of their interpretation has survived, and different manuscripts of any one piece rarely agree as to where they should occur.

The most comprehensive of all the sources is the *Fitz-william Virginal Book* (hereafter referred to as *FWVB*), a manuscript which now belongs to the Fitzwilliam Museum in Cambridge. It contains 287 pieces, often unique texts, by thirty-six named composers and others unnamed, ranging from Tallis and Blitheman of the *Mulliner Book* to the long-lived Thomas Tomkins. The manuscript was copied, together with two even larger anthologies of vocal and instru-mental ensemble music, by Francis Tregian the younger (1572–1619), a music-loving member of a Cornish family of Catholic recusants, who because of his religious beliefs was confined to the Fleet Prison from 1609 until his death ten years later. Thanks to the researches of Elizabeth Cole it is now known that almost everyone named in the book had Catholic sympathies, from the composers themselves to the nobles and commoners whose names appear in many of the titles. (It is significant that the Protestant Orlando Gibbons is meagrely represented.) A dozen of the pieces are dated, the earliest being Tallis's *Felix namque* of 1562, and the latest Sweelinck's *Ut, re, mi* of 1612. But there is no reason to suppose that later works than the latter were not included. Most of the forms used in the *Mulliner Book* reappear in the *FWVB*; but dances and popular-song arrangements, often supplied with 'divisions' (that is, variations), now greatly outnumber plainsong settings. The commonest dances are pavans and galliards (sometimes paired and sometimes single), almans, corantos and gigges (jigs). In Thomas Morley's *A Plaine and Easie Introduction to Practicall Musicke*, 1597, the first three are described thus: the pavan is 'a kind of staid music ordained for grave dancing'; the galliard is 'lighter and more stirring'; and the alman 'a more heavy dance than this, fitly representing the nature of the people whose name it carrieth'.

The three composers represented in *Parthenia* were out-

standing among the virginalists, and the greatest of them
was William Byrd (1543–1623). A pupil of Tallis, he
became a Gentleman of the Chapel Royal in 1570, where
he shared the post of organist with his master until 1572, and
where he remained, in spite of his Catholic faith, until his
death. He was a prolific composer, who besides much vocal
music wrote at least 125 virginals pieces. More than half of
these are pavans and galliards, often grouped in thematically related pairs. The lighter dances, such as almans,
corantos and gigges, are less numerous, as one would expect
of a composer whose style was predominantly serious. Byrd
also wrote plainsong and hexachord fantasies, magnificent
sets of variations on popular songs such as *Walsingham*
(*FWVB*, No. 68), illustrative pieces, and grounds. A
combination of the last two can be found in *The Bells*
(*FWVB*, No. 69), an astonishing *tour de force* in which a
vivid sound-picture is built up on a foundation of 138 repetitions of a tiny ground-bass consisting only of the notes C and
D (or G).

The keyboard output of John Bull (*c.* 1563–1628) is even
larger than Byrd's, though he wrote comparatively little for
any other medium. He was a pupil of Blitheman, and a
Gentleman of the Chapel Royal from 1585/6 until 1613,
when his Catholic sympathies obliged him to find refuge in
the Netherlands. His style is as brilliant as Byrd's is restrained, and even at times inclined to be superficial. Both
characteristics will be apparent if his setting of *Walsingham*
(*FWVB*, No. 1) is compared with that of Byrd. Nevertheless it would be unfair to suggest that this tells the whole
story, for Bull could on occasion strike a deeper note. His
Pavana and Galiardo: St Thomas, wake! (*Parthenia*, Nos. 10,
11) have a grave nobility that make them one of the finest
dance pairs in the whole literature. Bull's harmonic and
rhythmic experiments are also at times remarkable, as can
be seen from the modulating *Ut, re, me* (*FWVB*, No. 51)
mentioned earlier, and the *In Nomine* (*FWVB*, No. 119)
written with masterly assurance in a most unusual eleven-
beat rhythm:

The *In Nomine* theme appears in the bass, each note repeated four times.

Besides these large-scale works Bull wrote delightful miniatures such as *A Gigge: Doctor Bulls My Selfe* and *Dr Bulls
Juell (FWVB,* Nos. 263, 138). One version of the latter is
dated 12 December 1621 and inscribed to Jacques Champion, father of the first great French harpsichordist, Jacques
Champion de Chambonnières (see below, under France).

The last of the 'three famous Masters' is Orlando
Gibbons (1583–1625), who became organist of the Chapel
Royal at the early age of twenty-one. He wrote less keyboard music than either Byrd or Bull; yet it must have been
extremely popular, judging by the number of manuscripts
in which it is preserved. Temperamentally he is akin to Byrd
rather than Bull, for in spite of the florid passage-work in
some of his pieces, he never indulges in display for its own
sake. Even his dances have a curiously unsmiling quality
that reflects the gentle, withdrawn expression shown on his
portrait. That he could reach great heights, however, is
proved by the magnificent *Fantazia of Foure Parts* and the
passionately elegiac *The Lord of Salisbury his Pavin* with its
accompanying *Galiardo (Parthenia,* Nos. 17, 18, 19).

In comparison, Giles Farnaby (*c.* 1566–1640) is a minor
composer, though his virginals music remains outstanding.
Yet it cannot have been widely known during his lifetime,
for all but two of his fifty-odd pieces occur only in the
FWVB. To judge by their technical demands, he must have
been an accomplished player; but an amateur's hand is
sometimes betrayed by awkward details of part-writing or
harmony, and by his inability to sustain the interest through
long fantasies. He is at his enchanting best in short pieces
like the *Meridian Alman (FWVB,* No. 291); in the little sets
of variations on *Loth to depart* and *Tell me Daphne (FWVB,*
Nos. 230, 280); and in the wholly individual character
pieces *Giles Farnaby's dream, His rest* and *His humour (FWVB,*
Nos. 194–6). In the last of these he slyly introduces recondite chromatic progressions and a hexachord *cantus firmus,*
as though to prove he could be learned as the next man
when he wished. His *Alman (FWVB,* No. 55) is the only
known piece for two virginals.

Of lesser virginalists one of the earliest was Byrd's pupil, Thomas Morley (1557–c. 1602), the author of *A Plaine and Easie Introduction*. Apart from some rather stolid pavans and galliards, two fine sets of his variations have survived: *Nancie* and *Goe from my window* (*FWVB*, Nos. 9, 12). The latter is masterly in its cumulative effect, and one of the finest sets of virginals variations. Curiously enough, it reappears, with an extra final variation, as *FWVB* No. 42, where it is attributed to John Munday (c. 1560–1630), who also wrote the slight but charming *Munday's joy* and a set of variations on *Robin* (*FWVB*, Nos. 15, 282). The latter is almost certainly the tune of 'Bonny sweet Robin is all my joy', sung by Ophelia in *Hamlet*. Martin Peerson (1572–1650) should be mentioned for the sake of his two exquisite miniatures of spring and autumn, *The primerose* and *The fall of the leafe* (*FWVB*, Nos. 271–2); and the elusive William Tisdall because his five *FWVB* pieces – including the splendid *Pavana chromatica* (No. 214) – are the only certain evidence we possess of the existence of this accomplished composer.

Thomas Tomkins (1572–1656), another pupil of Byrd, was virtually the last of the virginalists. His style is conservative; but it lacks Byrd's strength and vitality, and reminds us all too often that every great tradition ends in a decline. Nevertheless, Tomkins could on occasion be truly eloquent, as when the execution of Charles I moved him to write *A sad pavan, for these distracted times* (C.E., No. 53). He also wrote one of the only two known duets for two players on one virginals: the impressive *Fancy: for two to play* (C.E., No. 32). The other, a rather dull piece, is *A verse: for two to play on one virginal or organ* by his friend Nicholas Carlton.

If Tomkins belonged to the past, Matthew Locke (c. 1630–77) looked towards the future. His treatise *Melothesia: or certain rules for playing upon a continued-bass*, 1673, includes seven of his organ voluntaries and four harpsichord suites, the latter consisting basically of an almain, corant and saraband, with one or more movements added. Other of his pieces appeared in a small anthology, *Musicks hand-maide*,

1663, published by John Playford, which proved so successful that Playford's son Henry brought out a sequel entitled
The second part of musick's hand-maid, 1689. This included
several harpsichord pieces by John Blow (1647–1708) and
his great pupil Henry Purcell, both of whom held the post
of organist at Westminster Abbey. In all, six suites by Blow
were published during his lifetime, while other keyboard
works remained in manuscript. Like Farnaby, he seems at
times an inspired amateur: for though he has beautiful and
original ideas – the almands of his suites are invariably fine –
he rarely manages to maintain a consistent level throughout
a whole work.

There was nothing of the amateur about Henry Purcell
(*c*. 1659–95). His mastery is as apparent in his comparatively
small-scale harpsichord pieces as in his more ambitious
works for stage, court and church. His eight suites, together
with some miscellaneous pieces, were published posthumously by his widow Frances in a small volume entitled
A choice collection of lessons for the harpsichord or spinnet, 1696.
Most of them include a prelude, alman and corant, and are
rounded off by either a minuet, a saraband (a quicker
movement then than later), or a hornpipe. As some of the
additional movements are arrangements of his stage music
it has been suggested that the suites were left unfinished by
Purcell and completed with whatever lay to hand by either
his widow or his younger brother Daniel. This is far from
certain, however, for at least five similar arrangements are
included among his eighteen pieces in *The second part of
musick's hand-maid*, which was 'revised and corrected' by
Purcell himself. The suites are remarkable for their variety,
ranging from the delicacy of No. 1 in G, through the
passion of No. 2 in G minor, to the brilliance of No. 5 in C;
while the miscellaneous pieces pass effortlessly from charming sixteen-bar song-tunes and minuets to intensely moving
grounds – a form that generally brought out Purcell's finest
ideas. A good example is *A new ground* in E minor (C.E.,
vol. 2, p. 4), an arrangement of the song *Here the deities
approve* from the ode *Welcome to all the pleasures*:

Ornaments: \ = appoggiatura from above; // = shake; ⚠ = mordant.

Note the unexpected three-bar length of the ground itself, and the typical way in which the melody overlaps its beginning and end (bb. 4 & 7).

The well-known *Trumpet tune* and *Trumpet voluntary* so often ascribed to Purcell are, in fact, by Jeremiah Clarke (*c.* 1673–1707), another pupil of Blow. Clarke's rather colourless suites were published posthumously as *Choice lessons for the harpsichord or spinett*, 1711, and some of his miscellaneous pieces appeared in *A choice collection of ayres*, 1700, which also included works by yet another of Blow's pupils, William Croft (1678–1727). Though Croft was an uneven composer, he is the most individual and interesting of Purcell's followers; and at least one of his pieces, the Ground in C minor, is so striking that it has been attributed to Purcell himself.

The rest of the eighteenth century in England was dominated by the titanic figure of Handel (see Chapter 2, below), who settled in London in 1711 at the age of twenty-six. His influence on native music was almost over-whelming; yet publications such as the *Eight suites of lessons*, 1728, by Thomas Roseingrave (1690–1766), an ardent admirer of Domenico Scarlatti, and the *VIII Sonatas or lessons*, 1756, by Thomas Augustine Arne (1710–78), show that some English composers managed to retain a certain individuality and to write solo keyboard music that has genuine freshness and charm, if no pretensions to greatness.

IBERIA AND THE NETHERLANDS

When the future King Philip II of Spain visited Italy, Germany and the Netherlands during the years 1548–51, and the Netherlands and England in 1554–6, he was accompanied by his private chapel and by his court organist and clavichordist, the blind Antonio de Cabezón (1500–1566). As this great Spaniard was also an outstanding keyboard composer it is tempting to speculate on how much he influenced, or was influenced by, the colleagues he must have met during his travels – near-contemporaries in Italy such as Marco Antonio Cavazzoni, his son Girolamo, and Andrea Gabrieli; and Retford and Tallis in England. Possibly it was less than at one time imagined, for the style and technique of all these composers must have been well established by the time of the visits.

The greater part of Cabezón's instrumental music was published posthumously in 1578 by his son Hernando. Though entitled *Obras de musica para tecla arpa y vihuela* (Compositions for keyboard, harp and lute), they are designed primarily for keyboard. The forms used include *tientos* (ricercars), *fugas*, various pieces based on either sacred or secular vocal originals, *diferencias* (variations) and dances. The predominantly severe style is best suited to the organ, but the dances and variations sound well on harpsichord or clavichord. A particularly fine set is the *Difer-*

encias sobre el canto llano del caballero (*Variations on the simple
song of a caballero*) (C.E., vol. 3, p. 61), in which the borrowed melody appears in each of the four voices in turn,
while the remaining parts weave free, flowing counterpoint
around it.

Cabezón influenced lesser composers in Spain and
Portugal, one being Rodriques Coelho (born *c.* 1583),
organist of the royal chapel in Lisbon. But no other major
figure appeared in either country until 1724, when Domenico Scarlatti arrived from Italy to join the household of the
music-loving Princess Maria Barbara of Braganza (see
below, under Italy).

Musical contacts between the Netherlands and England
were less fugitive and more fruitful. The two countries not
only traded together, but each sheltered the religious refu-
gees of the other –the Protestants who fled from the Netherlands and the Catholics from England. One of the latter, it
will be remembered, was John Bull, who found refuge in
Brussels in 1613 and became organist of Antwerp Cathedral
four years later. Another was the less distinguished virgin-
alist Peter Philips. As a result of this cross-fertilization, works
by the Dutchman Sweelinck appear in the *Fitzwilliam
Virginal Book*; while he in turn made settings of pavans by
Philips and the lutenist John Dowland, and other composers
of the Netherlands used English tunes such as *Daphne*, *Mal
Sims* and *Fortune my foe*.

The earliest known collection of Netherlands virginal
music, the *Susanne van Soldt Manuscript* of 1599 (British
Museum, Add. ms. 29485), is another example of this inter-
change. It belonged to the twelve-year-old daughter of a
Dutch refugee in London, and was probably her instruction
book since it contains explanations of notation, as well as
thirty-three fairly easy anonymous pieces, mainly dances
and settings of metrical psalm tunes. The later *Anna Maria
van Eyl Manuscript* of 1671 (Amsterdam, Toonkunst-Biblio-
theek) is a similar collection and equally well suited to the
capabilities of its fifteen-year-old original owner.

Passing reference has already been made to Jan Pieters-

zoon Sweelinck (1562–1621), who was by far the most outstanding composer of keyboard music in the Netherlands.
He was taught by his father, the organist of the Oude Kerk
in Amsterdam, and at the age of sixteen went to Venice to
study with the famous Italian theorist Gioseffe Zarlino
(1517–90). During his two-year stay he would have come
into stimulating contact with the works of the two Cavaz-
zonis, Andrea Gabrieli, and Claudio Merulo, and he is
almost certain to have known at least Giovanni Gabrieli,
who was only five years his senior. As a result, an Italian
influence is as apparent in his fantasies and toccatas as the
English influence in his dances and variations on popular
tunes. On his return home he took over his father's post in
Amsterdam, where his growing fame made him one of the
most sought-after teachers in northern Europe (see below,
under Germany).

None of Sweelinck's works was published during his lifetime, yet their popularity is shown by the number of
manuscripts in which they appear. The modern complete
edition contains 13 chorale settings (including variations)
which are essentially organ music; 14 fantasies, 2 preludes
and 15 toccatas, all playable on either organ or harpsichord;
and 5 dances and 7 sets of variations on popular tunes that
are clearly intended for harpsichord. The best of the dances
is a setting of Dowland's famous *Lachrime pavan* (C.E., No.
66), which was also set by Byrd and Farnaby, while
probably the finest of all Sweelinck's keyboard works is the
set of six variations on the hymn *Mein junges Leben hat ein
End'* (C.E., No. 60.)

ITALY

The recent rediscovery and re-examination of the Faenza
Codex of *c.* 1420 (Faenza, Biblioteca Comunale, 117) has
shown that Italian keyboard music existed at least a
century earlier than at one time supposed. This manuscript
of over a hundred pages contains some sections of keyboard
Organ Masses, and arrangements of secular vocal works by

Italian and French composers of the fourteenth and early fifteenth centuries, including Landini, Bartolino da Padova, Jacopo da Bologna, Machaut and Pierre des Molins. The music is in two parts throughout, the top voice being 'coloured' or embellished in a similar way to that used in the motets of the Robertsbridge Fragment (see above, under England).

A hundred years elapsed before the appearance of the first known printed source of Italian keyboard music: the *Frottole intabulate da sonare organi*, 1517, published by Andrea Antico in Rome. (A *frottola* is a type of secular song for three or four voices.) The book contains twenty-six anonymous arrangements of four-part songs, most of which are by Bartolomeo Tromboncino. The beginning of one of these arrangements, *Non resta in questa valle* (C.E., vol. 1, p. 7*), is printed overleaf together with the original, to show how such vocal works were embellished to make them suitable for the keyboard. Though the title-page specifies organ, an accompanying illustration shows a young man playing the harpsichord – a significant indication of how readily one keyboard instrument could be substituted for another at this period.

The first printed volume intended specifically for harpsichord and clavichord, to the exclusion of the organ, is the anonymous *Intabolatura nova di varie sorte de balli*, 1551, which was issued by Antonio Gardane in Venice, the home of Italian music printing. It contains twenty-five short dances – mainly galliards, passamezzos and saltarellos – whose simple texture and strongly marked rhythms fit them admirably as an accompaniment to dancing, and reasonably well for the harpsichord. Truly idiomatic writing for stringed keyboard instruments long remained the exception rather than the rule in Italy, and was restricted almost entirely to dance music until well on in the seventeenth century.

The first known printed volume by a named composer is the *Recerchari, motetti, canzoni*, 1523, of Marco Antonio Cavazzoni (*c.* 1490–*c.* 1570), also known as Marcantonio da

(Note-values halved)

Vocal original

Ex.6

Keyboard version

Non res - ta in ques - ta val - le

Al - tro cha-more e pa - ce   cho - mo tran-

quil - - - - - - - - la iace

Bologna. It contains two long and amorphous ricercars, their associated motets, and four arrangements of French *chansons* employing the type of contrapuntal embellishment found in the earlier *Frottole intabulate*. Marco Antonio's son, Girolamo Cavazzoni (*c.* 1510–*c.* 1580), was a far more accomplished composer. From his father's rambling ricercars he evolved the clearly defined form in dovetailed sections that became the standard pattern for such works. His compositions were published in two volumes in 1543 and ?1543, and consist of ricercars, hymn and plainsong settings, and two canzons based on French *chansons*. The latter, unlike those of the *Frottole intabulate*, are virtually new compositions. For example, the lively *Il est bel et bon* (C.E., vol. 1, p. 17) uses no more than the first bar and a half of the four-part song by Passerau on which it is allegedly based. The canzons by both father and son sound well on the harpsichord, though their other pieces are better suited to the organ.

As the Cathedral of St Mark in Venice was one of the most important centres of music in the whole of Italy, it is not surprising that several of its organists were also famous composers. One of the most influential was Andrea Gabrieli (*c.* 1520–86), best known for his pioneering compositions for antiphonal groups of singers and instrumentalists – works that were particularly suited to the architectural layout of the Cathedral. His solo keyboard music is less striking, and at times seems austere to the point of dullness; nevertheless, there is considerable formal interest in his use of paired movements, such as the canzon and ricercar on 'Pour ung plaisir' (C.E., vol. 4, pp. 27, 29), in which the first of the pair is an arrangement of a *chanson*, and the second an original composition where each section is based on the same theme as the corresponding section of the first piece. Andrea was succeeded at the second and first organs of St Mark's by his brilliantly gifted nephew, Giovanni Gabrieli (1557–1612), who between 1593 and 1605 prepared his uncle's keyboard works, together with some of his own, for publication in a six-volume comprehensive edition.

Besides motet arrangements, ricercars, canzons and toccatas by both composers, it includes two groups of *intonazioni*, the short preludes that were used by organists during the course of the liturgy to give the pitch to either priest or choir. The longer of these are not unlike miniature toccatas, and it is easy to see from their use of contrasted material how the larger form developed from the smaller. As an example of Giovanni's use of forms descended from the motet (see above, under Forms), his light-hearted *Canzon quarta* (C.E., vol. i, p. 35) may be cited. So far as is known, it is an original piece and not an arrangement of a vocal work. The opening section, A, consists of fifteen bars:

Section B begins where this leaves off, is three times as long, and is made up of a number of dovetailed clauses of different lengths. Most of them start with some rhythmic variant of A's first four notes, then blossom out into other clearly defined thematic elements. The last one closes into a recapitulation of A in its original form, and the whole enchanting piece is rounded off with a seven-bar coda based on a new quaver-figure.

This is a fairly sophisticated version of the motet type of form. Elsewhere each clause of B in the above might be based on an entirely fresh subject (i.e. B,C,D,E. . .), thus producing a less closely knit structure; other sections than A might be recapitulated; or there could be no recapitulation at all. The possibilities were endless.

Another famous composer–organist at St Mark's was Claudio Merulo (1533–1604), whose birthdate falls between the Gabrielis. His keyboard works cover a repertory similar to theirs; but though originally published in six volumes between 1567 and 1611, they still await a modern complete edition. Merulo's contemporary fame was spread by his pupil Girolamo Diruta (born c. 1550), who wrote the earliest Italian treatise on keyboard playing, *Il Transilvano*, Parts I and II, 1593 and 1608. Besides recommending his readers to study the ornamentation in Merulo's canzons, and to use it as a pattern whenever they had to extemporize embellishments of their own, he prints several complete works by Merulo in his treatise. Also included are compositions by the Gabrielis and himself, and by other contemporaries such as Banchieri, Bell'haver and Luzzaschi. Of these, Luzzascho Luzzaschi (1545–1607) is notable as being the teacher of Frescobaldi.

Girolamo Frescobaldi (1583–1643) is one of Italy's two greatest keyboard composers, and the most outstanding of all whose style was suited equally to organ and harpsichord. After studying with Luzzaschi in his native Ferrara and briefly occupying a post in Rome, he spent a year in the Netherlands, where the forty-five-year-old Sweelinck was at the height of his powers. In 1608 he returned to Italy to become the widely acclaimed organist of St Peter's in Rome; and there he spent the rest of his life, apart from a six-year stay in Florence as organist to Ferdinand II, Grand Duke of Tuscany.

Frescobaldi's keyboard works were published in a series of ten volumes, of which some are revised and enlarged editions of others. Among the earliest and latest are, respectively, *Il primo libro delle fantasie*, 1608, written before his visit to the Netherlands; the *Fiori musicali*, 1635, devoted to liturgical organ music – Bach possessed a manuscript copy of the work – and the posthumous *Canzoni alla francese*, 1645. Of greater interest to harpsichordists are the three definitive collections, *Il primo libro di capricci, canzon francese e recercari*, 1626, and the *Toccate d'intavolatura di cimbalo et organo* with its companion *Il secondo libro di toccate*, both of 1637. (The first two of these contain important prefaces by the composer concerning the interpretation of his works.) The ricercars in the 1626 volume still lean towards the severe style of the earliest book of fantasies; but the canzons and some of the capriccios breathe a freer air – notably the *Capriccio cromatico* and the *Capriccio di durezze* (C.E., vol. 2, pp. 34, 36) with their expressive use of chromaticism and suspensions. The other two volumes include a variety of pieces besides toccatas: partitas (i.e. sets of variations), canzons, capriccios (one an unexpectedly jejune battle-piece), and dances. Among the latter are two interesting small groups, each consisting of a balletto, corrente and passacaglia, of which the second and third movements are variations of the first (C.E., vol. 3, pp. 72, 75). Some of the partitas are particularly successful, including those on the airs entitled *Romanesca*, *Ruggiero* and *Follia* (C.E., vol. 3, pp. 46, 60, 67) – though oddly enough the last has nothing to do with the *Folia* theme mentioned on p. 16. Most of the toccatas suit the harpsichord admirably. The beginning of No. 9 (C.E., vol. 3, p. 32) gives some idea of the loosely imitative texture so often employed in the reflective sections:

In this particular work it is followed by a more brilliant section of semiquaver passage-work; and the two contrasting moods, using different themes at each appearance, are alternated throughout. Here and elsewhere the intended effect is improvisatory; yet in spite of the looseness of structure the works are always held together convincingly by Frescobaldi's superb sense of rhetoric.

After the death of Frescobaldi half a century was to elapse before the appearance of a comparable genius. Plenty of keyboard music was written in the interim, but it rarely transcended its immediate purpose of providing undemanding entertainment or instruction. Nevertheless, significant changes were taking place. Composers were beginning to turn away from music based on counterpoint and the equality of parts, and to favour a different type, derived ultimately from simple dances and more sophisticated operatic arias, in which the top line was all-important, the bass secondary, and the inner parts wholly subsidiary.

The two styles can be seen side by side in the works of Michelangelo Rossi (*c.* 1600–*c.* 1660), the old in his toccatas and the new in his *corrente*. In addition, there was a growing awareness of how to write idiomatically for harpsichord and clavichord as distinct from the organ. This is apparent not only in collections of dances, like Giovanni Picchi's *Intavolatura di balli*, 1621, but also in the more varied harpsichord works of composers such as the French-influenced Alessandro Poglietti (d. 1683), and Bernardo Pasquini (1637–1710) who was one of the first to apply the title *sonata* to his solo keyboard music. As yet the word meant no more than a 'sound piece', for it was given to toccatas, fugues, airs, dances, suites and anything else. But significantly enough it was also used for solo works in more than a single movement that are clearly influenced by the contemporary ensemble sonatas of Corelli and his followers.

The keyboard music of Alessandro Scarlatti (1660–1726) is less interesting than might be expected of the immensely influential leader of the Neapolitan school, who was himself the composer of over a hundred operas. His many toccatas are superficially brilliant, but lack variety, depth, and sheer power of invention. Indeed, they are mainly memorable for the fact that they were written by the father of the remarkable Domenico.

Domenico Scarlatti (1685–1757) is the second great figure in the history of Italian keyboard music, and one of the most outstanding of all harpsichord composers. Born in the same year as Bach and Handel, he spent his early manhood in various posts in Naples and Rome, where he composed operas and church music, all virtually unknown today. He appears to have been overshadowed at that time by the powerful personality of his father, for the full flowering of his genius did not begin until he left Italy at the age of thirty-nine to become *maestro* of the Portuguese royal chapel in Lisbon. After a final visit to Italy in 1724–8, during which his father died, he returned to the Iberian peninsula; thenceforth his home was in Spain, where his former pupil, Princess Maria Barbara of Braganza, was

now married to the Prince of the Asturias, later King
Fernando VI.

The only Scarlatti harpsichord works to be published
under the composer's supervision were the [30] *Essercizi per
gravicembalo*, 1738, which were issued, surprisingly enough,
in London. The greater part of his vast output of 555 single-
movement sonatas has survived only in manuscript copies,
for not a single autograph has so far been traced. In the
modern edition edited by Longo these have been grouped
into arbitrary suites; but originally, as Ralph Kirkpatrick
has pointed out in his definitive study of the composer,
more than two-thirds of them were grouped in pairs, or
occasionally in threes, according to key. Kirkpatrick also
suggests that the majority was written from 1752 onwards:
that is, after the composer had reached the age of sixty-
seven. Whether this astonishing hypothesis is correct or not,
there is no doubt that Scarlatti evolved an entirely new
keyboard style, some of whose features can be seen in the
following extract from the Sonata in D minor, L. 215:

Typical are the wide leaps at speed, the crossing of either
hand with the other, the harmonic clashes used to achieve
tension and accent (bar 20, left hand beats 2 and 4), the
unexpected phrase-lengths, and the sparkling brilliance of
the whole style. Less familiar but equally important is the
more introverted side of Scarlatti's genius, as shown in such
sonatas as the poignant B minor, L. 33, the gently reflective
D major, L. 183, and countless others that should be better
known. His works have, indeed, a far wider emotional range
than is generally realized; and though he may never aim
for the heights reached so effortlessly by Bach, he extended
the technical possibilities of his chosen medium in a way
unmatched by any other composer.

Scarlatti had an immediate disciple in the Spaniard
Antonio Soler, and, as we have seen, an ardent admirer in
the Englishman Thomas Roseingrave, who published an

edition of forty-two of the sonatas in 1739; but as an expatriate he influenced Italian music scarcely at all. Composers such as Benedetto Marcello (1686–1739) and Domenico
Zipoli (1688–1726) continued to produce minor keyboard
works in the tradition of Pasquini; but the main initiative
in keyboard composition had already passed to Germany
and Austria. There was one man, however, who provided a
link between the past and the future, for Giovanni Battista
Martini (1706–1784), besides being a composer and
theorist of international fame, was the Padre Martini who
met and encouraged the fourteen-year-old Mozart when
that astonishing boy and his father visited Italy in 1770.

FRANCE

While the six pieces in the Robertsbridge Fragment of c.
1320 may well have been French in origin (see above, under
England), two more certain sources of arrangements of
French music are the Faenza Codex of c. 1420 (see above,
under Italy), and the *Buxheim Book* of c. 1460 (see below,
under Germany). Thereafter, nothing is known of keyboard
music in France until 1530/31, when Pierre Attaingnant of
Paris published seven small books of anonymous arrangements 'for organ, spinet, clavichord and suchlike musical
instruments'. Three are devoted to keyboard versions of
chansons, two to plainsong settings from the Mass and
Magnificat, and one each to motets and dances – the latter
consisting mostly of pavans and galliards, but also including
some *branles* and *basses dances*. As might be expected, the
dances are the works best suited to the harpsichord.

The mid seventeenth century saw the emergence in
France of a true harpsichord idiom based on the arpeggiated
and richly ornamented lute music of composers such as
Adrian le Roy and the Gaultier family. (Jacques Gaultier,
the eldest of the clan, was court lutenist in England from
1619–47, and thus provided a link between the virginalists
and France.) Broken chords and profuse ornamentation
remained typical features of the style; but whereas the lute

could only hint at complex harmonic and contrapuntal textures, the harpsichord was able to present them in full. The organ and harpsichord repertories were more clearly differentiated there than elsewhere, for plainsong settings belonged exclusively to the organ, while dances of the court and theatre, illustrative pieces, and preludes were the province of the harpsichord. One type of prelude, known as 'unmeasured', is peculiar to France. It consists of a long series of semibreves (occasionally other note-values are included) without either time-signature or barlines. No contemporary treatise describes how such preludes should be performed; but their prototype is clearly the similar lute prelude, in which the rhythmic interpretation was left to the taste of the performer, and therefore varied from performance to performance. Dances are generally grouped into suites, or, as François Couperin called them, *ordres*, their four basic movements being the allemande, courante, sarabande and gigue, with other dances or character pieces added as fancy directs. The courante is the only one of these that calls for a definition, for the French *courante* differs from the Italian *corrente* in having six crotchets in a bar instead of three. These are normally grouped into three beats of two crotchets each; but at cadences, and sometimes elsewhere, a characteristic rhythmic ambiguity is introduced by changing the grouping into two beats of three crotchets each.

From 1670 onwards printed sources in France abound, so manuscripts are less important than in England and Germany. Only one considerable keyboard composer, Louis Couperin, remained unpublished during his own lifetime, his works having come down to us in the so-called *Bauyn Manuscript* of *c.* 1660 (Paris, Bibliothèque Nationale, MS. VM[7] 674–5), named after the music-lover who originally owned it.

This manuscript also contains works by Jacques Champion de Chambonnières (*c.* 1602–*c.* 1672) which are not found in the two books of his pieces that were published in 1670. Chambonnières, who is rightly regarded as the founder of the great French school of harpsichordists, came

from a long line of musicians who had served the royal
household since at least the 1520s. His father, Jacques
Champion, was harpsichordist to Louis XIII, and (it may
be remembered) was given an inscribed piece by John Bull
in 1621. Chambonnières succeeded to the post in 1640, and
achieved such fame both as a performer and a teacher that
the majority of later players could trace back their musical
lineage to him, either through a master–pupil relationship
or through some official post in church or court. His music
consists almost entirely of dances. It is uneven in quality, but
at its best has the strain of nobility that is so apparent in the
refrain of the Chaconne in F major (C.E., No. 116):

The ornamentation is editorial, as there is none in the original manuscript sources.
⋔ = shake (beginning on the note above); ⌠ = upward arpeggio (beginning on the note nearest the hook).

In contrast to this, his command of a lighter vein can be seen in such pieces as the Courante in C and the lovely Rondeau in F (C.E., Nos. 65, 106).

Among Chambonnières's immediate pupils were the three Couperin brothers, Louis (c. 1626–62), François the elder (c. 1631–c. 1701) and Charles (1638–79) – the last two being respectively uncle and father of the great François. A contemporary writer, Titon du Tillet, tells how the brothers once serenaded Chambonnières, who was their neighbour in the country, and how the older man thereupon offered to teach them in Paris. Louis soon became organist of Saint Gervais, where, on his early death, he was succeeded by Charles. He too died young, leaving the upbringing of his eleven-year-old son François to the remaining brother. Neither François the elder nor Charles appear to have been composers, but the harpsichord works of Louis show outstanding originality and skill. Besides many dances he wrote fifteen unmeasured preludes, a number of delightful character pieces, such as La Piémontoise (C.E., No. 103), and a dozen particularly fine chaconnes and passacailles, including one, the Passacaille in G minor (C.E., No. 99), which is not the rondeau type, but a set of variations like the normal passacaglia of Italy and Germany. He also wrote some of the earliest pièces croisées: pieces in which the hands cross one another in such a way as to make a two-manual harpsichord essential for their performance.

Two less remarkable pupils of Chambonnières are Nicolas Lebègue (1631–1702), who became organist of the

Sainte Chapelle in 1678, and Jean Henri d'Anglebert (1635–91), who succeeded his master as harpsichordist to Louis XIV in 1664. Lebègue's eleven suites, each containing anything from five to fourteen movements, are not superficially dissimilar from Louis Couperin's; yet they have a curious awkwardness, as though their composer was not fully in command of his material. D'Anglebert's works, though uneven, are more rewarding. Of the sixty pieces he published, roughly a quarter are acknowledged as keyboard arrangements of operatic movements by Jean-Baptiste Lully (1632–87). His own compositions range from the charming little Menuet in G (C.E., p. 25) to the magnificent *Tombeau de Mr de Chambonnières* (C.E., p. 118). The latter was written in memory of his master, and is an early example of the type of memorial piece of which French composers from Louis Couperin to Ravel have always been so fond.

Little is known about Gaspard le Roux (*c.* 1660–1707) apart from his seven suites published in 1705. They are unusual in that le Roux includes an instrumental trio version of most of the pieces and a two-harpsichord version of several of them, the latter being the earliest known French compositions for this medium. The pieces are more adventurous and more accomplished than those of Lebègue or d'Anglebert; and occasionally they explore an altogether new mood of romantic sensibility, as in the aptly named *La Favoritte* from Suite No. 6 in F sharp minor (C.E., p. 40).

A slighter talent, though no less original, is Élizabeth Jacquet (*c.* 1664–1729), wife of the organist Marin de la Guerre. When only ten she played at the royal court, whereupon Mme de Maintenon, the king's mistress, made herself responsible for the child's further education. Fourteen of her harpsichord pieces, the only solo works to survive, were published in 1707 in an edition dedicated to Louis XIV. They are described as being also playable on the violin, but it is not at all clear how this would be practicable.

With François Couperin the younger (1669–1733) we

reach one of the two giants of the French school. After studying with his uncle, François the elder, and with Jacques Tomelin, he succeeded the latter as one of the four organists of the Sainte Chapelle. In 1693 he was ennobled by Louis XIV and appointed *Maître de clavecin* to the royal family. His complete harpsichord works were published in four exquisitely engraved volumes between 1713 and 1730. They contain twenty-seven *ordres*, or suites, each consisting of from four to as many as twenty-three movements, the longer suites being collections of pieces in a single key, rather than works to be performed complete. Couperin also published the didactic *L'Art de toucher le clavecin*, 1707, in which he set out his ideas on fingering, phrasing and interpretation, adding eight of his own preludes for good measure. His harpsichord pieces are generally small in scale; nevertheless, it is astonishing what an impression of sheer size Couperin at times achieves. This is shown not only by the majestic and well known Passacaille in B minor (Ordre No. 8) – arguably the greatest harpsichord work by any French composer – but also in movements such as the less familiar *La Convalescente* from Ordre No. 26:

Ex. 11

Ornaments: ⋙ = shake (beginning on note above; but if.slurred to preceding note as in left hand bar 3, beginning on main note); small note = appoggiatura on the beat (in this case they are all semiquavers); ⋔ = mordant.

Like many other titled pieces this is a dance in disguise (an allemande). Another work, *Les folies françaises, ou les dominos* (Ordre No. 13), appears at first sight to be merely a group of tiny pieces depicting the different characters and 'temperaments' in a carnival; but closer inspection shows that it is also a set of variations on a bass. Couperin's works are full of such surprises, and it is pleasing to think that Bach must have known and admired at least some of them, for he included the rondeau *Les Bergeries* (Ordre No. 6) in a Notebook that he prepared in 1725 for the instruction of his second wife, Anna Magdalena.

Though their output is small, three composers who must be mentioned are Marchand, Dieupart and Clérambault. Louis Marchand (1667–1723) published two small books of harpsichord pieces, each containing one rather undistinguished suite. He is better known for the unauthenticated story of his proposed contest in Dresden with Bach, from which he is said to have run away. He was widely famed, however, both as organist and teacher, and Bach must certainly have admired him, for he is known to have written out several of his works. Bach also copied at least two of the six suites of Charles Dieupart (died *c.* 1740), a Frenchman who spent the last forty years of his life in England. This is specially noteworthy since there is a surprising melodic resemblance between the Prelude of Bach's *English* Suite No. 1 in A, and the Gigue of Dieupart's Suite No. 1 in the same key. Louis Nicolas Clérambault published one small volume for harpsichord and another for organ. The organ

pieces are the more striking; yet the harpsichord Suite in
C minor – the better of the two included in the book – has
an individual flavour that makes it more rewarding than
anything by either Marchand or Dieupart.

The second great French harpsichord composer was Jean-
Philippe Rameau (1683–1764). He was taught by his father
and possibly later by Marchand, travelled in Italy, and
eventually settled in Paris after holding various organist's
posts in France. He achieved wide though controversial
fame with his first opera, *Hippolyte et Aricie*, 1733, and a less
qualified success two years later with *Les Indes galantes*. His
harpsichord works were published between 1706 and 1741
in four volumes, two of which contain important introductions concerning technique and interpretation. His keyboard writing is more adventurous and experimental than
that of any other French composer, Couperin not excepted.
The magnificent rondeau *Les Cyclopes* (C.E., p. 52) demands
a virtuoso performer even today, and when it first appeared,
the left hand part in the following passage was so unusual
that Rameau felt it necessary to explain in his Preface how
it should be fingered:

Ornaments: ᴧᴧ = shake (beginning on note above; but if slurred to preceding note, beginning on main note);) =mordant.

Another piece, *L'Enharmonique* (C.E., p. 92) contains such startling harmonies that a note is added stating that 'the effect ... may not perhaps be to everyone's taste immediately; one can nonetheless grow accustomed to it after some application, and even grow to awareness of all its beauty once the initial aversion ... has been overcome.'

Near-contemporaries of Rameau were Jean François Dandrieu (1682–1738), François Dagincourt (*c.* 1684–1758), and Louis Claude Daquin (1694–1772). The most striking of the three is Dagincourt, whose forty-odd pieces, grouped into four *ordres*, follow worthily in the steps of Couperin. His Ordre No. 4 in E is particularly fine, with its rich-textured allemande *La Couperin*, and its rondeau *Les Tourterelles* which so convincingly imitates the cooing of doves. The more prolific Dandrieu published three books of pieces. He is at his best when working on a small scale, as in *La Gémissante* (Book 1), *Les tendres reproches* and *La Lyre d'Orphée* (both from Book 2), all of which have an individual quality of sensitive tenderness. Daquin, the godson of Élizabeth Jacquet and a pupil of Marchand, is more of a light-weight. His keyboard pieces appeared in two books, one for harpsichord and the other, a volume of *Noëls*, for organ or harpsichord. (The second, in spite of its description, is primarily intended for the organ, as five of its twelve pieces require pedals.) the well known *Le coucou* is typical of Daquin's slightly superficial style; but the less familiar *La melodieuse* shows that he was also capable of finding a vein of true poetry.

Though harpsichord music continued to be published in France until the second half of the eighteenth century, this great school of keyboard composers was already in decline: for its output, like that of the English virginalists, was confined to a period of roughly three quarters of a century.

GERMANY AND AUSTRIA

The sources of keyboard music in Germany and Austria go back to much the same period as in Italy, that is, to the early fifteenth century; they are, however, more numerous. Three of the most important (though not the very earliest) are the *Tablature* of 1448 written by Adam Ileborgh, monk and rector of Stendall (Philadelphia, Curtis Institute of Music); a treatise on composition entitled *Fundamentum organisandi*, 1452, by Conrad Paumann (*c.* 1410–73), the blind organist of Nuremberg (Berlin, Staatsbibliothek, MS. Cim. 352b); and the comprehensive anthology known as the *Buxheim Organ Book*, *c.* 1460–70 (Munich, Staatsbibliothek Mus. MS. 3725), which is by far the most important source of all. The first two of these manuscripts contain two- and three-part arrangements of vocal works with the top part embellished; and, in addition, some short preludes which are the earliest known keyboard pieces that are entirely independent of any vocal model. The *Buxheim Book* covers a similarly varied though far more extensive repertory, for its 258 pieces include 18 preludes and 222 arrangements of vocal *chansons* and motets by German, French, Italian and even English composers. The majority are three-part settings, but there are also some two-part and a few four-part ones. Pedals are required for certain of the Ileborgh and *Buxheim* pieces, but this is no proof that the music is for organ since both harpsichord and clavichord were often fitted with pedals at this period in Germany.

The organ is specified and required for the earliest of all printed volumes of keyboard music: the *Tabulaturen etlicher Lobgesang und Lidlein uff die Orgel und Lauten* by Arnolt Schlick (*c*. 1455–*c*. 1525), published by Peter Schöffer of Mainz in 1512. Unlike the Cabezón works mentioned earlier, these pieces are not intended for organ *or* lute: there are fourteen organ pieces, three lute solos, and twelve songs with lute accompaniment.

Of more immediate interest to harpsichordists are the dozen or so sixteenth- and early seventeenth-century tablature books by Kotter, Ammerbach, the two Schmids (father and son), Paix, Löffelholtz, Nörmiger and others. They include a wide variety of dances and arrangements of vocal music, and are mostly suited to the amateur performer. The earliest are two manuscript volumes written by Hans Kotter (*c*. 1483–1541). They cover the period 1513–32 and contain, besides pieces by Kotter himself and anonymous dances, arrangements of vocal works by composers such as Paul Hofheimer (1483–1537), the most famous German organist of the day, and the two great Flemings, Heinrich Isaac and Josquin des Prés. The first of the printed collections is the *Orgel oder Instrument Tabulatur*, 1571, by Elias Nicolaus Ammerbach (*c*. 1530–97), organist of the Thomaskirche in Leipzig a hundred years before Bach. Typical of the dances found in these tablatures is *Wer das Töchter haben wil* from Ammerbach's book, which also shows how some dances are followed by a quicker triple-time variation called a *Nachtanz* or 'After-dance' (here *Proportio*, to describe the tempo relationship of *sesquialtera*, or three in the time of two):

Ex.13

Proportio

* In bar 13 the third bass note is F in the original, not A.

Subsequent composers of the pre-Bach era may conveniently be divided into two groups: those who worked in the Catholic south (including Austria), and those of Lutheran north and centre. The influence of Italy is apparent over-all; but as might be expected it was felt most strongly in the south, while the north and centre were more powerfully drawn towards the Netherlands school of Sweelinck and to the Lutheran chorale.

The earliest of these composers who may be counted as southern is also the most outstanding: Johann Jacob

Froberger (1616–67). Though born in Stuttgart in central
Germany, he became court organist in Vienna at the age of
twenty-one, and was sent to Italy almost immediately by
the music-loving Emperor Ferdinand III for a four-year
period of study with Frescobaldi. On his return to Austria
he remained in the service of the Emperor until 1657, when
he set off on a prolonged European journey that took him
to Germany, France, the Netherlands and England, and
only ended ten years later with his death at Héricourt,
where he had found refuge in the house of his pupil Sibylla,
Dowager Duchess of Württemberg. In Paris he is known to
have met Chambonnières and Louis Couperin, and in London he encountered Christopher Gibbons, son of Orlando
and organist of Westminster Abbey. These visits resulted in at
least two compositions: a *Tombeau* on the death of the celebrated French lutenist Blancrocher (C.E., vol. 3, p. 110),
and a Lament written in London 'to dispel melancholy',
the cause of which is recorded on the only surviving manuscript. Apparently Froberger was robbed during the
Channel crossing and arrived in London penniless. He took
a job as organ-blower, but was so weighed down by his
misfortunes that he forgot to blow the organ and was
kicked out of doors by the enraged organist. The Lament is
the opening movement of the Suite No. 30 in A minor
(C.E., vol. 3, p. 112), and is in fact an allemande:

Ex. 14

*Froberger often relied on the player to add ties where required. Those crossed by a small stroke are editorial, as are notes within square brackets.

It is indicative of the romantic mood of most of Froberger's suites that the player should be instructed to perform this movement freely. Equally characteristic is the use of an almost impressionistic keyboard texture, better suited to the inflectional powers of the clavichord than to the harpsichord. His remaining works – toccatas, capriccios, canzons, fantasies and ricercars – are more Italian in style. The fantasies and ricercars are essentially organ music; but the rest are suited almost equally to harpsichord, clavichord or organ. They are found in many manuscript sources, but nothing of Froberger's was published until some twenty-five years after his death.

Two lesser keyboard composers of the south are G. Muffat and J. K. F. Fischer. Georg Muffat (1653–1704) – who should not be confused with his son Gottlieb Theophil – studied in Paris under Lully and in Italy with Pasquini, and later held various posts in Austria and Bohemia. His *Apparatus musico-organisticus*, 1690, contains twelve toccatas for organ (with the elementary pedal part customary in the south), and four harpsichord pieces of which two are outstanding: the large-scale Passacaglia in G minor, and the shorter but almost equally fine Ciacona in G. Both works have a power and solidity that is far more characteristic of

the north than of the south. The four collections of Johann
Kasper Ferdinand Fischer (c. 1665–1746), Kapellmeister
to the Margrave of Baden, are more typically southern in
their delicate sensitivity. The two devoted to harpsichord or
clavichord music, *Les pièces de clavessin*, 1696, and the
Musicalisches Parnassus, c. 1738, contain respectively eight
and eleven suites. Each of these begins with some sort of
prelude and continues with a group of dances or other pieces
not always including the usual allemande, courante, sarabande and gigue. The other two volumes, *Ariadne musica*,
1702, and *Blumen-Strauss*, c. 1733, contain miniature preludes and fugues. They are intended for organ, but many
of them sound equally well on harpsichord or clavichord.
The *Ariadne* set is of particular interest, for it foreshadows
Bach's *Forty-Eight Preludes and Fugues* in its wide range of
keys, and even in some of its themes – for example, compare
Fischer's Fuga VIII in E (C.E., p. 83) with Bach's Fugue
IX in E from the second Book.

Composers in Lutheran Germany were meanwhile lay-
ing the foundations on which Bach and Handel were later
to build. The school, which stemmed initially from
Sweelinck, was much influenced by the magnificent organs
that were being built in the north – instruments which
encouraged a more independent use of the pedals, and hence
a clearer distinction between organ and harpsichord music.

One of Sweelinck's most distinguished pupils was Samuel
Scheidt (1587–1654), a contemporary of the great Heinrich
Schütz who himself wrote no keyboard music. Scheidt was
born and died in Halle, where he served as organist to the
Margrave of Brandenburg. His keyboard works were
published in three parts entitled *Tabulatura nova*, 1624, of
which Part III is devoted to plainsong settings for organ,
while Parts I & II contain works some of which are suited to
organ, some to harpsichord, and some to either instrument.
The harpsichord pieces, like those of his master, include
dances, fantasies, and variations on both chorales and
popular tunes. One of the latter, the set entitled *Cantilena
Anglica Fortunae* (C.E., p. 126), is shared with Sweelinck,

who supplied three variations while Scheidt wrote five. The English song of the title, the well-known *Fortune my foe*, is one proof of the line of influence that extended from England through the Netherlands to Germany. It was also set by William Byrd (*FWVB*, No. 65), and was mentioned by Shakespeare, Jonson and other playwrights of the period.

The most influential of all the northern composers apart from Sweelinck was another foreigner, Dietrich Buxtehude (1637–1707). He was born in Helsingør in Denmark, studied there with his father, and at the age of twenty-nine was awarded the important post of organist at the Marienkirche in Lübeck, on condition that he married his predecessor's daughter – a neat arrangement that he later failed to impose on Handel. In 1673 he instituted the *Abendmusiken* in the city: performances that took place yearly on the five Sundays before Christmas, and to which the twenty-year-old Bach walked two hundred miles in 1705 in order to hear the aged Buxtehude play. Though primarily an organ composer (as far as the keyboard is concerned), Buxtehude's clavichord and harpsichord works are by no means negligible. They comprise twenty-nine suites, generally consisting of an allemande, courante, saraband and gigue, and some half dozen sets of variations. Specially beautiful are the short variations on the air *Rofilis* (C.E., p. 78) taken from Lully's *Ballet de l'impatience*, 1661. There is also an impressive dance suite in the form of variations on the chorale *Auf meinen lieben Gott*, which, though obviously a clavichord or harpsichord piece, is maddeningly included among the organ works of the modern edition(C.E., vol. 3, p. 37). The following extract from the courante, with the original melody printed above for ease of comparison, shows how a Lutheran chorale can turn up in the most unlikely context:

Three other composers who also influenced Bach were
Pachelbel, Kuhnau and Böhm, of whom only the last
worked in the north. Georg Böhm (1661–1740) was a
follower of Buxtehude, and organist at the Johanneskirche
in Lüneburg when Bach was a choirboy at the nearby

Michaelskirche. Bach's admiration for the older man long survived, for he included a minuet by Böhm in the book of pieces that he compiled for Anna Magdalena in 1725. Böhm's keyboard works are more evenly divided than Buxtehude's between organ and clavichord or harpsichord, both in quantity and in quality. The clavichord or harpsichord pieces consist of eleven suites containing from three to seven movements each, a less interesting Prelude, Fugue and Postlude in G minor (C.E., p. 23) and the isolated minuet mentioned above (C.E., p. 68). There are, besides, several sets of chorale variations, a Capriccio in D (C.E., p. 18) and a Prelude in F (C.E., p. 10), which sound equally well on organ or harpsichord. The suites are specially worth investigating – for example, No. 9 in F minor (C.E., p. 59) – for they have a warmth of feeling and an ease of harmonic movement that is rare in the pre-Bach era.

Before passing on to Pachelbel and Kuhnau, another central German composer may be mentioned briefly. He is Johann Krieger (1651–1735), who was born in Nuremberg and eventually occupied a post as organist in Zittau. His keyboard works were published in two volumes, the *Sechs musicalische Partien*, 1697, devoted to suites for clavichord or harpsichord, and the *Anmutige Clavierübung*, 1699, intended mainly for organ. The second volume is the more interesting; and some of its pieces, such as the Fantasie in D minor and the Prelude in G minor (C.E., Nos. 20 & 18 respectively), sound just as well on the clavichord or harpsichord as on the organ.

Johann Pachelbel (1653–1706) was also born in Nuremberg, and after serving in various posts elsewhere returned there for the last ten years of his life as organist of the Sebaluskirche. His influence on Bach was mainly in the direction of the organ chorale prelude, of which he published two books. A third volume, the *Hexachordum Apollinis*, 1699, contains six sets of variations for harpsichord, and is dedicated jointly to Buxtehude and Ferdinand Tobias Richter, court organist in Vienna. The best of the variations is the set in F minor on the *Aria Sebaldina*, named after the patron saint of his own church. Other works remained in manuscript during the composer's lifetime, such as the two harpsichord Ciaconas in C major and D major (of which the first is the more interesting), and the delightfully gay Fuga in A minor (C.E., p. 49).

The harpsichord works of Johann Kuhnau (1660–1722), Bach's predecessor at the Thomaskirche in Leipzig, appeared during his lifetime in four volumes: two books of *Clavier Uebung*, 1689/92, each containing seven partitas (suites); the *Frische Clavier Früchte, oder sieben Suonaten*, 1696, the earliest publication in which the title 'sonata' is given to a solo as distinct from an ensemble work; and the [6] *Musicalische Vorstellungen einiger Biblische Historien*, 1700, or 'Musical representations of some Bible stories'. The last volume is of particular interest since it contains some of the earliest examples of extended programme-music that attempts to describe subjects more varied than the formal battle-pieces of composers such as Byrd and Frescobaldi. Thus the fourth Sonata, *The mortal illness and recovery of Hezekiah*, has sections devoted to *The lament and prayers of Hezekiah* (symbolized by a setting of the chorale *O Haupt voll Blut und Wunden*), *His confidence in God*, and *His joy in recovery*. The approach may be naïve, yet it stimulated Bach in 1704 to write his witty and less earnest Capriccio in B flat, BWV 992, *On the departure of a beloved brother*.

The last composer to concern us in this chapter is Georg Philipp Telemann (1681–1767). Born in Magdeburg four years before Bach and Handel, who were both his friends, he was an immensely prolific composer and eventually became Music Director to the five principal churches of Hamburg. Handel admired his music sufficiently to borrow from it in his easygoing way. And Bach not only included Telemann's Suite in A major in the book of instructional pieces he compiled in 1723 for his eldest son, Wilhelm Friedemann, but also asked him to stand as godfather to his second son, Carl Philipp Emanuel. Telemann's keyboard compositions, of which some half dozen volumes were published during his lifetime, are never less than adroit, and occasionally strike a vein of grave beauty that is as unexpected as it is rewarding. Only four of the books have so far been reprinted, of which three are intended specifically for harpsichord: the [7] *Fugues légères et petits jeux*, 1730, where each two-part fugue is followed by a group of shorter pieces; the [*36*] *Fantaisies*, c. 1740, each consisting of two short movements, the first of which is repeated after the second to form an ABA structure; and the *VI Ouverturen*, c. 1745, where each overture in the French style is followed by a slow and a quick movement. The remaining volume, the *XX kleine Fugen*, 1731, shows Telemann at his best. It is intended for any keyboard instrument, and reverts unexpectedly to a use of the almost obsolete church modes. The fugues are never longer than two pages; yet within this framework each one manages to establish a mood that is as precise as its structure. They explain more easily than any of his other works why Telemann should have been so much admired by his two infinitely greater contemporaries, Bach and Handel.

(*Extracts from the same author's* Style and Interpretation, Early French Keyboard Music *and* Early Italian Keyboard Music *have been incorporated in this chapter by permission of the publishers, the Oxford University Press.*)

MODERN COLLECTED EDITIONS
OF EARLY KEYBOARD MUSIC MENTIONED
IN THE FOREGOING CHAPTER

England: Collections

The Robertsbridge Fragment (British Museum, Add. MS. 28550), etc: *Keyboard Music of the Fourteenth and Fifteenth Centuries*, ed. Willi Apel; *Corpus of Early Keyboard Music*, I; American Institute of Musicology, Dallas, 1963.
British Museum, MS. Royal App. 58 (10 pieces by Hugh Aston & Anon.): *Early Keyboard Music*, vol. I, ed. Frank Dawkes, Schott, 1951.

The Mulliner Book, ed. Denis Stevens: *Musica Britannica*, I, Stainer & Bell, (2nd ed.) 1954.
The Fitzwilliam Virginal Book, ed. Barclay Squire & Fuller Maitland, Breitkopf & Härtel, Leipzig 1899 (good cheap reprint by Dover Books, New York, 1963).
Parthenia, ed. Thurston Dart, Stainer & Bell, 1960.
Musicks Hand-maide, 1663, ed. Thurston Dart, Stainer & Bell, 1970.
The Second Part of Musick's Hand-maid, 1689, ed. Thurston Dart, Stainer & Bell, 1962 (2nd ed.).

England: Composers

Thomas Arne, *Eight Sonatas or Lessons*, facsimile ed. G. Beechey & T. Dart, Stainer & Bell, 1969.
John Blow, *Six Suites*, ed. Howard Ferguson, Stainer & Bell, 1965.
John Bull, *Keyboard Music*, I & II, ed. J. Steele, F. Cameron & T. Dart; *Musica Britannica*, XIV & XIX, Stainer & Bell, 1960/63.
William Byrd, *Keyboard Music*, I & II, ed. Alan Brown; *Musica Britannica*, XXVII & XXVIII, Stainer & Bell, 1969/71; *My Ladye Nevells Book*, ed. Hilda Andrews, Curwen, 1926 (good cheap reprint by Dover Books, New York, 1969).
Jeremiah Clarke, *The Contemporaries of Purcell*, vol. 5, ed. J. A. Fuller Maitland, Chester, 1921.
William Croft, *The Contemporaries of Purcell*, vols. 3 & 4, ed. J. A. Fuller Maitland, Chester, 1921.
Giles & Richard Farnaby, *Keyboard Music*, ed. Richard Marlow; *Musica Britannica*, XXIV, Stainer & Bell, 1965.
Orlando Gibbons, *Keyboard Music*, ed. Gerald Hendrie; *Musica Britannica*, XX, Stainer & Bell, 1962.
Matthew Locke, *Keyboard Suites* & *Organ Voluntaries*, ed. Thurston Dart, Stainer & Bell, 1959/57.
Thomas Morley, *Keyboard Works*, vols. 1 & 2, ed. Thurston Dart, Stainer & Bell, 1959.
Henry Purcell, *Eight Suites* & *Miscellaneous Keyboard Pieces* (together comprising the complete harpsichord works), ed. Howard Ferguson, Stainer & Bell, 1968 (2nd ed.).
Thomas Roseingrave, *Compositions for Organ & Harpsichord*, ed. Denis Stevens, Pennsylvania State University Press, 1964. Contains four suites, etc.
Thomas Tallis, *Complete Keyboard Works*, ed. Denis Stevens, Hinrichsen, 1953.

William Tisdall, *Complete Keyboard Works*, ed. Howard Ferguson, Stainer & Bell, 1958.

Thomas Tomkins, *Keyboard Music*, ed. Stephen Tuttle; *Musica Britannica*, V, Stainer & Bell, 1955.

Iberia & The Netherlands: Collections

Susanne van Soldt MS. (British Museum Add. MS. 29485), printed complete in *Dutch Keyboard Music of the Sixteenth and Seventeenth centuries*, ed. Alan Curtis; *Monumenta musica Neerlandica*, III, Vereniging voor Nederlandse Musiekgeschiedenis, Amsterdam, 1961.

Klavierboek Anna Maria van Eyl, ed. Frits Noske; *Monumenta musica Neerlandica*, II, Vereniging voor Nederlandse Musiekgeschiedenis, Amsterdam, 1959.

Iberia & The Netherlands: Composers

Antonio de Cabezón, *Obras de música para tecla, arpa y vihuela*, ed. Higini Anglès; *Monumentos de la música Española*, vols. 27–9, Instituto Español de Musicologia, Barcelona, 1966.
22 selected pieces in *Claviermusik* & *Tientos und Fugen*, ed. Macario Santiago Kastner, Schott, Mainz, 1951/58.

Manuel Rodrigues Coelho, *5 Tientos* & *4 Susanas*, ed. Macario Santiago Kastner, Schott, Mainz, 1951/58.

Jan Pieterszoon Sweelinck, *Keyboard Works*, fascicles 1–3, ed. G. Leonhardt, A. Annegarn & F. Noske; *Opera Omnia*, I, Vereniging voor Nederlandse Musiekgeschiedenis, Amsterdam, 1968.

Italy: Collections

Faenza Codex: to be published by the American Institute of Musicology.

Venice, Biblioteca Marciana, MS Ital. iv. 1227 (= 11699); the complete manuscript is printed in *Balli antichi veneziani*, ed. Knud Jeppesen, Hansen, Copenhagen, 1962.

Frottole intabulate da sonare organi, Andrea Antico, Rome, 1517; six of the twenty-six pieces are reprinted in Knud Jeppesen, *Die italienische Orgelmusik am Anfang des Cinquecento*, Munksgaard, Copenhagen (2nd enlarged edition), 1960.

Intabolatura nova di varie sorte de balli, Antonio Gardane, Venice, 1551; reprinted complete as *Intabolatura nova di balli*, ed. W. Oxenbury & T. Dart, Stainer & Bell, 1965.

Italy: Composers

Marco Antonio Cavazzoni, *Recerchari, motetti, canzoni*, 1523; reprinted complete in Knud Jeppesen, *Die italienische Orgelmusik am Anfang des Cinquecento*, Munksgaard, Copenhagen (2nd enlarged edition), 1960.

Girolamo Cavazzoni, *Orgelwerke*, I & II, ed. Oscar Mischiati, Schott, Mainz, 1959/61.

Girolomo Diruta: no complete edition.

Marco Facoli, *Intavolatura di balli*, 1588, ed. Willi Apel, American Institute of Musicology, Dallas, 1963.

Girolamo Frescobaldi, *Orgel- und Klavierwerke*, vols. 1–5, ed. Pierre Pidoux, Bärenreiter, Kassel, 1948/49.

Andrea Gabrieli, *Orgelwerke*, vols. 1–5, ed. Pierre Pidoux, Bärenreiter, Kassel, 1952.

Giovanni Gabrieli, *Composizioni per organo*, I–III, ed. Sandro Dalla Libera, Ricordi, Milan, 1957/59.

Luzzasco Luzzaschi, Benedetto Marcello, Giovanni Battista Martini: no complete editions.

Claudio Merulo, *Toccate*, I–III, ed. Sandro Dalla Libera, Ricordi, Milan, 1959. *Canzonen 1592* (Libro primo), ed. Pierre Pidoux, Bärenreiter, Kassel, 1954.

Bernardo Pasquini, *Collected Works for Keyboard*, vols. 1–5, ed. Maurice Brooks Haynes, American Institute of Musicology, Dallas, 1964–67.

Giovanni Picchi, *Intavolatura di balli*, 1621; reproduced in facsimile in the series *Collezione di trattati e musiche antiche in fac-simile*, Bollettino bibliografico musicale, Milan, 1934.

Alessandro Poglietti: no complete edition. The *Rossignolo* suite and some other pieces, ed. Hugo Botstiber, are published in *Denkmäler der Tonkunst in Oesterreich*, vol. 27, Jahrgang XIII/2, Artaria, Vienna, 1906, reprinted by Akademische Druck- und Verlagsanstalt, Graz, 1959.

Michelangelo Rossi, *Collected Keyboard Works*, ed. John R. White, American Institute of Musicology, Dallas, 1966.

Alessandro Scarlatti, *Primo e secondo libro di toccate*, ed. Ruggero Gerlin; *I classici musicali italiani*, vol. 13, Milan, 1943. [29]

Toccate per cembalo (the 'Higgs MS.'), ed. J. S. Shedlock, Bach, 1908–10.

Domenico Scarlatti, *Opere complete*, vols. 1–11, ed. Alessandro Longo, Ricordi, Milan, 1906 ff. Contains 545 of the 555 known sonatas; as the volumes contain no complete index it is essential to have the companion *Indice tematico* (*in ordine di tonalità e di ritmo*), Ricordi, Milan, 1937. A model edition is Scarlatti, *Sixty sonatas*, ed. Ralph Kirkpatrick, Schirmer, New York, 1953. A new complete edition is being prepared by Kenneth Gilbert for Heugel, Paris, 1971–.

Domenico Zipoli, *Orgel- und Cembalowerke*, I & II, ed. Luigi Ferdinando Tagliavini, Müller, Heidelberg, 1959. The harpsichord works are in vol. 2.

France: Collections

Pierre Attaingnant: of the seven books of keyboard pieces published by Attaingnant in 1530/31, vols. 1–3 (Chansons) are reprinted in *Transcriptions of chansons for keyboard*, ed. Albert Seay, American Institute of Musicology, Dallas, 1941; vol. 4 (Dances) in *Keyboard Dances from the Early Sixteenth Century*, ed. Daniel Heartz, American Institute of Musicology, Dallas, 1965; and vols. 5–6 (Mass-movements, Magnificats, etc.) & vol. 7 (Motets) in, respectively, *Deux livres d'orgue* & *Treize motets et un prélude pour orgue*, ed. Yvonne Rokseth, Société Française de Musicologie, Paris, 1925/30.

France: Composers

Jacques Champion de Chambonnières, *Œuvres complètes*, ed. Paul Brunold and André Tessier, Senart, Paris, 1925. Reprinted by Broude, New York, 1967. *Les deux livres de Clavecin*, ed. Thurston Dart, Oiseau-Lyre, Monaco, 1970.

Louis Nicolas Clérambault, *Pièces de clavecin*, ed. Paul Brunold and Thurston Dart, Oiseau-Lyre, Monaco, 1964.

François Couperin, *Œuvres complètes*, ed. Maurice Cauchie and others, Oiseau-Lyre, Paris, 1932/33. Vol. 1 contains the didactic work, *L'art de toucher de clavecin*, and vols. 2–5 the complete harpsichord works. An unlimited, revised reprint, ed. Thurston Dart, 1970. A new edition of the *Pièces de clavecin*, vols. 1–4, ed. Kenneth Gilbert, Heugel, Paris, 1969–71. *L'Art de toucher le clavecin,* ed. in French, German and English by Anna Linda, Breitkopf & Härtel, Leipzig, 1933.

Louis Couperin, *Pièces de clavecin,* ed. Paul Brunold & Thurston Dart, Oiseau-Lyre, Monaco, 1959. *Pièces de clavecin,* ed. Alan Curtis, Heugel, Paris 1970.

François Dagincour, *Pièces de clavecin,* ed. Howard Ferguson for the series *Le Pupitre,* Heugel, Paris, 1969.

Jean Henri d'Anglebert, *Pièces de clavecin,* ed. Marguerite Rœsgen-Champion, Société Française de Musicologie, Paris, 1934.

Louis Claude Daquin: no complete modern edition.

Charles Dieupart, *Six Suites,* ed. Paul Brunold, Oiseau-Lyre, Paris, 1934.

Elizabeth Jacquet de la Guerre, *Pièces de clavecin,* ed. Paul Brunold and Thurston Dart, Oiseau-Lyre, Monaco, 1965.

Nicolas Lebègue, *Œuvres de clavecin,* ed. Norbert Dufourcq, Oiseau-Lyre, Monaco, 1956.

Gaspard le Roux, *Pieces for Harpsichord,* ed. Albert Fuller, Alpeg Editions, New York, 1959.

Louis Marchand, *Pièces de clavecin,* ed. Thurston Dart, Oiseau-Lyre, Monaco, 1960.

Jean-Philippe Rameau, *Pièces de clavecin,* ed. Erwin Jacobi, Bärenreiter, Kassel, 1958.

Germany: Collections

Ileborgh Tablature, Paumann *Fundamentum,* and other early sources in *Keyboard Music of the Fourteenth and Fifteenth Centuries,* ed. Willi Apel, American Institute of Musicology, Dallas, 1963.

Buxheimer Orgelbuch, ed. Bertha Antonia Wallner; *Das Erbe deutscher Musik,* vols. 37–39, Bärenreiter, Kassel, 1958.

Wilhelm Merian, *Der Tanz in den deutschen Tabulaturbüchern,* Breitkopf & Härtel, Leipzig, 1928, reprinted by Georg Olms, Hildesheim, 1968. Includes 184 pieces from the tablatures of Kotter, Ammerbach, Schmid the Elder and the Younger, Paix, Löffelholtz, Nörmiger and Marechall.

Hans Joachim Marx, *Tabulaturen des 16. Jahrhundert; Schweizerische Musikdenkmäler,* VI, Bärenreiter, Kassel, 1967. Contains Kotter's two MSS. complete, and two lesser anonymous MSS.

Germany: Composers

Georg Böhm, *Sämtliche Werke für Klavier und Orgel*, vols. 1 & 2, ed. Johannes and Gesa Wolgast, Breitkopf & Härtel, Wiesbaden, 1952. Vol. 1 contains the works for clavichord or harpsichord.

Dietrich Buxtehude, *Klaver Vaerker*, ed. Emilius Bangert, Hansen, Copenhagen, 1944. Contains the pieces for clavichord or harpsichord. *Orgel-compositionen*, vols. 1-4, ed. Josef Hedar, Hansen, Copenhagen, 1952

Johann Kaspar Ferdinand Fischer, *Sämtliche Werke für Klavier und Orgel*, ed. Ernst V. Werra, Breitkopf & Härtel, Leipzig, 1901. Reprinted by Broude, New York, 1965.

Johann Jakob Froberger, *Orgel und Klavierwerke*, vols. 1-3, ed. Guido Adler; *Denkmäler der Tonkunst in Oesterreich*, VIII, XIII & XXI, Artaria, Vienna, 1897/99 and 1903. Reprinted by Akademische Druck- und Verlagsanstalt, Graz, 1959.

Johann Krieger, *Gesammelte Werke für Klavier und Orgel*, ed. Max Seiffert; *Denkmäler der Tonkunst in Bayern*, Band 30, Breitkopf & Härtel, Leipzig, 1917, reprinted 1968.

Johann Kuhnau, *Klavierwerke*, ed. Carl Päsler; *Denkmäler deutscher Tonkunst*, IV; Breitkopf & Härtel, Leipzig, 1901, reprinted 1958.

Georg Muffat, *Apparatus musico-organisticus*, 1690, ed. R. Walter, Coppenrath, Altötting, 1957.

Johann Pachelbel, *Klavierwerke*, ed. Adolf Sandberger; *Denkmäler der Tonkunst in Bayern*, Band 2, Breitkopf & Härtel, Leipzig, 1901, reprinted 1968. The *Hexachordum Apollinis*, 1699, is edited separately by Hans Joachim Moser and Traugott Fedtke, Bärenreiter, Kassel, 1964.

Samuel Scheidt, *Tabulatura nova*, 1624, ed. Max Seiffert and Hans Joachim Moser; *Denkmäler deutscher Tonkunst*, I, Breitkopf & Härtel, Leipzig, 1892, reprinted 1958. Also as vols. VI and VII of Scheidt's *Werke* ed. Christhard Mahrenholz, Ugrino, Hamburg, 1953.

Arnolt Schlick, *Tubulaturen etlicher Lobgesang und Lidlein*, 1512, ed. Gottfried Harms, Ugrino, Hamburg 1957.

Georg Philipp Telemann, [6] *Fugues légères et petits jeux*, c. 1730, ed. Martin Lange, Bärenreiter, Kassel, 1929. *XX kleine Fugen*, 1731, ed. Traugott Fedtke; in *Orgelwerke*, II, Bärenreiter, Kassel, 1964. [36] *Fantaisies pour le clavessin*, c. 1740, ed. Max Seiffert, Bärenreiter, Kassel, 1935, reprinted by Broude, New York [n.d.]. *VI Ouverturen, c.* 1745, ed. Hugo Ruf, Schott, Mainz, 1967.

ANTHOLOGIES

Willi Apel, *Keyboard Music of the Fourteenth and Fifteenth Centuries*, American Institute of Musicology, Dallas, 1963. Contains the earliest known keyboard music.

Louis Diémer, *Les clavecinistes français*, vols. 1–4, Durand, Paris [n.d.]. Seventeenth century. A good selection of pieces, but over-edited.

Aristide & Louise Farrenc, *Le trésor des pianistes*, vols. 1–23, Philipp, Paris, 1861–72. Sixteenth to mid nineteenth century. The most comprehensive anthology, now out of print.

Howard Ferguson, *Style and Interpretation*, vols. 1–4, 1963–4. Vols. 1 and 2 are concerned with early keyboard music in, respectively, England & France, and Italy & Germany. *Early French Keyboard Music*, vols. 1 and 2, 1966. *Early Italian Keyboard Music*, vols. 1 and 2, 1968. *Early German Keyboard Music*, vols. 1 and 2, 1970. *Early English Keyboard Music*, vols. 1 and 2, 1971. All published by the Oxford University Press, London. These volumes aim to supply a clean text, and contain many of the works mentioned in the present chapter.

Hans Fischer & Fritz Oberdörffer, *Deutsche Klaviermusik des 17. und 18. Jahrhunderts*, vols. 1–9, Vieweg, Berlin-Lichterfelde, 1960. Devoted to works that are not difficult technically.

Walter Georgii, *Keyboard Music of the Baroque and Rococo*, vols. 1–3, Arno, Cologne, 1960. A well-edited selection, with the editor's additions clearly differentiated from the original.

Macario Santiago Kastner, *Cravistas portuguezes*, vols. 1 and 2, Schott, Mainz, 1935/50. Early Portuguese keyboard music.

Louis Oesterle, *Early keyboard music*, vols. 1 and 2, Schirmer, New York, 1932. A good selection of pieces from Byrd to Scarlatti; but the texts are over-edited and at times unreliable.

Gino Tagliapietra, *Antologia di musica antica e moderna per pianoforte*, vols. 1–18, Ricordi, Milan, 1931–33. Second to Farrenc in comprehensiveness; but the texts are over-edited and very often unreliable.

Luigi Torchi, *L'arte musicale in Italia*, vols. 1–7, Ricordi, Milan, 1897–1907. The keyboard music is in vol. 3.

2

Bach and Handel

CHARLES ROSEN

*

By the early eighteenth century the *clavier* – the keyboard, in whatever form – had become the fundamental musical instrument and the centre of musical life. It was a position which it held for perhaps two hundred years, only to lose it at the beginning of the present century. Its tyranny was never greater than during the High Baroque period, the age of Bach and Handel; in its role of continuo it bound together and directed the performance, not only of operas and concertos, but even of polyphonic vocal motets. The great Renaissance composers had been trained as singers, but Handel, Bach, Scarlatti and Couperin were all basically keyboard performers. In theory, eighteenth-century musical education was founded (as today's still is) on a codified and degenerate version of sixteenth-century vocal counterpoint; in practice, it consisted in the realization of figured bass and the playing of counterpoint on a keyboard. I do not mean to call in question the vocal origin – always latent and always capable of being recalled – of eighteenth-century counterpoints, but by 1700 the linear nature of vocal writing had been completely translated into instrumental terms. Even vocal ornaments had been transformed and returned to singers in an instrumental form less suited to the voice; Bach often treats his singers only as another instrument in an orchestra.

It is time to return to the old evaluation of Bach's keyboard music as the centre of his work. The fashionable placing of the cantatas as Bach's principal achievement has only been harmful: it has led to an over-emphasis on extra-musical symbolism, reinforced by Schweitzer's tendentious aesthetic, and to an unhappy view of Bach's musical imagination, which was fantastically rich and yet predominantly non-dramatic. Even when the emotion expressed is as terrifying and as powerful as in the opening chorus of the *St Matthew Passion*, the procession to Golgotha, the means of portrayal are still essentially those of meditation, raised, certainly, to an intensity that music had never known before. Handel's simple and often brutal juxtaposition of masses, his use of the elements of music almost in block form, was rarely attempted by Bach, whose largest forms arise always from a concentration on the smallest details and the fullness of their expressive power. This conception of musical composition as a meditative art is particularly suited to keyboard style. Only a keyboard instrument affords at once the spontaneous intimacy of improvisation and the possibility of polyphonic texture Both are essential to an art that derives its greatness from the latent expressive force of even the most commonplace and most ordinary musical detail, and it is in this way that Bach's art appears to be so personal even with the most impersonal material. To understand this art, we must remember that, although Bach was one of the most famous improvisors of his age, he could never begin a series of improvisations with one of his own themes – he had to start from the idea of another composer – and he disapproved of composition at the keyboard itself. Improvisation recollected in tranquillity was at the heart of his musical sensibility: free of the pressure of the occasions and circumstances for which the cantatas and some of the large chamber works were written. The keyboard music reveals with the greatest directness the movement of his thought.

A division of Bach's keyboard works into those with pedal and those without pedal is essentially an artificial one, for such a distinction would have had little significance for Bach himself. Within thirty years of his death, however, keyboard music had become exclusively manual; when Mozart called the organ 'the king of instruments' he knew he was expressing an old-fashioned opinion, but Bach even had a set of pedals at home to be used with a clavichord. The *Well-Tempered Keyboard* contains one work – the A minor fugue of the first book – that, indeed, cannot be played as written without the use of a pedal keyboard. Much of Bach's music was not intended to be played on any specific keyboard instrument. The clavichord, harpsichord, organ and, at the end of his life, the pianoforte were all available to him, and we know that he used them all; many of the preludes and fugues of the *Well-Tempered* would go equally well on any one of them. Even the requirement of two keyboards does not automatically rule out the clavichord; as one could, and very often did, put one clavichord above another and play double-manual pieces on them. Essentially the clavichord was the inexpensive practice instrument for home use, while the harpsichord, far more costly even in its simplest form, was suitable for public, or semi-public occasions. From its invention around 1720, the pianoforte was an answer to the problem already discussed at that time that the most refined nuances of tone, dynamics and even phrasing that one had learned practising at home on the clavichord were inaudible in public and useless on a harpsichord. (The organ, prohibitively expensive for the home except in the form of a small *positive*, inapt for the playing of most of Bach's works, was, in Germany at least, rarely used for the performance of secular music.)

It is for this reason that the old controversy about which instrument the six great trio sonatas, the C minor Passacaglia and many other works were intended for is largely meaningless; it is not a question that could have been asked in the early eighteenth century. The trio sonatas, in particular, are essentially practice pieces, études, in short. They would have been studied on whatever instrument with a pair of keyboards and a set of pedals was handy – at home, it would most likely have been a clavichord. This does not rule out their performance on an organ when the occasion afforded one; that would be like forbidding a performance of a modern piano work on a nine-foot concert grand. The trio sonatas, like the Chopin studies, are not only finger exercises, but great music and great display pieces as well. But practising on an organ was not as simple a matter in the eighteenth century, in pre-electric days when manpower as well as an organist was needed to produce a sound; furthermore, occasions for the public performance of secular, non-operatic music were rare at that time. The trio sonatas are not so clearly intended for use during a church service as the toccatas and fugues. It would be wrong, however, to conclude that the sonatas were written only for clavichord; there was, indeed, very little specific literature for the clavichord before Bach's death in 1750. This basic interchangeability of instrument for most keyboard music of the time must be accepted before we can begin to understand the relatively limited number of works intended for a specific instrument. It was not indifference to instrumental sound on the part of the composers that gave rise to this large repertory of keyboard music adaptable to any keyboard instrument of the time, but the impossibility of control over the conditions of performance. There were, of course, no recitals in any recognizable sense of the word; keyboard music was private.

This fundamental privacy is one source of the greatness of Bach's keyboard style; he was as essentially a private composer as Handel was a public one. The nature of this inwardness has been most often misconstrued; it is not an early nineteenth-century composer's expression of emotions too personal for completely public revelation (as in many of Schumann's and Brahms's works, which half display and half repress their sources), and even less is it the disdain and precious avoidance of public effect of some twentieth-century composers like Satie. Bach's meditative keyboard style is at once subjective and objective, and it arises from a triumphant and profound comprehension of the musical conditions of his age. Not only were most composers of the time keyboard performers, but almost every professional keyboard performer was, in the most

literal sense, a composer. The teaching of music largely
entailed the teaching of composition; not only the grammar
of music – harmony and counterpoint – and the technique
of ornamentation, reading figured bass, and improvisation,
but the actual writing of music. Singers might escape the
practice of composition, although even Handel's cook, who
sang in his opera company, knew counterpoint*; and many
string and wind players may not, perhaps, have used their
knowledge. But there can have been very few keyboard
players – even amateur players – who did not compose a
few pieces. After 1720, almost all of Bach's keyboard music
became didactic, or was arranged in pedagogic form; he
even called most of his published works 'Keyboard Exercises'. They are, however, exercises to develop techniques
not only of playing but also of composition, models of form
that can stimulate, the works of a composer speaking to
other composers.

   That this was Bach's avowed intention is stated firmly in
his own hand on the title-page of the Inventions, which
proclaims that his purpose was only partially to provide
'honest instruction' in playing music in two and three parts;
it was also to teach 'lovers of the keyboard . . . not only to
have good inventions, but to develop them well, and . . .
also to obtain a strong foretaste of composition'. The Well-
Tempered Keyboard is, in fact, the greatest pedagogic work in
the history of keyboard technique; it has been a fundamental part of the education of practically every pianist
since the death of Mozart. Even before it had been published,
Beethoven made his reputation as a young boy by playing
it. Yet it is as much or more a treasury of musical form, a
textbook of composition, as a work of keyboard instruction, and in acknowledgement of this, Chopin began his
own great set of studies, op. 10, with a bow to the Well-
Tempered Keyboard, an imitation of the first Prelude in C
major.†

   *There is no reason, as Tovey has pointed out, not to take Handel's
joke ('My cook knows more counterpoint than Gluck') quite seriously.
   † 'Practise Bach for me' was Chopin's way of writing 'Yours sincerely'
in his letters to pupils.

This integral relationship between composition and 'keyboard practice' (style and technique) makes Bach's keyboard music seem so personal and yet so objective. It is, indeed, written to act on the emotions, to move, even to dazzle; but it is not directed at an audience. It is the performer that the music is written for, and to him that the composer is speaking – the performer, who was at least half a composer himself at that time, a student of composition, or already a connoisseur. 'For the young musician who wishes to learn and for the pleasure of those already skilled': the title of the *Well-Tempered Keyboard*, like the title-pages of all the published volumes of Bach's *Keyboard Practice*, asserts the ancient classical tie between the pleasure and the profit of art. 'Keyboard Practice to Refresh the Spirit of Music-Lovers' was not an empty title. It cannot be sufficiently emphasized that the keyboard works are written above all for the pleasure of the performer. One small detail will show to what an extent this aspect of musical life changed within thirty years of Bach's death. When Mozart rediscovered the music of Bach and began enthusiastically to compose fugues himself, he said that fugues must always be played at a slow tempo, as otherwise the successive entrances of the theme would not be clearly heard. Nevertheless, it is remarkable how often Bach tries to hide the entrance by tying the opening to the last note of the previous phrase, how much ingenuity he has expended in avoiding articulation, in keeping all aspects of the flowing movement constant. Yet though many of the entrances in Bach's fugues are, in Mozart's terms, inaudible, there is one person – the performer – who is always aware of them. If in no other way, he can always sense them through his fingers. The physical (or, better, muscular) pleasure in playing Bach is equal to that found in any other composer, and it is closely related to the purely musical qualities of the work by the sense of a genuinely tactile tracing of a musical line.

The very reproach often levelled at the keyboard – its blending, even confusion, of separate contrapuntal lines –

made it the ideal medium for Bach's art. This inability of
the instruments to make in practice the clear-cut distinc-
tions that were made in theory embodied the tendency
towards a completely unified texture and the powerful
vertical harmonic force that characterized so much of the
music of the early eighteenth century; it is, in fact, the
equivalent of figured bass. Bach's career has often been
presented as a reactionary one, an attempt to retain the old
contrapuntal values that were going out of fashion. It was
more than that; it was a reconciliation of the most advanced
and most modern harmonic experiments with the traditional linear structure. What held these forces together was
his profound development of the main principle of animation of Baroque music, the use of generic motive from which
everything flows and takes its shape. No composer carried
this farther than Bach; even the large harmonic sequences
so typical of the period appear in his music to arise solely
from the single motive which characterizes each individual
work. It is this that makes the music seem like a kind of
improvisation; indeed, the trick of improvisation is to start
with a few notes and to draw an entire piece of music from
them.* Bach is the first major composer in history whose
art is so closely allied to improvisation, and only a keyboard
instrument allows for a complex improvisation controlled
by one mind. No work gives a performer the illusion of
improvising – of himself as composer – so strongly as a work
of Bach, and perhaps this is why his music has given rise to
so much gratuitous rewriting by editors.

Once the intimate setting of this art is accepted, many of
the problems of playing it either disappear, or are seen in a
new light. Most of Bach's keyboard work was written to be
played for oneself or for a few other musicians; some of it
was written almost as much for meditation as for listening.

---

* The forms and the textures of the early eighteenth century altogether
are closer to improvisation than those of any other time in Western music
before jazz; in spite of Mozart's and Beethoven's fame as improvisators
their 'planned' forms differ radically from their 'improvised' ones, as
we can see from written cadenzas and from their fantasias.

Many of the more complex details can be appreciated fully only by the performer – they can be heard, but their significance can never be entirely grasped until one has felt them under one's fingers. This implies that much of the calculation of dramatic effect necessary for public performance was never intended for the greater part of Bach's keyboard music – except in the large organ works, it tends to be felt as an excrescence, an intrusion of the performer. Even the shaping of structure and its elucidation are not crucial in private, and performances of a Bach fugue in which the theme is consistently emphasized to the detriment of the other voices can only be a travesty of a work whose chief glory lies in the relation of the voices to each other and in their interaction; it must, however, be granted that it is exactly this sort of relation that is much easier for the performer to hear (since he knows it is there) than for the listener.

The much-debated problem of added ornamentation loses a great deal of its importance when the nature of music written above all to be played for oneself is considered. The public genres of eighteenth-century music, like the Handel operas, are skeletons that need to be fleshed by improvised ornament; the conditions of public performance, indeed, demanded a continuously varying and ever more elaborate ornamentation. But very little of this applies to Bach, principally because when he grew older, as we can easily see from the successive versions of his works, he tended to write out the ornaments in a fairly complete form – it was a contemporary complaint that he left nothing to the performer.* The later works, too, are so conceived as to make ornamentation superfluous; while it is possible to ornament the repeats of the dances in the early suites, it is far more difficult to find a varied ornamentation for the repeats in the *Goldberg* Variations that would not seem intrusive, so

* 'Every ornament, every little grace, and everything that one thinks of as belonging to the method of playing, he expresses completely in notes.' Scheibe, 1737 (*The Bach Reader*, ed. Mendel and David, New York, 1966, p. 238).

much do the original ornaments seem an indissoluble part of the conception of the melodic arcs. With *The Musical Offering* and *The Art of the Fugue*, the question of ornamentation has, in most cases, become irrelevant.

Bach was not the first composer to write out the ornaments in full – there were precedents for this, cited by his defenders in answer to the attacks during his lifetime. This full notation springs, in part, from the nature of Bach's music: its display of art, its classic combination of instruction with pleasure. But it is also related to Bach's situation as *Kapellmeister* of a provincial town. Leipzig, the most important of the cities in which he was employed, had not even the prestige of the musical culture of Dresden. Handel, on the other hand, was accustomed in London to performances by international virtuosi; his singers would have been outraged by any attempt to prescribe too closely their style of performance and the ornaments they employed. We must not, however, assume that only the notation of Bach's music is the result of his reliance upon provincial musicians, and that we can perform it today with quite the same freedom as Handel's; the essence of the music itself lies in that fuller notation. If improvised ornament received such a definitive form under his hands, we can only be thankful for his failure to obtain a more illustrious post. A great part of what we know about early eighteenth-century performance comes, indeed, from Bach's fully notated scores.

We do not know exactly how many of the later works of Bach were begun earlier, and only revised, arranged and collected later; many of them exist in several versions, and we have certainly lost a great many of the early manuscripts. Even the theme of the *Goldberg* Variations, published in 1742, was written by 1725 at the latest; it would be impossible to prove that none of the variations was written many years before publication. What is certain is that the last thirty years of Bach's life were spent in ordering his entire musical output, collecting old works and putting them

together with newly-written ones to fill out the monumental
schemes that he had drafted. He revised old cantata movements and set them side by side with new compositions to
form a Mass, and he rearranged a series of chorale preludes
as a complete Mass as well. In these schemes no distinction
was made between old and new works; some of the pieces
in the second book of the *Well-Tempered Keyboard*, collected
in 1744, were almost certainly written before many of those
from the first book, dated 1722. An attempt to trace a
strict chronological development of Bach's keyboard works
would be highly problematical at best, and the results
more than doubtful. It would not justify upsetting Bach's
own order.

Bach's great systematic arrangements have a musical
value in themselves, in spite of the fact that the ordering has,
in general, very little to do with performance of the music;
even the Mass in B Minor may have been as little intended
for performance at one sitting as the Organ Mass (or Part
III of the *Keyboard Practice*), for which 'anthology' would be
the closest description. Not that Bach was incapable of the
creation of an organic work of massive dimensions, as the
great *Passion according to St Matthew* can testify, but neither
the B Minor Mass nor the *Well-Tempered Keyboard* are such
works. In one sense, however, 'anthology' does not do
justice to the full significance of the ordering, which indeed
transcends the individual parts. How little this significance
has to do with actual performance, however, can be seen
from the original edition of the Organ Mass, framed by the
E flat Prelude at one end and the fugue (the *St Anne*) at the
other; the fact that these two pieces belong together in
performance gives meaning to the device of printing them
so far apart with the Mass between them. Of course,
performance – private, not public – was not out of the
realm of possibility for many of Bach's great collections; he
himself was known to have played through the entire
Well-Tempered Keyboard for a pupil. It would, however, be an
absurd distortion of the work to claim that it was principally intended for such a unified performance, although it

exists as a unity even if it takes one year to play through it, and draws part of its meaning from that unity.

We must beware of calling such orderings intellectual or even theoretical; the existence of musical significance which transcends the immediate audible experience is essential to Bach's style. I do not imply anything mystical, or anything that is beyond our ordinary experience of music; only that some of the most important forces in the development – the actual movement through time – of a work of Bach are latent in its material without becoming audible until the moment that he chooses to make them so. The forces shaping the movement of a work by Beethoven or Mozart are far more immediately audible. The dissonance in the seventh bar of the *Eroica* audibly implies the modulation to F major that Beethoven only makes when he repeats the passage hundreds of bars later; the movement to G flat major in the slow movement of Mozart's G minor Symphony begins in the second bar. The material of the great classical composers is directional – we can hear the opening of the *Eroica* moving towards something, even if we cannot name it, and its arrival, presented as a surprise, is also a logical satisfying of a dynamic tonal impulse, the resolution of a tension.* But if what is to happen in a work of Mozart and Beethoven is already to some extent audible in its opening, there is absolutely nothing about the theme of the Fugue in B flat minor from the *Well-Tempered*, Book II, that allows us to *hear* that it can be played in stretto at the ninth at the distance of one beat:

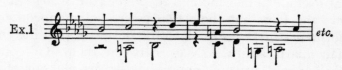

Ex.1   etc.

Yet this quality of the theme, together with the even more complicated possibility of playing it in stretto with its own inversion in double counterpoint at the tenth, is essential to

*This is not mere hindsight: it is only harder to appreciate tonal relations after a century of chromaticism and a half-century of atonality and blurred tonality.

the shape of this fugue. All this is latent in the theme, but not audibly active when we hear it. Static as this kind of structure essentially is, the stretto has an impressive and exciting musical effect comparable to the most dynamic structures of the later classical period. In this comprehension of these latent musical relationships, in his ability to draw from them all their power and significance, Bach was without equal in the history of music. The great collective structures – his arrangement of a considerable part of his life's work into formal musical patterns – are the large-scale equivalent of these latent relationships.

Many early works were, however, left uncollected, perhaps many more than have come down to us. One of the earliest, written when Bach was nineteen, is the *Capriccio on the departure of a beloved brother*, one of the freshest and most delightful works by a young composer. Although there are a few moments of awkwardness, it has a naïve, spontaneous humour that appears only rarely in Bach's later work; with its picturesque qualities, its tone pictures, its gaiety, it is the work of a young talent that could have developed a much more popular manner. Another beautiful work is the so-called Fantasy in C minor, which is really a movement in early 'sonata-form' (i.e., with the tonal structure and thematic pattern of a dance-movement, but with a more dramatically expressive character): this short but powerful work was to be the prelude to a fugue, which remains in fragmentary form (was it really never finished, or is the only manuscript that has come down to us an incomplete fair copy?) The unfinished fugue has some of Bach's most daring harmonic progressions. In addition to these better-known works, there are a number of early toccatas, most of them vigorous, splendidly imaginative and prolix. A little-played but concise and impressive work is the Fantasy and Fugue in A minor (BWV 904); the massive sonorities of the opening and the long melodic line of the fugue are as suited to the organ as to the harpsichord.

The most important, and the most astounding of these

isolated works is the famous *Chromatic Fantasy and Fugue*. As Forkel, the first biographer of Bach, wrote, the 'fantasia is unique, and never had its like'. In spite of its size and the passion that fills it, it may have been written specifically for the clavichord, perhaps the only work of Bach intended for the clavichord alone. In some ways it is the most advanced of Bach's keyboard works, the closest in style to the expressive clavichord pieces of the 1760s and 1770s, the ancestor of the passionate, mannered and fantastic improvisation of Philipp Emanuel Bach. The expressive recitatives are particularly effective on the clavichord with its capacity to reproduce vocal nuances; the final burst of octaves at the end of the fugue is the only example of such an effect in Bach, and suggests a keyboard instrument where no doubling was possible.* The fugue, however, has the spacious structure and the public brilliance of the great organ fugues and is as inexorable in its movement as the fantasy is varied.

Some of the collective works were published by Bach himself, but there would be little point in considering them as in any way distinct from the unpublished sets. The engraving of Bach's music was not a profitable venture; many works may have come into being in the hope of publication, and were then left expediently in manuscript. In any case, wide circulation in manuscript was very common throughout the eighteenth century, for literature as well as music. There are more eighteenth-century manuscript copies of the *Well-Tempered Keyboard* still in existence today than there ever were sold first-edition copies of *The Art of the Fugue*, and there were certainly hundreds more that have been lost; it was a famous work long before its first printing in 1801.

Pupils who came to study with Bach were started on the two- and three-part Inventions (or Sinfonias, as he himself called the latter). They are, indeed, the most deliberately

---

*This, however, is not conclusive evidence that only a clavichord was intended. Scarlatti's works are full of octaves, and there is no doubt that they are for harpsichord.

instructive of all his works. They were arranged by the composer in different orders, the most interesting being the original one: first, all the tonalities that have tonic chords with only white keys, in ascending sequence (C major, D minor, E minor, F major, G major, A minor); and then, in descending order, the other tonalities easily playable by a young musician (B minor, B flat major, A major, G minor, F minor, E major, E flat major, D major, C minor). In this way, the problems of fingering would go from the easy to the more complex.*

The Inventions appear for the first time in the little book for Wilhelm Friedemann, Bach's eldest son, and this is the only manuscript of Bach to give us some of his indications of fingering (although in other pieces than the Inventions). Bach has, indeed, been given the main credit for modern keyboard fingering, a claim that goes too far, for others had used the crossing-under of the thumb before him, and the examples we have of his fingering are not as advanced as some (his son, Philipp Emanuel, in particular) would like to have us believe. These fingerings were written down when Bach was over thirty-five years old, an age after which he is not likely to have changed his technique.

With all their clearly technical purpose, no other finger exercises in musical history – not even the Chopin Studies – have the unaffected grace and sweetness of the Inventions. Only a gentle gravity betrays their didactic intention. They were explicitly written to foster not a virtuoso technique, but a singing style of playing. The ornamented versions of several of them were written later; there is no reason to doubt that the ornaments were added according to the capacity of the student, and it is by no means certain that an unornamented performance would not have been completely acceptable. It must be remembered, too, that the art of improvising ornament was an essential part of musical education.

* Chopin's belief that F sharp major is the easiest of the scales and that one should start with it is an exceptional view, although a wise one, and based on more modern ideals of virtuosity.

Throughout, the two- and three-part writing theoretic-
ally remains absolutely pure: there are never more than two
(or in the Sinfonias, three) notes played or held at the same
time. But this apparent purity is in fact doubly corrupt
(both through the larger harmonic movement, and the
inner implications of each voice), and the corruption is the
source of the rich power of these works. The two and three
voices are not genuinely independent, and they rarely imply
less than four-part counterpoint. The way the theoretical
independence is offset by the imposition of what may be
called an anti-polyphonic conception of musical form can
be seen in this passage from the E major Sinfonia:

where the melodic line appears – but in *notation* only – to
cross from voice to voice, starting in the treble and going to
the bass. In reality, it is heard as a completely integral
line; it moves from one voice to another only when it
touches the notes of the main harmony, and these notes are
then successively held down, so that the melodic line acts
to provide its own figured bass. In short, this is not true
three-part writing, but a melodic outline accompanied by
three- and four-part harmony. The retention of theoretical
purity, however, is not just a display of ingenuity, but an

inner contradiction; the interplay between these forces informs every measure of these works.

The richness of harmony comes from Bach's ability to imply two and even three voices with only one. In the history of music only Mozart has equalled him in the art of using a single vocal line to trace the fullest harmonic sonorities. Bach's mastery can be seen in the briefest quotation:

Ex.3

Here, the upper voice is really three voices, and the A sharp in the right hand is not continued until several notes later; it lingers in our ears after it has stopped sounding because it is an unresolved dissonance. It is, in fact, dissonant to its own next note, for a single line of Bach provides its own tensions and resolutions. This is the technique that makes the solo violin sonatas such convincing works. It has often been noticed that Bach's fugue themes provide their own bass, and they very often provide perfectly worked-out inner voices as well. That is why they are so expressive and so complete in themselves.

In other words, the individual voices work within a larger system of harmonic movement which transcends their integrity; and, in addition, this integrity is broken down from within by the same system. Yet the ideal of contrapuntal purity in the Inventions (and in other works, like the *Goldberg* Variations and *The Art of the Fugue*) does not thereby lose in power. It gains instead a pathos – an unattainable goal that is kept alive by the pretence of achieving it. Bach's career was an unavailing protest against the powerful harmonic forces represented in Rameau's new theory, forces of which he was himself such a master. In the

Inventions, we are carried along by the surge of these forces with a movement that is consistent and unified: almost in direct opposition, the thin, pure integrity of the individual lines is eloquently sustained as if against heroic odds.

The *Well-Tempered Keyboard* is a monument to the ambiguity of tonal relations. It is not only the fact that all twenty-four major and minor keys are each represented here by a prelude and fugue that makes equal temperament indispensable; even if every piece were transposed into C major and C minor, they would still not be possible in just intonation. There is no space here to discuss just how equal Bach's system of tuning a keyboard really was, for this is a complex and perilous subject. But there is no doubt that he demanded enough equality in all his works – keyboard works or any others – for the ear to confuse E natural and F flat, for example, for the most far-reaching enharmonic effects to be possible. Tonal harmony is, of course, partly based on the natural physical series of overtones, and partly developed independently as a symbolic language. Bach's harmony is, in one sense, not only unnatural but anti-natural; it insists on confounding what nature has kept separate, and in so doing, incomparably enriches the expressive range of music. The great advance in musical style is not the possibility of playing in any key, but the possibility of passing rapidly from one to another – above all, the possibility of blending flat and sharp modulations (i.e. modulations at the limit of the subdominant and dominant directions).

Experiments with equal temperament date back at least to the sixteenth century, and many Renaissance pieces assume a certain amount of equality in order to be sung or played at all intelligibly. Nor is the *Well-Tempered Keyboard* the first collective work to exploit equal temperament; there were already precedents before 1720. But Bach's music is the first to make consistent and continuous use of the complete range of expressive modulation that comes from the falsification of just intonation. The *Well-Tempered Key-*

board is the celebration of this new-found 'unnatural' power.

The encyclopaedic nature of the work is not just a consequence of its didactic purpose, but a demonstration of the freedom that comes from equal temperament. The first book was compiled in 1722 from works, uneven enough in style (although not in mastery) to imply that they were written over a period of many years. There are fugues as concentrated and subtle as the C sharp minor, coarse and dramatic as the A minor, abstract and enchanting as the A major, lyric and loosely organized as the D sharp minor. The range of the preludes is certainly as great, from the pure improvisation of the first in C major and the rambling grandeur of the E flat major, to the profound Sarabande in E flat minor, and the delicate charm of the F sharp major. Both preludes and fugues are essentially 'character pieces'; vivacity of sentiment is their reason for existing.

The *Well-Tempered Keyboard* is so familiar to us today that it is difficult to realize how it opened up the entire field of tonal musical expression. Indeed, Bach's contemporaries and immediate successors did not fully comprehend this in spite of the innumerable copies of the work which circulated, and of its fame and importance for keyboard style and teaching. Music took a different turn, towards the rendering not of sentiment, but of dramatic action. Only by the late 1770s, when both Mozart and Haydn were trying to recapture the lost richness of the polyphonic style, was the importance of the *Well-Tempered Keyboard* finally understood; not only did Mozart study the work, he even arranged several of the fugues for string trio and string quartet – music was at last becoming more public, and the intimacy of these pieces was not considered a hindrance to concerted performance. By the early nineteenth century, they had become part of the foundation of the first Romantic generation's style, as important for the music of Chopin as for Schumann and Mendelssohn.

The second book of the *Well-Tempered* was compiled twenty years later, and differs only in being generally a little more sober, more inward, less ostentatious and, perhaps, less various as a whole. It is equally glorious: the great Ricercar in B flat minor, the double counterpoint at the tenth and twelfth of the Fugue in G minor, the rich chromaticism of the Fugue in A flat major may have peers but no superiors. There is little point in singling out individual pieces from collections where each one gains so much from its presence in the larger framework. I should not wish, however, to endorse the theory that the order of the preludes and fugues was set with an eye to performance; beyond the calculated improvisatory simplicity of the first two preludes of Book I, the place of any work in the ordering does not seem to me to have in any way determined its character. The order is not a temporal one – the twenty-fourth prelude and fugue does not really come *after* the first one – but a simultaneous radiation from a central idea. The order not only transcends performance, but has nothing to do with it – all of which, however, does not take away from the magnificent effectiveness for performance of each individual piece.

The first works that Bach chose for publication were the harpsichord Partitas, one of three sets of six dance suites for keyboard that he put together at some time during the 1720s. The other two sets are the *English* Suites and the *French* Suites; it would be unprofitable to ask which came first – claims of precedence have been advanced for both, and some of the Partitas, as well, must be dated years before their publication. The *English* Suites, so called, it seems, because they were written for an English nobleman, are no less French than the *French* Suites – more so, in fact, as their courantes have the characteristic 6/4 against 3/2 opposition of the French form (a cross-pulse rather than a cross-rhythm), while the courantes of the *French* Suites are in the smooth-running Italian style. The *French* Suites are, in general, less elaborate, beginning directly with the allemande without any introductory piece; they are also easier and less brilliant. We know that Bach used the suites for teaching: students were given them when they had mastered the Inventions, probably beginning with the French and going on to the English. The six Partitas exhibit the greatest variety of organization and of style.

The suite is the most useful and most characteristic form of court music. Did Bach choose a set of six for his first publication in order to further his attempts to exchange his post at the Leipzig Church of St Thomas for a court appointment such as he had had previously at Cöthen, where he spent the most fruitful years of his life? The dance suite is the closest the High Baroque came to public, secular music for a solo keyboard; although keyboard recitals, of course, did not yet exist, the popular dance-forms permitted the suite to bridge the gap between private, learned music and the larger concerted forms, and they were indispensable at semi-private musical occasions. Bach's suites turn, in fact, both ways: they are often as fully and as richly worked out polyphonically as the fugues of the *Well-Tempered*, and they attain easily the variety and even the orchestral effects of the concerto grosso.

The basic outline of the suite was a simple succession of dances to which, as suited the additive sensibility of the Baroque composer, other dances could be attached or inserted. The fundamental skeleton was allemande, courante, sarabande, minuet and gigue. A gavotte or a bourrée could be inserted, generally after the minuet; a great variety of other dances or dancelike movements were possible: passepieds, badineries, rondos, airs, etc.; and variations (or doubles) of the dances could be added. The basic order has something of the slow–fast–slow–fast arrangement of the baroque four-movement sonata. It is out of this very loose form that the later eighteenth-century sonata develops, more influenced by the articulated dance forms than by the more fluid movements of many of the sonatas of the first half of the century.

The allemande and the courante generally belong together, often beginning with the same melodic pattern.*

* Sometimes whole suites were unified in this way, but it was not a practice of Bach.

The allemande is always a smooth, evenly flowing piece –
the French style of performance, with its tendency to add a
lilting irregularity of rhythm, was expressly forbidden by
Couperin in his allemandes, and this dance has always the
air of a quiet prelude. The French courante with its elaborate rhythmic oppositions and its texture could be replaced
by its Italian namesake, with a brilliant, rapid and even
motion. The sarabande was generally the expressive centre
of the work, and the minuet has the place that it retained in
the late eighteenth- and nineteenth-century quartet and
symphony. The forms of all these dances are, almost
without exception, that of early 'sonata form' in two
sections, each repeated, the first going from the tonic to the
dominant, and the second from the dominant back to the
tonic. The pattern of the second part is largely symmetrical
to the first, although it is most often somewhat more
elaborate, with the melodic fragmentation and the rapid,
sequential half-modulations of a development section
combined with the repetition of the pattern, generally
before the return to the tonic. Speaking with historical
hindsight, the dance forms were the most modern and the
most progressive of the time.

In most respects, Bach's treatment of these forms was the
reverse of progressive. He consistently avoided the articulation of phrasing that Scarlatti used so brilliantly, and that
was to become so fundamental in the style of the second
half of the century. There is, indeed, periodic and symmetrical phrasing in Bach, but it is generally hidden under
the overlapping and continuous rhythmic flow. The articulation of form is also minimal; while the move to the dominant is often marked by new melodic patterns, and even by
a subtle increase of motion, the return to the tonic is never
a dramatic effect, rarely set off from what precedes it, but
is rather a gradual drift as part of a seamless structure. The
last quarter of each dance is often not the resolution that
the later classical style was to find so indispensable, but the
occasion for some of Bach's most poignant harmonic effects.
The symmetry of the two halves is also High Baroque, with

inversion playing an important role, although here Bach often begins to work out something like the later classical form, using the inversion of the theme as a development, and reintroducing the original form with the return to the tonic – in this respect he even outpaces Scarlatti in his anticipation of later developments.

In general, however, the articulation of phrase and structure natural to the dance which, emphasized and dramatized, led to the great achievements of the late eighteenth century, was a facet of the suite that Bach was chiefly concerned to minimize in his concern for a unified and always expressive ebb and flow that is rarely allowed to disturb the continuity of movement. The climactic tensions do not often rise much above the general, compared with the dramatic strokes in the minuet of a Haydn or Mozart symphony, but the constant intensity in the piece as a whole is much greater. Only after his mastery of part of Bach's contrapuntal technique did Mozart occasionally attempt and achieve this consistently high level of intensity throughout a work.

Bach's most original contribution to the keyboard suite was his development of the opening movement; five of the six partitas, and five of the six *English* Suites have massive and brilliant first movements. Many of them transfer to the single keyboard not only the grandeur but the specific effects of contemporary orchestral style. The following passage from the splendid opening movement of the *English* Suite in G minor shows how a Baroque composer could achieve a crescendo before the Mannheim orchestra had trained themselves for their famous effect:

To use the two keyboards of a harpsichord when playing a piece like this is to ruin Bach's conception, which is not 'terraced dynamics' at all; the contrast between solo and tutti sections is built into the writing, when it is played simply on one keyboard, by the simple thickening of sound. Pianists frequently make similar nonsense when they equalize all the dynamics and forget that on a harpsichord four notes are louder than two, and that Bach was relying on this to make his point.

The typical Baroque sonority, in any case, is not 'terraced dynamics', as is so often thought; except in the concerto grosso, a contrast of loud and soft is the exception rather than the rule, a luxury rather than a necessity. The most common dynamic system at that time is a consistent level with the small but subtle range of nuances that both the clavichord and the harpsichord (used with unchanging registration) were capable of. Registration stops were changed manually in Bach's time (except, perhaps, for a few harpsichords in England which introduced pedals for that purpose). An assistant to pull the stops, used for the more elaborate organ toccatas and preludes, would have been ridiculous for playing a suite of dances. The range of stops available on even the most expensive harpsichords was small; the sixteen-foot was not widespread until Bach's death. I do not imply that the style of music followed the nature of the instrument: quite the reverse. It is a change in style that forces the invention of new instruments. Not only are all of Bach's orchestral effects ideal in most of these opening movements with the relatively unified sonority of one keyboard of a harpsichord; they are also only distorted by the gratuitous addition of a second dynamic system.*

These grand openings – the Sinfonia of the C minor Partita, the Overture in French style of the D major Partita, the concerto forms of many of the *English* Suites – completely transform the keyboard suite. Before Bach, suites were often anthologies, grouped by key, from which one could play as few or as many dances as one liked. Bach may have treated his own that way – the A major *English* Suite has two courantes, the second of which has two doubles; a selection may have been intended here. In any case, some of his suites were written by accretion, and earlier versions have fewer movements. But the new, massive introductions of these works announce a new conception of unity, answered by the complementary development of the finale. The gigues take on a completely novel brilliance and weight, and are often fugues as rich and serious as any that Bach wrote. Some of these virtuoso gigues are also harmonically among his most daring essays, with dissonances that reach anything else his century attempted, and they have a rhythmic fury that is almost unique in his work.

How exceptional 'terraced dynamics' were is shown in Bach's second publication, Volume II of *Keyboard Practice*,

* However, one copy of the A major *English* Suite suggests the use of two manuals in that work.

devoted only to works for double keyboard, the *French* Overture and the *Italian* Concerto – both open imitations of orchestral style. Separated by this requirement from the six Partitas (Volume I of *Keyboard Practice*), they were intended to form a group with them, as Bach transposed the original version of the *French* Overture from C minor to the less convenient B minor so that the eight works of the two volumes should cover all the keys of A, B, C, D, E, F, G and H.* Even with the most courtly of his works, the encyclopaedic purpose was not absent. In addition to the basic tonalities, he also covers the opposing national styles of the eighteenth century. These eight works are, like almost all of Bach's keyboard music, intended as exemplars. The extraordinary variety of forms in the Partitas was as much for instruction as amusement – not that the two were very different for Bach.

In the works of Volume II, a double-keyboard harpsichord is used for a contrast between solo and tutti sections in concerto style, for echo effects in the *French* Overture, and for imitating the sound of a solo line over accompanying instruments in the *Italian* Concerto. Bach's command of the ornamental grandeur of the orchestral French style did not always require two manuals: the opening of the D major Partita is also in French style, and needs only one manual. And it is amusing to note that the echoes at the end of the *French* Overture are not naturalistic, but decorated echoes. The two keyboards are here an essential part of the decorative conception of the work. With the *Italian* Concerto Bach not only recreated a convincing opposition of solo and tutti, in concerto grosso form, but surpassed all his Italian models. All the Vivaldi concertos he had arranged for keyboard in his youth had taught him the style, but no Italian contemporary was capable of the combination of unity and imaginative vigour, of consistency and variety displayed by the outer movements, and, above all, of the immensely long

*B in German is B flat, and H is B. (The transposition to B is less practical on the harpsichord than C as the lowest note on the instrument is a G. This put the low dominant of B, i.e. F sharp, out of reach.)

sustained arabesque of the slow movement, one of the most profound creations of the century.

The concerto grosso form of the central fugue of the *French* Overture and of the outer movements of the *Italian* Concerto – the alternation of a short orchestral tutti with solo episodes derived from it – is the natural form of the High Baroque. The contrast between ensemble and solo sections was never intended to be an emphatic one; it was an art that developed its effects cumulatively, with a slight and continuous rise and fall of intensity, rather than one with a clear dramatic outline. This alternation of ensemble and solo sections is also the shape of most chorale preludes, which move between the *cantus firmus* and derived or contrasted episodes. Even Bach's fugues fall into this form: it is reported that he insisted on the need to embellish a fugue with episodes, and the alternation of these episodes with the entrances of the themes is his most characteristic form, closely related in shape to the concerto grosso.

The polarity of the Italian and French style is at the heart of Bach's work; as a German, he was in the enviable position of being able to balance their claims equitably. The difference between Italian and French styles is chiefly rhythmic. Italian rhythm looks outward: it falls into simple, even groups, which are then contained in larger units. The *Italian* Concerto opens immediately with two absolutely clear four-bar phrases; the periodic grouping by phrases imposes a broader pulse on the basic one, and a large-scale dramatic movement is possible within this framework. French rhythm looks inward: it subdivides, and there is a consequently heavy use of syncopation, reinforced by lavish ornament. French style is, therefore, relatively static compared to the more vigorous Italian manner, which, indeed, carried the seeds of the future within it. Bach is the only composer who represents a genuine synthesis of both national styles (apart from religious music, the German tradition had very little strength at that time). Even the other great German, Handel, while his mastery of the French tradition was undeniable, relied principally upon

Italian forms. Bach was able to combine the expressive ornamental weight and grace of French style with the sustained line and dynamic rhythm of Italian music; except for the operatic field, where Handel and Rameau were supreme, and the still infant proto-classical 'sonata' style, Bach summed up the entire musical life of his time. The *French* Overture and the *Italian* Concerto are a declaration that he assumed the role consciously. Bach's aesthetic was an exhaustive one, as if he were driven in all that he did to cover everything, to work out all the possibilities: all the tonalities, all the genres, all the styles, all the permutations. His daemon is a key to the magnitude of his achievement, as well as to its form. The great cycles are not only an ordering of his life's work but of his era as well.

The third volume of *Keyboard Practice* came out in 1739 and contained largely organ music: chorale preludes based on the words of the Mass. But it also contained the Four Duets, examples of pure two-part writing which, in daring and sophistication, surpass the Inventions. Nothing can better emphasize Bach's consideration of all his keyboard music, with and without pedals, as a unity than their publication here.

In the last ten years of his life, Bach's style became intensely concentrated; the great collective works now developed from a tiny kernel, each one drawn from only a single theme. He wrote four variation sets for keyboard; the *Goldberg* Variations for harpsichord with two keyboards, *The Art of the Fugue* for single keyboard (except for one fugue for two keyboards, four hands), the Chorale Variations on *Vom Himmel Hoch* for organ with two keyboards and pedals, and *The Musical Offering*, in which the two ricercars are for single keyboard without pedals. These four sets are at once the most personal and the most generalized of Bach's works, models of contrapuntal ingenuity and composition that still speak to anyone that plays them with an intimacy and an expressive directness that have no parallel elsewhere in the eighteenth century.

The elegance of the *Goldberg* Variations is its glory: it is the most worldly of Bach's achievements, with the *Italian* Concerto. The theme dates back to a little practice-book that Bach compiled for his second wife many years before, a sarabande, richly ornamental and deeply expressive. The thirty variations are on the bass of the theme, and they come in triads: one brilliant variation for crossing hands, one canon (starting with a canon at the unison, and going through all the intervals until the ninth) and a 'free' variation – a siciliana, a fugue, a French overture, or an accompanied solo. The final variation, in place of the expected canon, has a *quodlibet*: two comic songs combined over the bass of the theme. At the end, the sarabande is repeated. The two central canons, at the fourth and the fifth, are each inverted canons; the last canon, at the ninth, provides its own bass, and does not need a third voice. The variety of mood, rhythm, style and sonority is dazzling.

If Goldberg's birth certificate is read correctly as 1727, he must have been fourteen years old when, as one of Bach's pupils, this greatest of all Baroque virtuoso works was written for him to play for his patron, Count Kaiserling. Essentially a creation of the comic spirit, it also contains some of the most moving passages that Bach ever wrote. A survey of most of the forms of secular music of Bach's time, an encyclopaedia like most of Bach's published works, it represents the art of ornamentation at the highest point it ever reached. Baroque variation is above all the art of ornamentation, and here everything is written out, every grace made manifest.

Even if the variations were intended to be treated only as an anthology, even if Bach's age would have offered no public, and few semi-public, occasions for playing the composition as a whole, no large keyboard work of comparable size before Beethoven achieves such unity in the modern sense. The minor variations are strategically placed to vary the harmony. A massive French overture opens the second half of the work. The use of two keyboards offers a variety of sound effects, particularly in the accompanied solos (in the other double-keyboard variations for crossing hands no great contrast is intended*; the virtuosity provides its own interest). Above all, there is a real sense of a finale; after the profoundly tragic twenty-fifth variation, the music gradually increases in brilliance until the great comic *quodlibet*, and the quiet return of the theme. Except for the *St Matthew Passion*, in no other work is the depth of Bach's spirit so easily accessible, and its significance so tangible.

On 7 May 1747, at Potsdam, King Frederick the Great personally condescended to play on the pianoforte a theme of his own for Bach to improvise into a fugue. The Silbermann pianoforte was the King's favourite instrument; he is reported to have acquired fifteen of them. Bach improvised a three-voice fugue, and was later asked by Frederick for the seemingly impossible: a fugue on the same theme in six voices. Bach hesitated – the royal theme was too complex for such improvisation – and improvised a six-voice fugue on a theme of his own. On returning to Leipzig, however, he took up the King's challenge in the wonderful, long six-voice ricercar of the *Musical Offering*, the *Prussian* Fugue, as he himself called it. It is a miracle of art, in its compression of the richest and most elaborate harmonies in six real parts into the space of two hands.† Architecturally, it is at the same time the simplest – no stretto, no inversion, no counter-theme, nothing but the six entrances, and six further playings of the theme, once in each voice, embedded in the most varied and expressive episodes – and the most imposing of all Bach's fugues. All the majesty and lyricism of Bach's art are concentrated in this work.

The three-voice ricercar is generally assumed to represent at least in part, the first fugue that Bach improvised for the King: its character is indeed improvisatory, lighter and

---

* Several of these variations even bear the indication 'for one or two keyboards': to play a real forte on Bach's harpsichord, one had to couple the keyboards by pulling one on top of the other and pressing down two keys at once. The direction told the player to play these variations on only one keyboard if he had the strength and the agility.

† It was one of Philipp Emanuel's proudest boasts about his father that this fugue was for two hands alone.

more colourful than its great companion, but with several striking harmonic effects. Both pieces were published in *The Musical Offering*, along with a trio sonata and several canons, all based on the theme; the *Prussian* Fugue, although written on two staves, was printed in score to display the perfection of the part-writing. The two ricercars are the only works of Bach that pianists are entitled, with any historical justification, to claim as their own. We must remember, however, that the eighteenth-century piano had a thinner and clearer sound than the modern one, and that there was nothing about the style of the music or the practice of the time to preclude playing them on any other keyboard instrument. One important quality of the *Prussian* Fugue is veiled on the organ: the expressive attack or accent when five or six voices move together; and there are many places in this work which are beautifully calculated to this end. Harpsichord, clavichord and pianoforte do more justice to this great work, and it is only fair to add that Frederick the Great, to whom it was dedicated, would have listened to it played on a pianoforte. Pianists should be more jealous of their first masterpiece, still one of their greatest.

It is by now generally recognized that *The Art of the Fugue* was also intended for the keyboard – eighteen of the most complex contrapuntal works do not fall only by chance within the compass of two hands (the one exception – a three-voice mirror-fugue – being arranged by the composer himself for two keyboards, four hands).* The only question is: was it also intended for anything except a keyboard? The publication in score proves nothing; the preface added by Marpurg in 1752 to the original edition tells us that this was for the convenience of reading. Anyone who has read the work from score at the keyboard will testify to the great advantage of the score over the piano reduction, and its aid to clarity and understanding. Arrangements and transcrip-

---

* The theory that *The Art of the Fugue* is either abstract or intended for instrumentation is an early twentieth-century muddle; the first great biographer of Bach, Spitta, classified it as a keyboard work, as we do again today.

tions were certainly common enough during Bach's lifetime, and he himself transferred many pieces from one medium to another. It should be added, however, that these transcriptions were never concerned with fugues as fully worked out and severe in character as the *Prussian* Fugue or the similar ones in *The Art of the Fugue*. This kind of music was exclusively keyboard in character throughout the first half of the eighteenth century. The delightful and varied textures of the trio sonata from *The Musical Offering* show clearly what Bach, at that time of his life, thought ensemble music should be. All the fugues that Bach or Handel wrote or arranged for ensemble are in a more concerted and brilliant style, with far less of the serious or 'learned' character of most of the pieces in *The Art of the Fugue*. Works as meditative and as contrapuntally rich would have been lacking in decorum in the guise of ensemble chamber music (or orchestral – the difference was hardly visible then). There is no instance of Bach's writing this kind of contrapuntal work except for keyboard. Nor was there any place for such music in early eighteenth-century musical life, where anything even as semi-public as ensemble music was expected to have a lighter character; religious music was allowed its earnest side, but rarely the completely undramatic seriousness of the six-voice ricercar or *The Art of the Fugue*, which is, in genre, style and technique, keyboard music through and through.

What keyboard, as usual, does not matter. As in *The Well-Tempered Keyboard*, one fugue of *The Art of the Fugue* needs a final pedal note; one canon goes beyond the range of the average clavichord. None of this would have deterred any of the rare purchasers of the original edition (only forty people bought a copy), even if he had had only a single clavichord. He would have placed his copy on the music rack of whatever keyboard was available, and read through the work, grateful for the clarity of the printing in score. Is the music for study or for playing? This question, still posed by some writers, allows a false choice; *The Art of the Fugue* was meant to be studied by playing it, to have its marvels

seen, heard, and felt under one's fingers. Some of the fugues
are among Bach's most effective, and should take their place
in the concert hall, but it is inconceivable that the composer
ever intended a complete performance of twenty works in
the same key and on the same theme, most of them, too, in
the same rhythm. *The Art of the Fugue* was meant to be
played over a period of time (which does not in the least
detract from its unity). Apparently simple, subtly complex,
with the ease of a lifetime's experience in every line, it must,
indeed, be played many times before its deceptive lucidity
can be penetrated.

The work was never finished; its plan, basically simple,
was altered during composition, and the order of the first
edition is certainly wrong. Like a gigantic set of variations,
each piece is based on the same theme. There are (1) four
simple fugues (two on the inversion of the theme); (2) three
stretto fugues (the second a French overture in style, and the
third with the theme in augmentation, diminution, and at
the original speed simultaneously); (3) two double fugues
(double counterpoint at the tenth and at the twelfth); (4)
two triple fugues (the second with the themes of the first
inverted); (5) four canons; (6) two sets of 'mirror fugues'
(each fugue with its double, which completely inverts every
note of each voice); (7) and last, an unfinished quadruple
fugue (there was to have been a second quadruple fugue,
which was never begun). The final section of this fugue –
the combination of the first three themes with the main
theme of the work – was still to write; Bach became blind
as he finished ·the third part of the fugue based on the
letters of his own name. The manuscript breaks off just as
the composer had, in effect, put his signature to the work that
was the summation of his art.

The style of *The Art of the Fugue* is that of a counterpoint
exercise; the theme is simple, the textures largely unchanging, uncontrasted. There are almost no dramatic
effects; the most fantastic modulations take place discreetly,
and the sequences are continually varied with a delicacy
unparalleled in Baroque music. All the intensity lies in the

individual lines, severe and expressive throughout. The power of sliding through several tonalities – touching them lightly and quickly – is seen here with an ease afterwards lost to music until Chopin's chromatic polyphony revived it:

Ex.5

and the texture has a transparency that makes light of the contrapuntal ingenuity. In the following stretto:

Ex.6

there is all the melting smoothness of the finest Renaissance vocal writing, although not only are the soprano and alto in canon at the fourth, but the tenor and bass together are in strict canon at the octave with the upper voices at the distance of only one beat, an intricacy of relationship belied by the simplicity of effect. A few pieces have a more brilliant aspect: the stretto fugue in the French manner, the mirror fugue arranged for two keyboards; but in general there is a unity of style that Bach never attempted in his other collective works, as if here everything were concentrated on the single details, the subtlety of the accents, the purity of the linear tracery. There is no more deeply moving music.

If Handel's keyboard music has so small a place in our estimate of his achievement, that is in part because he wrote so little of it down. Famous as a harpsichordist and as an organist, he left few pieces for keyboard alone, and even fewer of these can lay any claim to being in a finished state. Of the sixteen suites, only the first eight were prepared for publication by Handel himself; the rest are a hodge-podge of pieces put together out of works composed for different reasons – for teaching or as the basis of improvisation – some sketchy, carelessly written, and only half finished. Among the works published without Handel's consent, there are, of course, a few beautiful things, including the lovely theme that Brahms used for a set of variations.

Handel was the greatest master of the public genres of the High Baroque: opera, oratorio, outdoor festive music. The genius of these works lies in the large conception and in the vigour and force of the details, rather than their refinement. To a certain extent, the subtlety and the nuances were left to the performers, the singers in particular. No composer before Beethoven had Handel's command of large-scale rhythm, which is perhaps why Beethoven thought him the greatest composer of all. Handel's music turns outward; it is written directly at the public, and his finest works have an unlimited, if sometimes coarse, power, and an exhilaration and an excitement that Bach never tried to attain. More than in any other music, Handel's supremacy has suffered from difficulties of performance: the need for larger ensembles than Bach demanded, a dependence on virtuosity. Nineteenth-century styles of playing and singing and, more recently, pseudo-eighteenth-century performance practice, have only served to obscure his greatness further.

The first book of Suites, published in 1720, remains his only major contribution to contemporary keyboard literature. The Six Fugues or Voluntaries of 1735 are, as the title indicates, more organ works than anything else, although there was nothing to prevent their performance on any other keyboard as they are entirely manual; they are vigorous, loosely constructed and effective. The first eight suites, however, are unduly neglected today, although some of the pieces in them, the E minor fugue which opens Suite IV in particular, are among the finest that Handel ever wrote. It is a pity that, of all these suites, only the one in E major, with the set of variations popularly called the *Harmonious Blacksmith*, is familiar to concert-goers.

Not even those suites are completely notated; the opening prelude of Suite I, for example, is merely a sketch for an improvisation. A great many of the dances need not only ornamentation, but inner voices as well, for only the bare outlines have been traced. However, in a few cases, Handel has written out a fully ornamented form as a guide. The opening adagio of Suite III is complete with every note of its luxuriant ornamentation; as decoration it has never been surpassed for grace and simple expressiveness, not even by Bach. The whole of Suite II is impressive, with its brilliant allegro, the dramatic and lavishly decorated recitative-like second adagio, and the final hornpipe fugue. It is less a suite in the modern sense than an early four-movement Italian sonata.

Unlike Bach, Handel generally followed the tradition of beginning the allemande and the courante with the same motive. His suites are less elaborate, with fewer movements, and the gigues, far from being severe fugues, are unashamedly popular in style. Some of the pieces date back to 1705, but the English influence is already evident in many of the dance movements which must have come somewhat later. The rhythmic sweep is remarkable throughout in the calculation of the sequences, which are used with an imaginative vitality superior to all Handel's Italian and French contemporaries, and in the brilliant use of octave displacement for surprise and accent, as in the following passage from Suite II

Ex.7

where the music is twice impelled urgently forward by the
unexpected leap to another register. Also beyond the grasp
of any other composer of the time is Handel's dramatic
juxtaposition of different kinds of texture:

Compared to the dramatic power of this phrase near the
beginning of the fugue from Suite VIII, Scarlatti's abrupt
changes of texture are more playful, and more refined.
Handel's boldness is never witty. In the opening adagio of
this F minor Suite, he is capable of sustaining a lengthy
slow-moving progression with all of Bach's intensity; no one
ever avoided a cadence more naturally or more convincingly than Handel, and he achieved breadth and grandeur
of phrase with a simplicity that has been the envy of all
composers.

With the death of Bach and Handel, the end of the High
Baroque synthesis came quickly; in their last years they

were almost alone in sustaining it. How the style fell to pieces, how musical thought became fragmented, can be seen with Bach's children. Three of them became fine composers, and they appear to have divided up the realm of style, each one cultivating only a small plot of ground. Wilhelm Friedemann, the eldest of Bach's children, continued an eccentric and highly personal version of the High Baroque; the forms and, above all, the rhythmic movement are uncontrolled but there are moments of a bold and passionate sensibility. Johann Christian, the youngest, is the hardest to appreciate, for his music seems bland in comparison to that of the great generations before and after him. But he is responsible for much of the exquisite balance of the later classical style. In Mozart's music, the symmetry – which lies under all he wrote – is delicately varied, sometimes hidden; but he would never have attained this without the model of Johann Christian, whose exemplary feeling for proportion was a creative force that was crucial in the change that came over European music. His clarity and feeling for the articulation of form were as important in the development of the late eighteenth-century sonata as were the works of his more appreciated brother, Carl Philipp Emanuel.

The latter, is, to us, the most interesting of the Bach children, the master of a style which we may call, for lack of a better name, North German mannerism. His keyboard works are almost all entirely for the clavichord – specifically so, full of an ardent, intimate sensibility suited to that instrument. His music is dramatic, his feeling for tonal relationships bold, striking, and not quite coherent. His rhythmic organizations are still less satisfactory, and he passes abruptly – sometimes with a splendid, but momentary, dramatic effect – from a baroque sequential continuity to a classical periodic articulation. What is most dated in his music is the ornamentation, almost always applied, and rarely growing from within; he tried to do with decoration what Haydn, who was so indebted to him, was to learn to do with structure. Philipp Emanuel's forms have corresponding virtues and vices; they are daring, imaginative, and illogical. His conception of the rondo is an improvised fantasy on one theme that wanders·through several keys, with striking effects. He helped free the dramatic sensibilities of the next generation, and his eccentricity kept alive the ideal of serious expression at a time when music threatened to become only pretty, forcedly naïve, or comic. The end of the slow movement of the Sonata in D minor (written in 1766, but not published until 1781) is an example of this exacerbated sensibility:

The dissolution of the rhythm at the end is as remarkable as the violent contrasts of texture and the dramatic control of the line. His large output of keyboard music – fantasies, rondos, and sonatas – disappoints only because it creates and implies the highest standards; otherwise it gives nothing but pleasure. It is ironic to think that the development of a new, completely balanced and unmannered style (in the work of Mozart and the mature Haydn) was to coincide by a few years with the rediscovery of Sebastian Bach and Handel by Viennese musicians around 1780, after a generation in which Bach's children had each preserved a part of the tradition.

3

Haydn, Mozart and Their Contemporaries

EVA BADURA-SKODA

*

THE BACKGROUND

THE second half of the eighteenth century was a period of political and cultural ferment; the general instability was certainly reflected in its music. Even against a turbulent background – cultural revolution, the impact of the Enlightenment, social reforms in Austria and Prussia (including the abolition of serfdom and introduction of compulsory schooling), France's *ancien régime* and the events culminating in the Revolution, the Austrian wars against Prussia and Turkey – music history still appears vivid. Many diverse currents flourished simultaneously; among them affective expression (*Empfindsamkeit*), the felicitous galant style, early romanticism, the *Sturm und Drang* ('storm and stress') movement. Simultaneously in the final quarter of the century the Viennese classical style evolved with the consummate achievements of Haydn and Mozart, enhanced by mutual stimulus.

In the first decades of the century Baroque composers had still delighted in gestures of grandeur, flamboyance and intense pathos. Reacting against this, the next generation preferred music which was charming, effortless and entertaining, modest in scale and gratifying to perform, free of bombast and clever polyphonic devices. In Austria this period between the baroque and classical eras, often imprecisely termed the rococo, fell roughly between 1740 and 1770, and formed the background to the start of Haydn's composing career. After the middle of the century, however, expressive traits became increasingly conspicuous in instrumental music, until a more dramatic, profound and realistic mode of expression was championed in opera, and contrapuntal forms achieved a new respectability. This too was reflected in Haydn's output, for example in his *Sun Quartets*, op. 20, written in 1772 and notable for their fugal movements, and the great C minor Piano Sonata, UE 33 (Hob. 20). This work is a far cry from the lighter vein of the early sonatas, which are often little more than divertimenti; it attains new symphonic proportions and heightened expressiveness.

Italy still dominated the European musical scene in mid century, although chiefly on the operatic front; instrumental supremacy moved appreciably further north. No longer was the best orchestra in Europe to be heard at a Venetian orphanage, but at Mannheim and in Paris. Mid century Italian keyboard composers represented to perfection the attitudes of Rousseau's day; their work was pleasing, simple and galant, with a predominantly two-part texture of melody and accompaniment and a vocal approach towards melodic construction (singing allegro). Many of these keyboard writers are now virtually forgotten, but there is one exception outstanding in every respect: Domenico Scarlatti. His single-movement *Essercizi* were mostly written in Spain, and at first they were not in general circulation. It is doubtful whether Haydn, as a young man, knew any of Scarlatti's music at first hand; but he cannot have failed to encounter works by other better-known Italians in Vienna. All eighteenth-century Austrian composers display Italian influence to a more or less marked degree, among them G. C. Wagenseil (1715–77), a Viennese keyboard player and composer who was one of Haydn's most important precursors. This is hardly surprising: Vienna was not so very far from Italy and Italian had been its court language for over a century; it was politically connected with large parts of it and many of the performers and court musicians were Italians.

Berlin, the capital of Prussia, presented an utterly different picture during the reign (1740–86) of Austria's military antagonist, Frederick the Great. French was spoken at court and French music was in favour, though the king did condescend to acknowledge German achievements in instrumental music. His flute teacher, Quantz, wrote: 'When the best is selected, with due discrimination, from the musical tastes of various nations, the result is a composite taste which might very well, without overstepping the bounds of modesty, be described as German taste.' For decades Frederick the Great employed C. P. E. Bach, the foremost German keyboard composer of the post-baroque period. Bach created and developed the expressive clavichord style of northern Germany and wrote numerous keyboard sonatas, harpsichord concertos and a treatise on keyboard playing. Haydn claimed to have learned much from him, and Bach still exerted a detectable influence on Beethoven.

The baroque tradition in keyboard music was more tenacious in France than in Italy. Still the most important part of the repertory around 1750 were the suites of Couperin and Rameau, and these were only superseded by the advent of instrumentalists from Germany and Bohemia, and Italian singers and *opera buffa* composers. French composers scarcely wrote any keyboard sonatas; a sonata literature only developed as German composers began to settle in Paris in the fifties and sixties.

In England, the baroque style was cultivated for even longer, and not only because of Handel's dominating influence (died 1759); altogether the 'ancient style' conformed better than the galant rococo style to English conservatism. Italian musicians, however, had brought modern trends rather earlier to London. The 'Milanese' Bach, J. S. Bach's youngest son Johann Christian, finally achieved a break-through in London for the galant style shortly after Handel's death. London concerts were already thriving, and received further impetus from those organized by J. C. Bach and the German cellist Abel. Many music-publishing houses and instrument makers flourished in

London, testifying to widespread and active interest in music and ensuring an important place for London in the international scene.

Throughout Europe there developed an enormous demand for amateur chamber music which composers and publishers strove to meet, often with arrangements clearly tailored to a particular market. This is reflected in the remarkable number of 'accompanied' keyboard sonatas, manuscript and printed, surviving in libraries. Works for *Clavicembalo ou pianoforte avec l'accompagnement de violon* (flute, cello, etc.), are frequently solo works in disguise, pieces in which the accompanying part is, in effect, *ad libitum*. It often merely doubles the right hand of the piano part, or is confined to purely accompanying harmonies, Alberti figurations or isolated harmony-notes on strong beats. Most works of this type (such as the sonatas by Rutini and Schobert) would suffer little if performed by a pianist alone – unlike Mozart's later violin sonatas, some of which were published under a similar designation. Similarly the cello parts of Haydn's exquisite piano trios were often, in fact, more like *ad libitum* additions to sonatas for piano and violin. Furthermore, eighteen of Haydn's piano sonatas were issued in London in 1784 with a violin accompaniment by Charles Burney. Music for two performers, on one or two pianos, also falls into the category of chamber music and cannot receive treatment here, though Mozart's Sonata in D for two pianos, K.448, and above all the finest of his five sonatas for piano duet – the F major, K.497 – are virtuoso masterpieces almost without parallel in his solo keyboard works.

INSTRUMENTS

One perennial question must be raised before proceeding further; it concerns the instruments for which the keyboard works of this period were written. In 1750, harpsichord and spinet were still to the fore, followed by the clavichord (especially in northern and central Germany), with the pianoforte or *Hammerklavier* in third place. For although Cristofori in Florence had built a piano by 1709, or possibly even earlier, it was at least half a century before the mechanism had been sufficiently improved to earn it general esteem rather than isolated enthusiasm. In Berlin in the 1750s Quantz and C. P. E. Bach were writing about the fortepiano (pianoforte) in a way which presupposes knowledge of the instrument on the part of their readers. In fact, about fifteen Silbermann pianos had been supplied to Berlin (or Potsdam) by that time. No less an authority than C. P. E. Bach was insisting, in 1753, that the clavichord was still preferable to the piano, whose 'touch is difficult and requires thorough study'. However, in the second part of his treatise, which appeared in 1762, he did concede the piano equal rights with the harpsichord and clavichord. Indeed, some important technical improvements in piano construction do appear to be concentrated between the years 1753 and 1762. Piano-making enjoyed an unexpected boom, especially in southern Germany and shortly afterwards in England. Experiments by the Augsburg instrument maker Johann Andreas Stein resulted soon after 1755 in his escapement action, and later in a reliable damping mechanism as well. Mozart encountered this on his visit to Augsburg in 1777, and his enthusiastic response is well known. Stein also travelled to Paris in 1758 with the young Augsburg pianist and composer Eckard, who settled there shortly afterwards, publishing two sets of sonatas from 1763 onwards. He was the first to specify use of the piano for performing his own music. Surprisingly, there is no proof that pianos were used in the public *concerts spirituels* in Paris earlier than 1768. At about the same time in London J. C. Bach was giving public performances on the piano for the first time. Its late advent as a concert instrument was due partly to the slow evolution of a tradition of public concert-giving, partly to the fact that the harpsichord was still stronger in tone and therefore better suited to the concert hall, and even more to the fact that piano music of this period remained, quite literally, chamber music, intended for a small circle of listeners. Haydn's first key-board sonatas, with their short, suite-like movements, were still intimate in character. Soon, however, he was striving for more spacious formal construction, greater sonority and expression, and by the late piano sonatas the dimensions have become Beethovenian. This trend, of course, can also be observed in the works of the other keyboard composers, e.g. Kozeluch, Mozart, Clementi, etc. Piano-makers had to keep pace with the composer's demand for an ever greater volume and richer tone and they succeeded. In 1788 Haydn wrote to his publisher Artaria: 'I had to buy a new forte-piano in order to write your three clavier sonatas really well . . .' This remark could imply either that he did not own one before or more probably, that an 'old' piano was no longer adequate. We know that Mozart acquired a first-rate piano soon after settling in Vienna in 1781. Mozart undoubtedly came into contact with pianos at an early period when he visited Paris in 1763–4 and came to know some of the music of Eckard, Schobert, Raupach and Honauer. In Salzburg, however, he still had no piano at his disposal in the seventies. This we can infer from a letter of his mother's, written to Mozart's father Leopold on 28 December 1777: 'Here [in Mannheim] his playing is very different from in Salzburg, for there are pianos everywhere, and he handles them incomparably . . .'. Earlier in the same year Mozart had written to his father: 'the last [of the three sonatas K. 282–4] sounds superlative on Stein's piano'. Thus, we should not be surprised at the quantity of *f*, *p*, crescendo and accent markings in the autographs of these early sonatas. Misleadingly, even later on Mozart often used to label the piano part *cembalo*, and does so in the last piano concerto, K. 595. This is often misconstrued; Mozart was merely conforming to a tradition, and the designation should be taken no more literally than those title-pages of early printed editions which specify *pour le clavecin ou pianoforte* – even including the first edition of Beethoven's sonatas op. 31. There is no historical justifica-tion for playing Mozart's mature sonatas on the harpsichord, however suitable it may be for early Haydn. Notably, the sonatas Hob. 14, 18, 19, 21 and UE 19* contain 'harpsichord passages'. However, as early as 1771 Haydn wrote dynamic markings in the C minor Sonata (Hob. 20), which cannot be fully carried out on the harpsichord. Since this particular sonata evidently was not conceived for the clavichord, the ideal instrument for this and many of the following sonatas seems to be the early fortepiano.

The choice of authentic sonority is less pressing for Haydn's larger-scale sonatas. Interpretation of classical piano sonatas depends less on specific tone-colour (and hence choice of instrument) than on the manner of performance, the vitality of expression and stylistic understanding (which will determine a suitable tempo), vivacious articulation, rich gradation of dynamics and tasteful execution of ornaments. It is possible, unfortunately, to play badly on a splendid early piano and conversely, a great artist may do justice to a Haydn sonata on the historically wrong keyboard instrument.

REGIONAL STYLES

We have mentioned (p. 113) some of the composers whose works Mozart came to know in Paris in 1763–4. Although almost totally forgotten today, they were celebrated in the eighteenth century both as virtuoso pianists and as composers for the instrument. They were responsible for introducing the expressive mid eighteenth-century style of northern Germany into France, and for marrying it with the galant trends of Italy and southern Germany. Between about 1750 and 1770 nearly all composers were striving after a 'natural' but heightened means of expression, in reaction against the formal mannerisms and conventions of the rococo. In Prussia, this took shape in the ideals of dawning romanticism; also in a predilection for clavichord music embodying *Empfindsamkeit* as well as for the impassioned idioms of the

* As different editions have numbered Haydn's sonatas in different ways a checklist has been added on pp. 164–5.

Sturm und Drang. Slow movements were often exaggerated in expression. C. P. E. Bach stands at the centre of this primarily North German repertory – a repertory hall-marked by its extremes of sensitivity and turbulent pathos. Together with this we find unconventional musical ideas, frequent use of startling harmonic progresssions and a taste for minor keys (which had seldom been chosen for the cheerful galant music of the rococo). There are passages in free rhythm, instrumental recitative punctuated by rests (C. P. E. Bach spoke of speech principles underlying music), and free improvisatory writing as well as strict. C. P. E. Bach's sonatas often include highly expressive slow movements. An andante from one early sonata (no. 1 of the *Prussian* set of 1742) begins:

Ex.1

A singing melody is set off against the even quaver move-ment of the bass. To be fully effective, it needs to be played with a true rubato. C. P. E. Bach refers to this in his treatise, and offers an example to illustrate it (see the English edition, translated by W. Mitchell, New York, 1949, pp. 1160–62). This is possibly as rigid a rubato as the one defined by Mozart for his own music: 'in an adagio in *tempo rubato*, they do not realize that the left hand should never be affected, for they let it fluctuate in speed.' By this he meant that the essence of true rubato is a stable tempo for the accompaniment, which should not reflect the gradations of speed applied to the melody.

The theme quoted above leads on to five bars of free recitative, followed by three further bars of the high-relief arioso theme, leading then to a fresh recitative entry with bold harmonic relations. The heightened expressiveness latent in these works, and even more evident in later ones, can only be brought out properly in an interpretation which is both stylistically correct and imaginative. Refinement of tone-quality is vital, and in fact we rarely hear convincing performances of C. P. E. Bach these days.

Bohemian and Austrian composers kept a certain distance from this subjective and elevated style, if indeed they were familiar with it at all. Besides a ready championing of Italian galant features, they display first and foremost a close contact with folk music, an instinctive popular touch, using familiar tunes and dance rhythms. Also often displayed is a remarkable mastery of their craft, based on baroque traditions and often encouraged by fierce competition.

How was Italian influence displayed? Most Italian keyboard works of the period are characterized by small-scale melodic formations, tuneful and charming, often based on the notes of the triad, which may be repeated entire or in part. The two-part texture (melody and accompaniment) is enlivened by breaking down the accompanying harmonies into rhythmically uniform figurations. This moving backcloth of sound was aptly described by Rousseau as '*un accompagnement contraint et continu, qui fit plutôt un léger murmure qu'un véritable chant, comme serait le bruit d'une rivière ou le gazouillement des oiseaux*' (a restrained and constant accompaniment, a gentle murmur rather than actual melody, like the sound of a stream or of birds warbling).

As a typical example of Italian rococo style, we may cite a sonata in B flat, which might be by Alberti, though it has been wrongly included in the complete edition of Pergolesi (1710–36), the brilliant Neapolitan composer who died so prematurely (volume XXI, p. 16):

Apart from the imitative opening bar, the movement is innocent of counterpoint, consisting throughout of a melody with simple harmonic accompaniment. The opening 'head'-motif is followed by a graceful figure, typically 'rococo', in bar 2. This, and the rhythmically identical one in bar 6, are among the numerous galant motifs which sound like a decorous inclination. The repetition on the next degree of the scale and the subsequent cadence in bars 3–4 underlines this graceful poise. The paired semiquavers in bar 3 recur in all conceivable forms as a distinctive feature of contemporary Italian style, and are found in J. C. Bach and Mozart too. They were later used by the Mannheim composers, especially in the descending form subsequently designated the 'Mannheim sigh'. The repetition of bars 2 and 3 (presumably intended as an echo effect) is equally characteristic; so is the symmetrical phrase-structure already apparent here. From bar 2 onwards, the accompaniment resolves into those broken-chord figures which Alberti is supposed to have invented, and which still bear the text-book label 'Alberti bass'. This type of accompaniment aimed to provide a harmonic backcloth enabling a cantabile melody to be heard to maximum effect and became extremely popular. Apparently Rousseau was referring to this with his 'gentle murmur'. In all piano music of this time which came under Italian influence these accompaniment figures crop up in various permutations – as alternating notes in pairs groups of three , or six . For his time, Haydn made rather sparing use of them, employing only the most common forms from his tenth sonata onwards (Hob. I = UE 10; we shall adopt the chronology of the UE – see the table at the end of this chapter). Mozart was from the beginning altogether more Italianate, and at an early date acquired the habit of using Alberti basses – from J. C. Bach. Examples can be seen in his first sonata, K. 279, in the A major Sonata K. 331, and in all three movements of the so-called *Sonata facile* K. 545, written in 1788. In the minor section of the slow movement, they are applied to increased harmonic movement over a descending bass progression, then to the diminished-seventh chords which make this passage sound so truly Mozartian:

Ex. 3

Here, obviously, we are worlds away from the simple textures of Italian rococo music proper. In the Italian Alberti basses the rate of harmonic change is less frequent, and each motif was subjected to at least one identical repetition.

A few further comments about forms of accompaniment and melodic construction are relevant at this point. Re-iterated quavers or semiquavers – a relic from basso continuo practices – were common in keyboard music of the period, especially in the form of 'drum' basses, as they came to be called, in allegro movements. Haydn sometimes made use of them in his early sonatas, but this progression is more in character for Haydn:

Ex.4

Two basic types of melodic formula crystallized in the Viennese classical period: the Italian 'open-ended' melody (rooted in baroque tradition), with a well-defined character-istic opening statement followed by motivic extension, usually sequential; and the French 'closed' or song type subjects. The opening motif in both cases is very often triadic, the phrase structure usually regular, with themes comprising 2 + 2; 4 + 4; 6 + 6; 3 + 3 + 2 (4) bars; or similarly regular subdivisions. Mozart's music often gives the impression of this same symmetrical flow, but internal arrangements can be astonishingly irregular; and in Haydn, regular symmetrical constructions are even rarer than in Mozart. A theme extended to nine bars, or thematic groupings with odd numbers of bars, in either composer's work appear, however, balanced and proportioned within themselves. Most deviations from the normal symmetrical forms of the time generate a dynamic vitality which markedly enhances our enjoyment.

What is it about the music of Haydn and Mozart which leads us to single them out as 'classics', where we would not apply that term to contemporaries, composers such as Dittersdorf and Kozeluch? One important feature is their indescribable sense of structure, regular in its irregularities; another their special approach to polyphony, their increasing cultivation of part-writing; however, most important are the wealth of ideas, the abundance of invention, which distinguish the music of Haydn and Mozart from that of their contemporaries.

HAYDN

In our time, Haydn's keyboard works have been seriously underestimated, and even Mozart's sonatas have been relegated to the shadow of Beethoven's. They have borne this handicap since the middle of the last century, when it became customary to evaluate the classical works of Haydn and Mozart as little more than stepping-stones towards Beethoven. Fortunately this attitude has recently taken a turn for the better.

The first serious attempt to edit all known piano sonatas by Haydn was made by Karl Päsler and issued shortly after the First World War by Breitkopf & Härtel. Päsler presented fifty-two sonatas in a chronological order which was taken over by Hoboken in his Thematic Catalogue of Haydn's Works, where they are listed in Group XVI. Since the Hoboken numbers are becoming better and better known we always shall refer to them, but feel obliged to mention also the numbers of the *Wiener Urtext Ausgabe*, edited by Christa Landon and issued recently by Universal Edition (UE), which not only contains newly discovered sonatas but also presents a revised chronology.

According to UE Haydn wrote sixty-two sonatas, but

seven of these survive only in the incipits from a thematic catalogue made by Haydn himself. At least one of the remaining fifty-five is of debatable authenticity. Haydn research has been so long neglected that it is not surprising that three previously unknown youthful sonatas were discovered only after the Second World War. More may yet turn up. The many sonatas which *are* undoubtedly genuine display astonishing formal and stylistic diversity, testimony to Haydn's urge to experiment and his knowledge of the different traditions of north and south.

The three UE volumes edited by Christa Landon are similar in size. Yet the third volume contains only ten sonatas, the middle volume seventeen and the first volume, of early works, has twenty-eight sonatas (nos. 1–35). This alone shows the extent to which Haydn enlarged the scope of his later sonatas as, of course, he also did in the case of his later symphonies and quartets. In the late eighteenth century there is a tendency not only to consolidate sonata form but also to expand it: this expansion reached its climax in Beethoven's *Hammerklavier* Sonata. At the other end of the scale, Haydn wrote some very short movements especially in those early sonatas which he still called partitas.

Taking the first volume of the UE edition, we find two four-movement works, UE 1 and 13 (Hob. 8 and 6), which defy precise dating, but might have been written by 1760 at the latest. Both have a delightful 'open-air' flavour characteristic of G major, the key of both sonatas, which according to Daniel Schubart was often used to represent 'country idylls'. Schubart's descriptions of 'key-colour' often seem a little far-fetched to us but it is understandable that choice of key often largely determined the mood of an eighteenth-century composition. No. 1 is remarkable chiefly for its light-heartedness and wittily short movements (e.g. the finale), while no. 13 is more ambitious. The first movement opens with a gay carefree melody with alternating duplets and triplets in Haydn's most characteristic manner. This is followed by a typically Austrian march theme in dotted rhythm of a kind common in Haydn's divertimenti. Although it is in the dominant key, D major, this idea does not necessarily qualify as a second subject. The sonata form of nineteenth-century textbooks, with its 'proper' main subject, transition and contrasting second theme, can anyway rarely be found in Haydn's sonatas. Sometimes his exposition contains several themes, but in many cases it is monothematic, all its main ideas being derived from the first subject. In such cases it is pointless to look for a second, contrasting subject. The second movement of this G major Sonata, a short minuet with a beautiful G minor trio, is surpassed in expression and intensity by the adagio in G minor which follows it. The right hand has an archaic concertante melody, with triplet movement and melodic appoggiaturas over the even pulse of the accompanying quaver chords, while the performer is left to ornament two cadence points. Despite all the differences in Haydn's treatment, the movement may well owe its inspiration to Wagenseil. In the B flat Sonata U E 11 (Hob. 2) the most impressive movement is again its highly charged slow movement (Largo), which is also in G minor.

Many of these early sonatas might owe their composition to Haydn's need to supply himself with new music while he had to support himself by teaching. We read in his autobiographical sketch:

When my voice eventually broke, I spent eight long, wretched years teaching youngsters. So many talents are crushed in the perpetual struggle for survival which deprives them of time to study; I suffered the same experience, and only achieved the little I did by composing at night . . .

The sonatas U E 12, 15 and 16 (Hob. 12–14) deserve special mention among the early works. The first of these was offered for sale in 1767 but may have been written much earlier. It opens with a shapely theme also found in a *Singspiel* aria of the mid seventeen-fifties, presumably by Haydn.* The almost incessant triplet motion of the first

* Printed in *Denkmäler der Tonkunst in Österreich*, vol. 64, p. 53. See bars 9 ff.

movement adds to the impression of an organically rounded form. Many things in this sonata recall the form of the late baroque suite: the development section, for example, remains in the compass of tonic and dominant keys. The second movement is a gay, innocent minuet. The rhythmic pattern of its A minor trio is reminiscent of J. J. Fux's vocal duets, which Haydn must have sung as a choirboy. It is remarkably polyphonic in its texture. The other two sonatas, in E and D, are more ambitious; the D major, in particular, starts with a melody built on a chaconne bass and radiates the spirit of the south German and Austrian divertimento. Here again the minuets have characteristic trios in the minor, and the presto finales are racy and effervescent.

A second group of sonatas, U E 29–33 (Hob. 19, 44–6 and 20), can be dated more closely – between 1766 and 1771. As with Haydn's symphonies and quartets of this period, a more serious approach appears in the piano sonatas. In general terms, Haydn reconciles the Austrian baroque and galant elements, thus creating a rather personal style. We might even claim that the weaknesses inherent in the galant style are overcome by him while recreating the larger-scale forms of the baroque. In his string quartets of this period, Haydn revives the church-sonata tradition at the expense of divertimento style, while in the piano sonatas the influence of C. P. E. Bach's concerto style is displayed. The splendid D major Sonata U E 30 (Hob. 19) already embodies concertante elements. The first movement seems to call for harpsichord tone, with its baroque bass line in steady quavers and the sharply-dotted rhythms of the first subject. The middle movement is even more concerto-like and highly individual in flavour, with its opening bass leap of three octaves and attractive A major theme. A final cadenza should be supplied, as so often in C. P. E. Bach. In places, this adagio sounds like a concerto for cello or baryton, with the melody down at the bottom of the keyboard among the accompanying harmonies. Could it, in fact, be an arrangement? One argument against this is the conscious exploitation of contrasting registers towards the end of this extended movement.

The concertante style is also in evidence in the sonatas in E flat, U E 29 (1766) and A flat, U E 31 (*c.* 1768), in G minor, U E 32, and C minor, U E 33: these mark the first climax of Haydn's keyboard composition and are fully-fledged masterpieces. The later sonatas do indeed often have broader dimensions, greater brilliance, and a more dramatic imposing quality. But these middle-period sonatas are in no sense dwarfed by their better-known successors.

The E flat Sonata U E 29 (Hob. 45), large-scale yet perfectly poised, must have come as something of a surprise to Haydn's contemporaries. Although it contains extreme contrasts, it comes over as a convincing entity. The first movement is a typical Haydn allegro moderato in sonata form, starting with a theme which embodies a rhythmically vigorous opening and a contrasting tune-like answering phrase. Apart from a few bars in three-part texture, a preference for two-part writing is still paramount, though this does not always take the Italianate form of melody and simple accompaniment. The beginning of the development is forward-looking (bar 45 f.), as is the passage starting at bar 44 in the middle movement. It is tempting to suggest that this latter passage, together with an interpolation in the very free recapitulation of the first movement, may have influenced Beethoven, who was not yet eighteen when the sonata was published, twenty-two years after its composition. The finale sounds rather traditional by comparison with some passages reminiscent of Wagenseil. But it is precisely this masterly stylistic integration of different trends which distinguishes the sonata. The lyrical andante in A flat with its arioso melodies, the contrapuntal interplay of its part-writing and the lovely minor touches (e.g. bars 20–21), presents a wealth of inspired innovations.

Somewhat akin thematically to this lyrical andante, and in the same key, is the first movement of the fine A flat Sonata U E 31 (Hob. 46), an extended movement with

fantasia-like interpolations in the manner of C. P. E. Bach.
It opens with an expressive motif:

This motif returns during the development in E flat major
and F minor, and in the recapitulation in A flat minor and
major providing elegiac points of repose in a richly inventive movement.

The middle movement of this sonata, a D flat major
adagio, is one of the most exquisite movements Haydn ever
wrote for the keyboard. The structure and harmony of its
opening have some affinities with J. S. Bach. A texture in
three parts is nearly always maintained and the soloistic
right-hand melody is sometimes almost bravura in its
imitation of twittering birds. The modulation to D flat
minor towards the end and the approach to a point where
a cadenza has to be improvised, are enough in themselves
to demonstrate Haydn's newly achieved mastery: he has
assimilated baroque and galant features and a personal
idiom of expression almost perfectly. The idiomatic outer
movements show clearly why this work is one of Haydn's
most frequently performed sonatas.

Another gem is the rather more subtle G minor Sonata
UE 32 (Hob. 44) which also dates from this period. It has
only two movements, on the Italian pattern, and is less
virtuoso than other works of this period, although nonethe-

less brimming with pianistic effects and, apart from the first
subject, quite different from the resigned melancholy of
most of Mozart's G minor music. The first movement, in
sonata form, has something of the mood of the theme of
Haydn's late F minor Variations in its sensuous opening:

Ex.6

The accomplished part-writing already apparent in other
sonatas of this group is even further refined here: for
example, at the marvellous build-up in the transition to the
recapitulation, bars 46–51. It is pure Haydn, yet reflects the
influence of C. P. E. Bach, and the movement has an
adagio cadenza just before the end which is reminiscent of
baroque practice.

Haydn also treads new and revolutionary paths in his only
C minor Sonata, UE 33 (Hob. 20), of 1771. Wyczewas
interprets the works written around 1772 as a reflection of
the *Sturm und Drang* movement in Haydn's work, coinciding
with a romantic crisis in his life. Against this much-quoted
view one might set that of Jens Peter Larsen, who describes
it, convincingly, as the climax of a long struggle towards
heightened musical expression rather than as a personal
crisis. But whatever the reason, the symphonically proportioned C minor Sonata does indeed have a powerful
intensity, especially in the first movement with its elegiac
theme doubled in thirds and sixths – a foreboding of

Brahms's song *Immer leiser*. This achieves added dramatic intensity in the development and recapitulation by reversing the roles of right and left hands, and by sequential extension (bar 73).

The long development is unusual, and influences the recapitulation of the first subject; another noteworthy feature is the prolonged dominant-ninth chord which concludes an adagio ornamental passage – rather like a cadenza – in the transition (exposition, bar 23: also in the minor-key recapitulation). The new broad canvas and symphonic spaciousness of thematic material are just as apparent in the central movement, an andante con moto in A flat. Its bold innovations include the exploitation of extreme registers and the wide spacing between the hands (almost four octaves) in bars 11 and 53, where the f''' seems to have been the highest note of the keyboard at that time. The copious use of written-out rubato (bars 14 ff., 31 ff. etc.) and the even-quaver accompaniment were traditional techniques, though turned to novel use in this movement. The solemn drama of C minor pervades the last movement as well as the first. It is another sonata-form movement, whose first subject recaptures the powerful intensity of the first movement, especially of the development. The finale is technically even more demanding than the preceding movements and is well able to hold its own with them in dramatic tension, musical content and formal cohesion.

It may be impossible for us to realize today how very advanced Haydn's sonatas of the period around 1770 must have sounded to his contemporaries. In any case, it is significant that Haydn did not see fit to publish them until the seventeen-eighties.

We see a more conventional side of Haydn in the next sonata in D major (UE 34, Hob. 33) which was published in 1778 but probably composed in the early seventies. It is followed by a set of six sonatas, written in 1773, dedicated to Prince Nikolaus Esterhazy and published in Vienna by Kurzböck the year after. This is the first of three sets of sonatas, all published between 1774 and 1780. The second set was probably composed in 1776 and was printed by Hummel in Berlin. The third set included the C minor Sonata of 1771 and was Haydn's first work to be published by Artaria, the leading publisher in Vienna from then onwards, and appeared in 1780.

All three sets contain the most varied musical components. Each set begins with a sonata in C or G major which is comparatively simple, musically and technically. The sonatas are graded in difficulty, culminating in the sixth sonatas of the second and third sets (in B minor and C minor); Mozart did the same in his set of six sonatas K. 279–84, maybe for commercial reasons.

The first set of sonatas UE 36–41 (Hob. 21–6) is relatively the least interesting. Its first sonata in C major consists of three movements in sonata form, and clearly reverts to the current divertimento style, with its Austrian march-rhythms in the first movement (which also occur in the third, fifth and sixth of this set) and the galant ornamentation of the finale. The second movement is an andante in the same vein and the same key (F major) as the corresponding movements in the last C major Sonata UE 60 (Hob. 50) and also the adagio in the first sonata of the third set, the well-known C major Sonata UE 48 (Hob. 35).

The second sonata, E major, is rather more adventurous. Its second movement, an andante in the tonic minor, begins, like the G minor movement of UE 13, with baroque melodic triplets, though in this case they are interrupted in bar 4 by a dotted figure and a rest. The finale takes the form of a cantabile variation rondo or French rondo, with episodes in the minor and rather varied appearances of the ritornello. It could be regarded as a double-variation movement (that is, one with two themes), but in no circumstances as a minuet, with which it has nothing in common beyond its tempo. The mixture of variation and rondo forms in the Viennese school, the variation-rondo, becomes increasingly more characteristic for those of Haydn's finales which are not in sonata form.

The third sonata, F major, is the most popular of this set. The sweet, intimate melancholy of the F minor siciliano theme points the way to Mozart, especially when it moves to A flat major in bar 5:

Undoubtedly it was in Mozart's mind when he composed the F major Sonata, K.280. The exuberant finale is pure Haydn and probably influenced many of Mozart's finales.

The fourth sonata, D major, is gay in its outer movements but altogether more traditional, especially in the baroque accompaniment of the D minor adagio, which ends on a dominant chord and is followed *subito* by a presto in free variation form. Haydn's new interest in counterpoint is reflected in the last two sonatas of this set, as it was in the op. 20 quartets. The highly original fifth sonata in E flat, in only two movements, has a canonic finale which is formally a minuet without a trio; and the middle movement of the lovely A major Sonata, the sixth, is a *menuet al rovescio** borrowed from Symphony no. 47. This movement is not in the autograph: Haydn may not have decided to add the borrowed movement until after composing the finale, perhaps because the finale seemed too short – a two-four presto of only twenty-six bars.

The next set, U E 42–7 (Hob. 27–32), opens with the short G major Sonata which is both musically attractive and easy to play. The unison tail-piece to the theme of the first movement recalls Mozart's G major Sonata K. 283 written in 1774 (presumably earlier than Haydn's). In the development the broken chords drive relentlessly forward before returning to G major. The remaining two movements have a delicious simplicity, a minuet with a G minor trio and a presto finale in variation form, with written-out minor repeats in the third variation.

Taken as a whole, this set could be seen as a reaction

* In other words, both the minuet and trio are so written that each is played first forwards and then backwards (*cancrizans*).

against conventional taste. The second sonata, in the festive key of E flat, is a demanding work, though its middle movement is another minuet: there is only one 'normal' slow middle movement in this set, the adagio of the third sonata. This Sonata in F is laid out on a comparatively grand scale, and the first movement is full of originality. A vigorous opening motif is followed by a cantabile phrase, familiar to us from its subsequent use by Paisiello and Mozart. The arpeggios and repeated notes which follow the pause in bar 14 are a further reminder of C. P. E. Bach, as also are the 'written-out accelerandos' (bars 22 f., 57 f., 80 f.). The interesting development begins dramatically:

The fourth sonata in A major is utterly different in character. The first movement, in two–four, opens in a merry, playful mood. Suddenly we hear the horn-like march rhythm ♩. ♪♫ ♩ in bars 13–14: Mozart often used this rhythm, especially in the piano concertos, in the form ♩ ♪♫♩ ♩ e.g. in K. 415, 451, 453, 456 and 459. The suggestion of horns is emphasized towards the end of the exposition (bars 55 f.):

The first movement leads straight into the adagio by means of a dramatic interrupted cadence on the dominant: the harmonies in this slow movement are exquisite, though in form it is really no more than a transition to the variation finale, a sort of accompanied recitative.

In the fifth sonata in E major it is the E minor middle movement which especially claims our attention. It maintains strict three-part writing, almost as though it were written for strings. The steady bass movement, sequences and contrapuntal part-writing are baroque in flavour, yet the sonorous descending chain of first inversions in bar 13 ff. is almost Schubertian, building up in the following bars to achieve maximum tension between extreme registers:

Abert has demonstrated the melodic relationships which exist in this set of sonatas between the themes of first and last movements. He claims that the relationship is especially clear in this case:

However, the finale also reminds one of the opening bars of the preceding sonata.

The last sonata, in B minor, is on a larger scale than the others in this group. Masculine and impassioned, with its virtuoso outer movements, it is a work of high dramatic tension, with a contrasting minuet in the bright key of B major, which embraces a trio in the tonic minor. This trio is – as so often in Haydn's sonatas – a weighty, dramatic movement. Most surprising of all is the sonata-form finale, containing an original first subject, whose upper and lower parts are contrapuntally exploited in a 'learned' development section. This finale generates a wild, almost scurrilous humour, culminating in the unexpected unison conclusion – a sharp contrast with the seriousness of the first movement. Haydn had not written a finale of comparable significance since the C minor Sonata.

Next, we come to the third series of sonatas, UE 48–52 (Hob. 35–9), which Haydn made up to a set of six by adding the C minor Sonata of 1771 (UE 33, Hob. 20). The first sonata is again a straightforward work, intended to attract amateurs:

The popular and attractive first movement makes modest demands on the pianist, but is by no means limited in its musical content, showing admirable economy in the varied use of material. The second sonata, in C sharp minor, is quite different in character. The unison opening of the first movement, like so many of Haydn's themes in minor keys, is virile and energetic; it continues as a dialogue.

Ex.14

There are unusual modulations in the development, and the recapitulation is anything but literal. A brisk scherzando in A major replaces the slow middle movement and is followed by a very fine minuet-finale.

The next sonata, in D major, is another favourite and well-known sample of Haydn's genius. The first subject of the first movement (allegro con brio) is superficially reminiscent of Scarlatti. Baroque idioms dominate the slow movement, a wonderfully powerful sarabande; after this, the naïve gaiety of the finale is well suited to its *innocente* marking. The fourth sonata in the set is again in Haydn's favourite key of E flat, and its exuberant first movement is teeming with new ideas – Haydn encompasses an incredible range of variety in the sonatas of this set. He achieves very special sonorous effects in this movement by exploiting the highest register (bars 22 f.). The fifth sonata (G major, Hob. 39) opens, unusually, with a variation-rondo using a theme already familiar from the scherzando of the C sharp minor Sonata. Haydn referred to this in his preface. The finale, an unparalleled prestissimo, is in sonata form.

After this set it would appear that Haydn restricted his sonata output. Apart from the fine E minor Sonata U E 53 (Hob. 34), the only sonatas Haydn wrote in the seventeen-eighties were three two-movement works: UE 54–6 (Hob. 40–42), dedicated to Princess Marie Esterhazy and published in 1784, and the sonatas UE 58 and 59 (Hob. 48–9) written a few years later.

The three two-movement sonatas are often underrated. Their unity is such that they should really be played as a cycle. Essentially they are chamber music; they were later issued as string trios, and might even have been conceived as baryton trios. The G major Sonata Hob. 40 is a (double-) variation movement which cannot fail to elate the performer. Haydn's contemporaries evidently felt this too, and one is reminded of Haydn's letter to an admirer:

It was indeed a most pleasant surprise to receive such a flattering letter from a part of the world where I could never have imagined that the products of my poor talents were known . . . You happily persuade me . . . that I am often the enviable means by which you, and so many other families sensible of heartfelt emotion, derive, in their homely circle, their pleasure – their enjoyment. How reassuring this thought is to me! – Often, when struggling against the obstacles of every sort which oppose my labours; often, when the powers of mind and body weakened, and it was difficult for me to continue in the course I had entered on; – a secret voice whispered to me: 'There are so few happy and contented peoples here below; grief and sorrow are always their lot; perhaps your labours will once be a source from which the care-worn, or the man burdened with affairs, can derive a few moments' rest and refreshment.'

The minor episode in the first movement of the G major Sonata is alternately tender and passionate. The presto finale in sonata form, chamber music in essence, is an ebullient movement nonetheless. The finest craftsmanship of the set can be seen in the B flat Sonata UE 55 (Hob. 42), especially in the second movement based entirely on the motif:

Ex.15

Another two-movement work otherwise rather different

in character is the better-known C major Sonata UE 58 (Hob. 48) of about 1788–9. Its first movement is more extended and shows an interesting structure which could be called an enlarged double-variation form with a pattern which features throughout the juxtaposition of major and minor. The rondo which follows is perhaps less complex, but shows contrapuntal ingenuity (e.g. bars 71 ff.).

The E flat Sonata UE 59 (Hob. 49), dedicated to Marianne von Genzinger, is an extended and demanding three-movement work. It starts with one of the finest examples of Haydn's mature handling of sonata form, showing a masterly economic use of motivic material and an interwoven style comparable only to that of the most mature works of Mozart and Beethoven. The opening motifs of the movement contain the germs of practically everything that follows:

The two motifs a and b also form the second subject (bar 26 ff.). Both of them are stretched out to four bars each. A new feature is the Alberti figure which forms the accompaniment of motif b of which the last part, the rhythmical figure ♪.♪♪, is used for an extended cadence. Two parts of motif b appear in melodic inversion in the interesting last bars of this subject. The closing section follows immediately (bar 42), using the parts b₁ and b₂ of motif b. An interrupted cadence, a dramatic silence and a hint of Beethoven's 'fate' motif ♪♪♪|♩ precede a short codetta.

The relationship between this and the motif b₁ is shown in the development section when b appears (bar 96 ff.), not with a broken triad for the upbeat b₁ as in bars 3 and 42 but now with three repeated notes. The codetta ends with an apparently new motif of five successive quavers going up with chromatic steps (bar 60 ff.) which, however, turn out to be familiar (bar 62, and in metric displacement 65 ff.) from the transition. The return to the recapitulation is noteworthy: Haydn, after a beautiful polyphonic section (bar 117 ff.), juxtaposes the 'fate' motif from the codetta with the motif a$_1$ and upsets the basic three-four metre by the rhythmic transformation of motif a$_1$ into downbeats:

This extraordinary movement concludes with a relatively extended coda of twenty-seven bars. It is followed by two equally admirable movements, the second in a varied and enlarged A–B–A form typical of Haydn, the third, a French rondo which has only the tempo in common with a minuet.

The final three sonatas are masterpieces unique in the piano repertory. It seems that Haydn, now at the peak of his career, was commissioned to compose them for Miss Teresa Jansen, a pianist living in London. He also wrote three piano trios for her and a piano duet (also preserved as a trio) called *Jacob's Dream*. The sonata U E 60 (Hob. 50) was printed in England around 1800 and, according to the title page of the first edition, was obtainable from Miss Jansen, who became Mrs Bartolozzi in 1795. The title ran:

'A Grand Sonata for the Piano Forte Composed Expressly
for and Dedicated to Mrs Bartolozzi by Haydn.'

No one else could have conceived the opening of this
C major Sonata. There is a tension in its single staccato
notes which gathers momentum and is finally released in a
forte outburst after a rest (bar 7):

As so often in Haydn's mature works the second subject is
a variant of the first, transferred to the bass part and the
dominant (bar 20). It returns to the treble at bar 30, and
parts of the theme are already 'developed' in the exposition.
The development itself contains some fine polyphonic work,
derived in part from the fugal style of his quartets. Yet other
aspects of the theme are exploited when it is played legato
in the left hand, *pp*, with 'open pedal', and again in A flat
(bar 73), soft, dark and sonorous. In the recapitulation the
open pedal effect sounds almost impressionistic (bar 120):

In this exceptional movement, there is much subsidiary material, often of high emotional intensity, and many subtle touches, such as the harmonies which underlie the polyphonic passage in bars 37–41. The lyrical F major adagio has an imposing quality absent in earlier comparable movements. All repeats are written out in the finale, which may well be the first classical piano work to use the wider compass of English pianos, requiring a''' in bars 103 and 171. If Beethoven had had access to a 'modern', wide-compass instrument in Vienna as his teacher Haydn did in England, he would clearly have been spared much irritation (see the first movement of op. 10, no. 3, bars 103–5).*

The well-known C major Fantasy, Hob. XVII/4, written in 1789 and published by Artaria, could very suitably be performed with this C major Sonata. The two are related thematically, and the Fantasy would effectively counterbalance the virtuoso finale. In any case, it is a vivid and breathtaking piece. (However, the marking 'hold until the sound is inaudible' [i.e. with the dampers raised], can only be taken literally on an early fortepiano. On a good modern grand piano one would have to wait much too long.)

The D major Sonata UE 61 (Hob. 51) again has only two movements, the first of which is an andante with a cantabile theme over Alberti figurations in triplets which could almost have been written by Schubert. In places this movement comes close to improvisation in the romantic manner: it is in fact in very free sonata form, without repeat

* This handicap was, however, often turned to artistic purpose, especially by Mozart.

marks in the exposition. The second movement is also advanced for its time, anticipating Clementi or Beethoven rather than Schubert.

Probably the last sonata which Haydn wrote is the E flat U E 62 (Hob. 52). Even the adagio makes virtuoso demands. Was it already the challenge of the young Beethoven? Unlike the D major, this E flat Sonata is an example of classical sonata form, though new in its formal spaciousness. One can sense its closeness in date to the *London* Symphonies – this sonata is no less rich in content. As in other late sonatas and symphonies, the first subject of the the first movement also forms the principal second subject in bar 17 and heads the concluding group in bar 33. There is a distinct second subject theme, at bar 27, accompanied by a horn figure. But the construction is monothematic in essence, and shows remarkable economy. Schubert was the next composer to adopt Haydn's technique, in his A minor Sonata D 845; whereas for Beethoven the dialectical principle of first and second subjects, thesis and antithesis, was more significant than Haydn's monothematic synthesis. Another remarkable feature is the orchestral treatment of the piano: bars 111–12 suggest horns, trumpets and drums, and the whole passage sounds like a piano reduction. This sonata is a landmark of the piano repertory, for the sound of other instruments is constantly implied in the piano writing.

The following adagio is one of Haydn's most beautiful and profound inspirations. The remote key of E major is a juxtaposition almost without precedent, although in this case it had been anticipated in the development of the first movement – an inspired touch. The main theme of the adagio is not unlike some of the themes in Haydn's masses, with their religious ethos. The third movement shows Haydn's supreme skill at combining free and strict styles in so-called *thematische Arbeit*, such as we also find in the symphonies of this period. The humour with which he handles the main theme is most aptly characterized by a remark of Furtwängler's to the effect that the joys of life are captured in handfuls in Haydn's music. (Heinrich Schenker published a penetrating analysis of this sonata in *Der Tonwille*, volume 3, 1922.)

Between his two London visits, Haydn wrote the famous F minor Variations in Vienna in 1793 (Hob. XVII/6). He appears originally to have planned this work as a sonata, starting as in Hob. 48 with a variation movement. The autograph is even headed 'sonata', whereas an authentic copy entitles it '*Un piccolo Divertimento*'. It may well be his most popular piano work, and uses one of his favourite double variation forms, in which two themes, presenting a minor-major contrast, are varied in alternation. The first variations give an impression of magically simple, tender melancholy, which is further underlined by the alternation between F minor and F major. In the coda, however, a storm bursts out: the bold harmonies retain their power to astonish even the modern listener.

J. C. BACH

Considering the fact that the first published set of the piano sonatas of Johann Christian Bach (1735–82) appeared as op. V as early as 1765, they are surprisingly consistent and advanced in style. J. S. Bach's youngest and by nature most gifted son was trained in Germany and Italy, and then lived mainly in London, where he championed the Italian galant style. He influenced Mozart in various ways, and one is tempted to state anachronistically that some of his sonatas begin with a 'Mozartian' idea. The readiness with which the young Mozart learned to imitate J. C. Bach has always given cause for amazement. As is well known Mozart also arranged three of the op. V sonatas (Nos. 2–4) as concertos (K. 107). He chose in the charming G major Sonata, op V/3, and in the even more enchanting E flat major Sonata, op. V/4, works very much in the line of his own thinking. However, the most admired of this set of J. C Bach's sonatas is the last one in C minor. It is fairly traditional in form, starts with an expressive *Grave* followed by a fugue, replaces the slow movement of the old church-sonata with a three-bar adagio improvisation and ends with a light dance-like allegretto. The fugue shows that J. C. Bach had studied counterpoint successfully, not only with his father as a boy but more so with Padre Martini in Bologna.

Altogether a more interesting set of sonatas are those published as op. XVII around 1780. Besides the graceful flow of melodic invention in the well-proportioned and charming Sonata in A major (No. 5) and the sensitive, beautiful C minor Sonata (No. 2), it is the Sonata in E flat major (No. 3) which deserves special attention. It is less 'Mozartian' than the others, consists of two movements only and contains some surprising harmonies. The second subject of the first movement, an allegro assai, reads as follows:

This is, of course, not as bold as many of the harmonic progressions in C. P. E. Bach's music. It reflects very much the general aesthetic attitude of the time, which Leopold Mozart expressed in a letter about J. C. Bach to his son:

The small is great, when it is written in a naturally fluent and easy, light style, and solid in composition. To compose in this style is more difficult than to write all the artificial harmonic progressions incomprehensible to most people, and melodies difficult of execution. Did Bach lower himself by this? Never! The correct setting [composition] and the arrangement, *il filo* – this distinguishes the master from the bungler, even in trifles.

Undoubtedly Leopold was referring to J. C. and not to C. P. E. Bach, who was famous in Germany but less known in London, where the Italianized music of J. C. had won greater acclaim. Nevertheless C. P. E. Bach developed a much more original style than his brother, due to a peculiarly subtle art of playing his favourite instrument, the clavichord, a molto espressivo style which might otherwise have been lost for ever. Apart from the sons of Bach, other successful contemporary keyboard composers, such as Galuppi, Wagenseil, Rutini and Eckard, would have deserved discussion if it were not for the vast gap that separates their works from those of Haydn and Mozart.

MOZART

Mozart's relatively late start in sonata composition* accounts for the remarkably assured consistency of style of his first set. The later sonatas, as one would expect, include some of greater importance, which are more extended and more personal in expression but these early sonatas effortlessly

*Not taken into account are the lost piano sonatas K. 33d–33g. The sonatas K. 46d and 46e (composed in 1768) were probably violin sonatas of which the violin part is lost.

combine thematic material of great diversity. Haydn, in his
sonatas, tended to use themes more economically than
Mozart so that the entire exposition, and hence the whole
movement, was very often derived from the component
cells of the first subject by means of sequential treatment and
various kinds of fragmentation. Mozart's miracles of form
are less easy to account for.

We may reasonably assume that Mozart knew Haydn's
Kurzböck Sonatas (Hob. 21–6) by the time he was composing
his own first six sonatas. But apart from these, J. C. Bach's
op. V sonatas may well have been his chief models, for, like
the latter, Mozart's six are all in three movements, with
middle movements in the subdominant (K. 279, K. 281,
K. 283 = K. 189d, f and h), the relative minor (K.280=
K. 189e) or the dominant (K. 282, K. 284 = K. 189g and
205b).*

The first sonata, K. 279 (189d), has all three movements
in sonata form, and is notable particularly for its lyrical
andante and fresh Haydnesque finale. The first movement,
with its ornate figuration, does not yet attain the melodic
richness of the following sonatas. The second subject of the
finale, which also opens the development, happens to be
rhythmically identical with the finale motif of Haydn's
F major Sonata Hob. 23: it should be played with brilliance.

The first movement of the F major Sonata K. 280 (189e),
is in three–four and, despite the marking 'allegro assai', the
first subject is a typically Mozartian cantabile melody,
with sighing Italian appoggiaturas in bars 5 and 6 and a
written-out rubato in bar 8. It anticipates two other F major
movements in three–four: K. 332 and K. 547 (originally
written for piano and violin). The first-subject group
contrasts the quaver and semiquaver movement of the first
twelve bars with the continuous triplets of the following
fourteen bars, though the latter could be regarded as
transition material. The adagio of this sonata, an F minor

*The revised K. numbers represent the improved chronology of
Alfred Einstein's edition of Köchel's catalogue.

siciliano, is one of the finest works of Mozart's youth, and could almost have been by Haydn:

Indeed, this is not at all unlike the siciliano in the same key from Haydn's F major Sonata Hob. 23. Further similarities between the two composers emerge as the movement proceeds: in both pieces, the original lament of the siciliano resolves into a warm A flat melody with a gently moving accompaniment. In Mozart's movement we have calm, even semiquavers, and in Haydn's rather more animated semiquaver triplets. Mozart achieves a smoother flow, but even in the major key is more poignant. The adagio marking classes this as the slower, more serious type of siciliano: it has affinities with the immensely sad slow movement of the A major Concerto, K. 488, which is likewise marked adagio instead of andante. The finale, a three-eight presto, then restores the joyful mood of the opening: it too is Haydnesque, but is more pianistic, longer, and richer in contrast than its precedents. All the movements of this sonata are thus in triple metre, a very rare occurrence.

B flat major, the key of the third sonata, K. 281 (189 f), seems to have been Mozart's favourite for piano music, since he used it for three sonatas and no fewer than four concertos. At the outset, the theme introduces a dualism between semiquaver triplets and demisemiquavers – another touch of Haydn? This admirably constructed movement deserves to be better known, and the two following movements fully live up to it. The andante amoroso is one of Mozart's loveliest early works; it should be played as an introspective devotion, not as a declaration of passion. The final rondo is in gavotte rhythm; if a little less polished in detail, it is nonetheless packed with high spirits and concerto-like effects, such as the short cadenza (bar. 43) and the return of the theme beneath a trill accompaniment (bar 114 ff.):

Ex.22

The rondo theme is binary, its second part being a 'varied repeat', to use C. P. E. Bach's term. The Italianate 'Mannheim sighs' in bar 3 recur in the first episode, which leads back to the theme through a chain of trills, a fermata and a rhapsodic transition. The theme is followed by an episode in the minor which, especially in its second half, introduces a hint of melancholy into the course of events, which the third episode also interrupts, this time with a loud, dramatically spread diminished-seventh chord (bars 102, 104). A free play of motifs from the rondo theme, a brilliant transition, and further quotation of the theme (this time complete) – and the movement comes to an end with a brief, playful coda. In form as well as in key the movement is related to the finales of the sonatas K. 333 and K. 570, and the concerto K. 238.

The lyrical E flat Sonata K. 282 (189g) opens with a slow movement (like the doubtfully authentic 'romantic violin sonatas' which similarly betray Italian influence).

This first movement is in sonata form and starts with an expressive theme in three-part writing:

This is followed by a contrasting melodic idea, with a motif repeated twice at different pitches, modulating to an imperfect cadence on the dominant. The gracious second subject begins in bar 9. Basically, this is a simple motif with two halves, which are repeated and merge imperceptibly into the concluding group. The development begins with a highly charged diminished seventh chord followed by two short crescendos and two bars of transition to the foreshortened recapitulation; the three-bar opening theme does not return until the coda. This movement shows early Mozart at his best – expressive, exquisite. He was meticulous in providing it with plenty of phrasing and dynamic markings. The next movement is a lively minuet with a relatively long trio section (labelled Minuet II), which clearly draws on Austrian dance traditions. Such folk or popular elements are rare in Mozart, but this movement is akin to the minuets of Beethoven's Septet op 20 and his Sonata op. 49, no 2. A two-four allegro in sonata form concludes a distinctly original work.

The fifth sonata K. 283 (189h), in G major, has more novel ideas, musically and pianistically. The diversity of its melodic invention is highly typical of Mozart: so is the clear-cut sonata form of the first movement. The opening theme is an interplay of question and answer

breaking characteristically into semiquaver movement. The ornamented unison passage which follows (bars 16–22) is superbly written for the pianos of Mozart's time, on which it sounds brilliant and full-bodied. This tutti effect was one of his favourites, and he also used it in later works, such as the Variations on a Theme by Gluck (K. 455) and the Piano Concerto K. 456.

The andante, in C major, is unpretentious, but the repeated notes require subtle shading in performance to be really effective. Unlike the first movement, which in place of a development section simply presents a new idea, followed by an extended transition to the recapitulation, the second movement contains a true development in the ninteeenth-century sense, presenting the subject first in the right hand (in D minor and C major) and then in the left. A scintillating presto concludes the sonata.

Sonata no. 6 in D major, K. 284 (205b), written for Baron von Dürnitz, is undoubtedly the best and the most technically demanding of these early sonatas. Mozart retained a special affection for it and continued to perform it himself. It was this sonata which, he said, sounded incomparable on Stein's pianos. The material is laid out on a more ample, orchestral scale, a departure from the intimacy of the earlier sonatas. The tremolo effect in bars 13–16 and the unison announcement of the first subject read very much like a piano reduction of an orchestral tutti. The second subject, a supple melodic line unaccompanied in its opening bar, incorporates a descending chain of first inversions – that favourite harmonic formula of the baroque and classical periods. (There are analogous passages in the subsidiary themes in Gluck's overture *Iphigénie en Tauride* and the slow movement of Bach's *Italian* Concerto.) This functions as a solo passage in contrast to the ensuing tutti entries in bar 30. The development describes a circle of minor keys before the recapitulation begins in bar 72.

Mozart called the second movement a *rondeau en polonaise*. The opening four bars form a kind of dialogue (as in the first movement of the preceding G major Sonata), and

Mozart subjects them to felicitous variations (bars 9 ff., 31 ff., where the dynamic roles are reversed, 39 ff., 70 ff., 78 ff.). The contrast between statement and counter-statement is heightened by Mozart's meticulous dynamic markings.

The last movement of this sonata is a pianistically reward-ing, cheerful set of variations, which up to the adagio variation has the character of a gavotte – the preceding 'rondeau' was also a dance movement. It shows Mozart's special gift for writing variations at its most brilliant. The superficial impression of a diffuse form does not stand up to closer inspection: it would not be at all easy to omit one of the twelve variations or add an extra one. The adagio variation has a special interest for Mozart scholars, for it gives us some insight into his concept of impromptu orna-mentation. The autograph is only modestly ornamented, and Mozart would presumably have embellished it in performance as his fancy dictated. But a richly ornamented version was published during Mozart's lifetime: it is most probably his own work, and illuminates his ideas on performance in general. Some modern editions give both versions.

The next two sonatas, K. 309 (284b) and K. 311 (284c), were probably written in Mannheim in 1777, and are more consistent, almost more 'classical', than the earlier sonatas. The first movement of the C major Sonata K. 309 is a model of text-book sonata form. With sonata form, as with Bach fugues, no formal dogmas underlie the process of composition, but each sonata varies anew a basic principle. For Mozart, this entailed strict adherence to certain funda-mental patterns without inhibiting his creative freedom. In his sonata movements in major keys he favoured a distinct second subject in the dominant, for example; a point at which Haydn, on the other hand, revelled in experiment. It may help to demonstrate Mozart's standard sonata form by means of a brief analysis, and the first movement of K. 309 is an ideal example.

The first subject is distinctive, a marcato opening

followed by a five-bar 'answer'. The falling fourth and rising sixth of the opening is one of Mozart's favourite melodic devices:

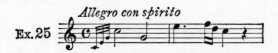

Ex. 25   *Allegro con spirito*

He often uses it in the minor as well as major, and it introduces many of his themes (e.g. the sonata K. 331/2, the B minor adagio K. 540, and the symphonies K. 114, K. 124, K. 319/2 and K. 551/2). The seven bars of the theme are repeated, lightly varied. Bars 15–21 conclude the first-subject group with an answering phrase (3 + 3 bars). The transition consists of new material and then, in bar 35 (after two bars of preparation) comes a second, cantabile theme in the dominant (G major) comprising 2 × 4 bars, which is also repeated and proceeds to a spirited closing theme (concluding group) using passage-work (bar 43) and incorporating a delightful diminution of bars 35–6 in bar 45. The exposition ends with five bars of codetta. The development presents the opening motif, first in G minor, and then works out the various ideas of the first subject, keeping much more closely to text-book principles than Mozart usually does. Two further statements of the opening motif lead back to the recapitulation in bar 94. The second subject, now in the tonic, has surprisingly changed places with its accompaniment. The opening is recalled again in an effectively assertive coda.

The second movement of this sonata is an introspective 'andante un poco adagio'. Mozart stated his desire to make the andante of this sonata match the character of the young pianist for whom he wrote it, Rosa Cannabich: 'she is a sweet, pretty girl, just like the andante. For her age she is sensible and level-headed; she is serious, and doesn't talk too much, though what she does say is pleasing and sympathetic.' An elegant and smoothly flowing rondo concludes this sonata.

The first movement of the D major Sonata K. 311 (284c) is an orchestral 'brio', like the earlier D major *Dürnitz*

Sonata; both works radiate with Mannheim exuberance. The second movement might be described as a sonata movement without a development. Its song-like eleven-bar theme* − 4 + 4(3½) + 3(3½) − is followed by an episode and a wonderfully varied return of the theme in D major (bar 25) instead of a contrasting second subject. The recapitulation starts in bar 39. The finale is one of Mozart's 'hunting' rondos in six-eight, so common in the piano concertos.

Suddenly, with the A minor Sonata K. 310, a new world opens up. Einstein may well have been right in assuming that the sonata was written under the weight of Mozart's grief at his mother's death in Paris. The first movement is marked 'allegro maestoso', and the opening theme is indeed truly majestic: dotted rhythms were formerly understood to imply majesty. The texture is orchestral in fullness, and the relentless pulsing of the accompanying chords suggest majesty of a demonic and sinister kind:

* An example of overlapping phrases; the theme is, however, incomplete without the resolution in the twelfth bar. (D.M.)

The first movement constantly alternates between remonstrance and resignation. For the cantabile second theme (from bar 23) we have consistent semiquaver movement, followed by two-part counterpoint for the left hand from bar 28. The last five bars of the exposition recall the dotted rhythm of the first subject. A storm breaks in the development; this passage is without parallel or precedent. The sudden dynamic contrasts between *ff* and *pp*, and *ff* again which Mozart prescribes here foreshadow Beethoven's outbursts. The two diminished-seventh chords in bars 126–7 heighten the expression of tragedy – a typical classical implication of this chord.

The second movement of this sonata (in F major) is marked 'andante cantabile con espressione'. This eloquent movement is basically lyrical, but it should be played with dignity, for it displays a restrained passion unlike the warmth and grace of Mozart's usual major-key slow movements. A second theme (bar 15 f.) recalls the second subject of the second movement of the Symphony K. 201. The development grows in intensity up to the climax at bars 43–9 – a parallel to the development of the first movement – before the return of the solace of the first subject.

The third movement, presto, reverts to the foreboding of the first movement, but instead of the 'orchestral' drama it gives a subdued image of the underlying mood of tragedy. Mozart, unlike Beethoven, rarely resolved his minor-key works into radiant major finales; he seldom allows joy to conquer tragedy.* Most of his minor compositions return to

* The major-key endings of Mozart's G minor Piano Quartet and String Quintet, and D minor Piano Concerto, and the tragic finales of Beethoven's sonatas op. 27 no. 2, op. 31 no. 2, and op. 57, are famous exceptions. (*D.M.*)

the spirit of the opening, as here. The presto is one of the darkest movements Mozart ever wrote, with its remarkable fluctuations between resignation and defiance, and only a single subtly illuminating shaft of A major, a fleeting *Fata Morgana*.

The next sonata, K. 330, probably also written in Paris, is a total contrast, with no trace of melancholy. The first movement is exuberantly gay and is followed by an intimate andante cantabile with a beautifully expressive minor episode and fine contrapuntal part-writing in the episode's A flat section. The numerous phrase marks and careful dynamic indications testify to Mozart's own fondness for this sonata. The last four bars are not in the autograph. They were added by Mozart when the sonata was engraved. What a blissful afterthought! The andante is followed by a cheerful, sturdy allegretto finale in sonata form.

The A major Sonata of 1778, K. 331, has always been one of Mozart's best-loved pieces, beginning with its intimate and elegant andante theme with variations:

This work differs from a usual sonata, having not a single movement in sonata form; it is more akin to the divertimento. Yet even here, the movements are bound together by strong melodic and formal affinities. It is no accident that the crossing of hands in the trio of the minuet is anticipated in the fourth variation, that the A minor finale key is prefigured in variation 3, while the A major ritornello of the Turkish march is alluded to in bars 5 and 6 of the allegro variation. The irregular phrase-structure of the minuet is typically Mozartian. The double octaves in bars 20–24 of the minuet trio make pianistic demands unusual for the period; this is the only occasion on which Mozart prescribes them. The delightful rondo alla turca, with its imitation of Turkish music in the A major section, is justly famous. Here an early piano with a percussion stop would be ideal.

The F major Sonata K. 332 has a three–four first movement, like K. 280 in the same key. The cantabile opening measures are followed by an unusually long answering phrase containing a wealth of melodic ideas, many of which are reminiscent of Haydn (bar 13 ff.). This is not a textbook example of sonata form, though the main landmarks are present – the threefold division into exposition, development and recapitulation, and the broad outlines of the key scheme, although there is a stormy D minor passage and a modulation to C minor before the entry of the second subject in the regular key of C major. There are many other touches which demonstrate Mozart's freedom in handling sonata form, such as the hemiola rhythm in bars 64–5, and the new thematic material introduced at the beginning of the development. The B flat adagio displays his skill in varying repeats and typifies his practice of enriching the ornamentation prior to publication. The last movement is a rollicking virtuoso allegro assai in six–eight.

The B flat Sonata K. 333 takes us into new realms of lyricism – we might say this is inherent in the choice of key. The first movement opens with a cantabile theme which no one else could have written:

According to Schubart's aesthetic theory, E flat, the key of the middle movement, was the key 'of love, prayer, intimate converse with the Almighty, signifying the Trinity with its three flats' – a characterization which does seem to apply, for once, to this rather solemn and prayerful andante cantabile. It is in sonata form, and in places could have been conceived as a string trio. One of the boldest moments is the beginning of the development with its biting dissonances, all the more telling after the preceding euphony. The sombre ethos of E flat is dispelled by a concertante rondo finale in B flat, although this good-humoured movement does retain a touch of seriousness – a sufficiently weighty conclusion to this fine sonata. The introduction of a full-scale cadenza (bar 171) into a sonata movement is most striking, and this one is only rivalled in the concertos and far surpasses those in Haydn's sonatas. Several features suggest that this is a concerto movement in disguise, not least the tutti entry preceding the cadenza (bar 168).

After this, Mozart wrote no more sonatas until the great C minor Sonata of 1784, K. 457. Meanwhile he had emancipated himself from his father and from the Salzburg court, and was writing and performing piano concertos – five in quick succession in 1783–4 (K. 449, 450, 451, 453 and 456) – for his subscription concerts in Vienna, which at first were highly successful. It is no wonder, then, that the virtuoso brilliance on which his success depended can be detected in his compositions. But the C minor Sonata offers more than this: a shattering expression of personal anguish, and a new language which sets it at the beginning of an epoch. This is the work which made the deepest impression on Mozart's direct contemporaries and successors, especially on the young Beethoven. Discounting Haydn's quite different C minor Sonata (Hob. 20), it is the first truly monumental work in the sonata repertory, designed for acoustics more spacious than those of drawing rooms. It is tragic to the core, although written when Mozart was at the peak of his worldly success in Vienna, in 1784. He gave more than twenty concerts of his own works that year, all of which were fully booked: even in our modern 'concert industry' it is quite exceptional for a virtuoso, or even a composer, to make twenty successive appearances in a single city. Yet it was just at this time that tragedy, objective and subjective, took grip on Mozart's life, ending in his death in poverty. The C minor Sonata is the first of a series of tragic works in minor keys, culminating in the unfinished Requiem of 1791.

From the assertive opening

Ex.29

the first movement is a sustained cry of protest, yielding at the end to a consoling adagio, one of Mozart's finest inspirations. It may be more than accidental that the A flat major theme of the second episode is almost identical with the adagio theme of Beethoven's *Pathétique* Sonata. But the tragedy will not be stemmed, and returns with shattering force in the final rondo. Lamentation, protest, resignation, breathless terror and despair are constantly interrupted by silences which render the cries vain and hollow. Yet classical form is not undermined by all this subjective expression. Mozart's music achieves greatness through the conquest of personal tragedy by inner order and discipline, and on this level he is Beethoven's peer. In the first movement the opening unison statement and its answer – like the themes of the K. 491 Piano Concerto and the K. 475 Fantasy – lead us to a profundity which language is powerless to fathom.

Although he wrote the great C minor Fantasy – where he effects a unique blending of funereal C minor with demonic chromaticism – two whole years after the sonata, he endorsed the intrinsic connexion between the two works by publishing them together. This fantasy might well be ranked Mozart's most significant single piano composition. Like the sonata, it opens in unison: like the concerto, it is chromatic:

The chromatic steps around the fifth (F sharp, G, A flat) seem to convey a sense of impending doom, as it does in the concerto. The Fantasy seems freely constructed, but is nevertheless most tightly-knit. The overall shape is a succession of slow, fast and slow sections, with a return of the first theme towards the end. The chromatically descending bass in bars 10–16 supports bold harmonies, with their almost Schubertian modulation from C minor to B minor.

After this, there is a turning-point in Mozart's sonata output. His writing assumes more subtlety, and a more pronounced inclination to contrapuntal writing – as in the second movement of the F major Sonata K. 533. (Mozart himself later added the F major Rondo K. 494 as a third movement for this sonata.) The first movement opens rather conventionally: yet he builds up tension in the development from the simplest raw material. The recapitu-

lation brings a further surprise by turning towards the
remoter minor keys. The second movement, andante, is
resigned and melancholy – undoubtedly the best movement in the sonata. Unlike the more short-winded first
movement, it spans a great melodic arch which never sags
throughout the first subject group, right down to the half-
close at bar 22. The anguished dissonance in bar 2 of the
theme is quickly resolved, giving way to a sublime cadence
on B flat with a hint of resignation:

The polyphonic writing is meticulous, and the themes are
fundamentally related as well as being contrapuntally
viable (see the beginning of the development). The cumulative dissonant suspensions towards the end of the development (bars 60–72) still perplexed musicians in the nineteenth century, and even today we can only marvel at the
dramatic suspense of this linear part-writing. The F major
Rondo affords a point of repose after this andante. Despite
Mozart's extension of rondo form by a contrapuntal
cadenza, and despite a wonderful episode in F minor, it
lacks the tension which distinguished the previous movements, particularly the second.

Mozart's C major Sonata K. 545 is considered easy to
play, a 'sonata facile' ideal for teaching purposes. While this
is true, we must bear in mind that Mozart, like Bach and
Schumann, maintained the highest standards when
writing for students. The rondo is perhaps the most childlike movement, and the innocently graceful G major
andante has already furnished us with an example of
resourceful use of Alberti patterns (ex.3).

Many of Mozart's later works in B flat are characterized
by gentle, sombre resignation; among them are the K.

595 Concerto and the Sonata K. 570. Compared with the rhythmically similar opening of the F major Sonata, K. 332, this B flat major Sonata is lacking in energy and drive, and the beginning of the first-subject melody swings like a pendulum around the tonic. As in many of his late works Mozart makes ample use of counterpoint in a galant manner. This movement has no well-defined contrasting theme, but approaches the monothematicism of many Haydn sonatas. Nor is Mozart the dramatist totally absent in this lyrical movement: the development plunges us abruptly, and with great effect, into D flat major. Tension mounts as the second part of the theme rises in pitch and volume (bars 84–94), leading to a G major bass entry, *piano*, of the first subject. The thematic economy of this movement and the skilful exchanging of material between the hands are somewhat reminiscent of Haydn: not so the introspective E flat adagio. It expresses resignation but without bitterness: a sublimated farewell, music free from earthly trammels. It is in rondo form and its first episode in C minor is closely related to the C minor passage in the central movement of the K. 491 Piano Concerto, bar 14 being an almost literal quotation.

Less other-worldly in character is the last of Mozart's piano sonatas, K. 576 in D major. It is often known as the *Hunt* Sonata; its key and six–eight time signature set the mood vividly. Mozart told his creditor Puchberg in a letter of 1789 that he intended to write six simple sonatas for Princess Frederica of Prussia in order to raise some money. This is the only one he completed and, far from being easy, it demands a high standard of finger technique. As in so many works of his last years in Vienna, this sonata features subtle contrapuntal interplay of deceptively simple material. In the development the theme enters in new canonic imitations, first a bar apart (bars 63–4), later only half a bar (bar 70), leading to an impressive climax with a modulation to F sharp major (bar 77 ff.), and a return through the minor keys (F sharp minor, bar 83; B and E minor). The recapitulation starts in bar 99 after a brief transition; it rearranges and modifies the exposition material in true Mozartian fashion.

The A major adagio is a straightforward ternary movement with a middle section of sweet melancholy in the relative minor:

Ex.32

Mozart may originally have devised this as a four-movement sonata, on the lines of his string quartets and symphonies, in which case the fragmentary Minuet K. 355 (594a), the chromaticism and polyphony of which is closely related to this sonata, was probably intended as the third movement. The rondo finale is more contrapuntally conceived than a superficial impression would suggest. Particularly impressive are a canon in reverse using the rondo theme and its inversion (bars 34 ff.) and a canon in the fifth in the development section (bar 103).

The F major Sonata K. 547a is an arrangement of two movements from a sonata for violin and piano (K. 547), plus the third movement of the C major Sonata K. 545 transposed to F major: Mozart can hardly have been responsible for it. Some adaptations of wind divertimenti, published under the title of 'Viennese Sonatinas', are also pianistically unrewarding, though there is no valid reason to doubt the authenticity of the original divertimenti (KV. Anhang 229).

Of Mozart's individual piano compositions, the late ones in minor keys are among the finest: the A minor Rondo K. 511 and the B minor Adagio K. 540. Both are models of formal perfection while full of personal expressions. The rondo has copious expression marks and attains a remarkable level of subtlety and technical refinement – the chromaticism of the first subject is arresting and, indeed, pervades the whole work. The atmosphere is never theatrically coarsened, even by the downwards leap of a seventh in bar 156: but although gentle, the sadness is despairing. The movement ends with chromatic ornamentation (B flat, A, G sharp) of a low-pitched tonic, answered finally by the opening motif at the high fifth. As Mozart put it in a letter – apparently the last he wrote to his father:

I have now made a habit of being prepared in all affairs of life for the worst. As death, when we come to consider it closely, is the true goal of our existence, I have formed during the last few years such close relations with this best and truest friend of mankind, that his image is not only no longer terrifying to me, but is indeed very soothing and consoling!

But Mozart's continuation is also characteristic:

I thank my God for graciously granting me the opportunity (you know what I mean) of learning that death is the *key* which unlocks the door to our true happiness. I never lie down at night without reflecting that – young as I am – I may not live to see another day. Yet no one of all my acquaintances could say that in company I am morose or disgruntled. For this blessing I daily thank my Creator and wish with all my heart that each one of my fellow-creatures could enjoy it.

The B minor Adagio, a solitary movement in sonata form, is another subjective utterance, yet the form is classic in its balance and consummate in its beauty. The atmosphere of lyrical sorrow is still to be detected in the more dramatic passages, such as the dialogue between bass and treble, *f* and *p* (bars 11 f., 24, 27 etc.) or the richly dissonant lead-in to the recapitulation (bars 31–4): even the tender D major melody at bar 15 is sorrowful. The beauty of the B minor melody (Schubart's key of 'gentle lament') is intensified rather than weakened by repetition. The B major coda is an example of 'smiling through tears', which only Franz Schubert could convey with the same poignancy.

There is no space to explore Mozart's other piano music more closely. We must ignore the enchanting Rondo in D major, the little contrapuntal Gigue K. 574, the two Fantasies (K. 396 in C minor, a fragmentary work completed by Abbé Stadler, and K. 397, the popular D minor Fantasy): but we might single out the C major Fantasy and Fugue K. 394 (383a) for special mention, since it is relatively little known. It was prompted by Mozart's study of Bach, and he wrote to his sister as follows, referring to the three-part fugue: 'I have specially marked it "andante maestoso" so that it shall not be played too fast', and, writing about the fantasy-like prelude in the same letter: 'it's rather confusing: the prelude belongs first, the fugue afterwards. . . . But the reason for this is that I composed the fugue first, and wrote it down while I was thinking out the prelude'. The prelude shows no signs of its haphazard composition.

A short, solemn adagio is followed by a stormy, toccata-like section which exploits piano sonorities and technique to the full, and contains figuration that, at times, is almost Lisztian. As an expression of radiant power, this is un-paralleled in Mozart's piano writing. The beginning of the fugue is a welcome point of repose after such an outburst. The well-poised subject undergoes various contrapuntal devices: augmentation, diminution and stretto.

Of Mozart's variations, it is those on themes by Gluck (K. 455) and Duport (K. 573) which are best known, and deservedly so. The *Sarti* Variations, K. 460, and the set on *'Ein Weib ist ein herrlich Ding'*, K. 613, are two less well-known works which are, however, also brilliant and rewarding.

Few keyboard works by Mozart's lesser contemporaries are publicly performed today. Among the few really worth reviving, apart from those of C. P. E. and J. C. Bach, are some works of the Bohemians Kozeluch and Dussek and Domenico Scarlatti's Spanish pupil Padre Antonio Soler. Muzio Clementi (1752–1832) is one of the brighter stars in this constellation, and well deserves the growing interest in his work, though most of his more valuable sonatas date from the later years of his long life-span, making him more important as a contemporary of Beethoven than of the precocious Mozart. But it is hardly possible to go as far as the assertion, in Grove's *Dictionary of Music and Musicians* (Fifth Edition), that Clementi was 'the first completely equipped writer of sonatas' and that 'he may be regarded as the originator of the proper treatment of the modern pianoforte, as distinguished from the harpsichord'.

Abbreviations

UE	= Universal Edition: *Wiener Urtext Ausgaben* (Editors K. H. Fuessl and H. C. Robbins Landon) *Joseph Haydn: Sämtliche Klaviersonaten*, in three volumes, edited by Christa Landon, Vienna, 1963–4.
Hob.	= A. van Hoboken, *Joseph Haydn: Thematisch-bibliographisches Werkverzeichnis*, vol. I, Mainz, 1957.
Peters	= Forty-three Sonatas in four volumes; six Divertimentos (abbr. Divt.), edited by C. A. Martiensson, Edition Peters.
Br. & H.	= Breitkopf & Härtel: Urtext Edition (edited by Hermann Zilcher), forty-two Sonatas in four volumes.
HU	= Henle Urtext Edition of twenty-one selected sonatas, edited by Georg Feder, Duisburg, 1963 and 1965.

UE	Hob.	Key	Peters	Br. & H.	HU
1	XVI/8	G major	Divt. 4	—	—
2	XVI/7	C major	Divt. 5	—	—
3	XVI/9	F major	Divt. 6	42	—
4	XVI/G 1	G major	—	—	—
5	XVI/11	G major	Son. 11	31	—
6	XVI/10	C major	Son. 43	—	—
7	XVII/D1	D major	—	—	—
8	XVI/5	A major	Son. 23	41	—
9	XVI/4	D major	Divt. 3	—	—
10	XVI/1	C major	Divt. 1	—	—
11	XVI/2	B flat major	Son. 22	40	—
12	XVI/12	A major	Son. 29	28	—
13	XVI/6	G major	Son. 37	36	—
14	XVI/3	C major	Divt. 2	—	—
15	XVI/13	E major	Son. 18	18	—
16	XVI/14	D major	Son. 15	14	—
17	—	E flat major	—	—	1
18	—	E flat major	—	—	2
19	—	E minor/ (E major)	—	—	—
20	XVI/18	B flat major	Son. 19	19	—
21–7	—	Themes of the lost works	—	—	—
28*	XIV/5	D major	—	—	—

* Fragment

UE	Hob.	Key	Peters	Br. & H.		HU
29	XVI/45	E flat major	Son. 26	25		—
30	XVI/19	D major	Son. 9	9		3
31	XVI/46	A flat major	Son. 8	8		4
32	XVI/44	G minor	Son. 4	4		6
33	XVI/20	C minor	Son. 25	24		5
34	XVI/33	D major	Son. 20	20		—
35	XVI/43	A flat major	Son. 41	11		—
36	XVI/21	C major	Son. 16	16		—
37	XVI/22	F major	Son. 40	39	Set of six	—
38	XVI/23	E major	Son. 21	21	published in	7
39	XVI/24	D major	Son. 31	32	1774	—
40	XVI/25	E flat major	Son. 32	—		—
41	XVI/26	A major	Son. 33	—		—
42	XVI/27	G major	Son. 12	12		8
43	XVI/28	E flat major	Son. 13	13	Set of six	—
44	XVI/29	F major	Son. 14	14	published as	—
45	XVI/30	A major	Son. 36	35	'op. 14' in	—
46	XVI/31	E major	Son. 30	29	1776(?)	—
47	XVI/32	B minor	Son. 39	38		9
48	XVI/35	C major	Son. 5	5	Set of six (including	10
49	XVI/36	C ♯ minor	Son. 6	6	UE 33 as	11
50	XVI/37	D major	Son. 7	7	no. 6) pub-	12
51	XVI/38	E flat major	Son. 35	34	lished as	—
52	XVI/39	G major	Son. 17	17	'op 30' in 1780	—
53	XVI/34	E minor	Son. 2	2		13
54	XVI/40	G major	Son. 10	10	Two-move-ment works	14
55	XVI/41	B flat major	Son. 27	26	dedicated to Princess	15
56	XVI/42	D major	Son. 28	27	Marie Esterhazy	16
57	XVI/47	F major	Son. 34	33		—
58	XVI/48	C major	Son. 24	23		17
59	XVI/49	E flat major	Son. 3	3	Written for Marianne von Genzinger	18
60	XVI/50	C major	Son. 42	22	Written for Mrs Teresa Bartolozzi	21
61	XVI/51	D major	Son. 38	37		20
62	XVI/52	E flat major	Son. 1	1		19

4

Beethoven, Schubert, and Brahms

DENIS MATTHEWS

*

FROM this point on – roughly half way through the present survey – the problems of the editor and his contributors become more and more complex. By the end of the eighteenth century the piano (pianoforte, fortepiano, call it what you will) had established itself as *the* keyboard instrument. This is a plain statement of fact, and in no way disparages the work of the later revivalists, the twentieth-century champions of the harpsichord and the clavichord. The piano cannot do full justice to Scarlatti and Couperin, and the harpsichord takes its rightful place in modern society, thanks to pioneers like Landowska – and not only as an archaic instrument to satisfy the purists. But the assets of the piano were overwhelming: instant dynamic response and tonal gradation, a singing quality, and a carrying power sufficient for a large concert-hall. This is, of course, jumping ahead a little; the age of public recitals had yet to come, and the piano of Beethoven's op. 2 sonatas (1796) was a far more intimate affair than the iron-framed concert grand that grew out of it. Nevertheless the growth of the instrument and its popularity were rapid. In 1767 it made its first public appearance in England; by 1795 it had replaced the harpsichord in the King's Band – a real status symbol! The German maker, Zumpe, produced square pianos for domestic use, forerunners of the ubiquitous 'upright'. In the nineteenth century, and well into the twentieth, no drawing-room, however humble, was complete without a piano – until it, too, was partly ousted by the further march of science: records, radio, and television, the arch-discouragers of amateur music-making. Yet to this day it is still the most popular solo instrument, largely if not wholly because of the richness of the repertoire that descended on it. The piano's growth in range and brilliance was matched by vast ramifications of its literature. Haydn wrote his last sonata in 1794. Another thirty years encompass the complete piano works of Beethoven, four more take us to the late sonatas of Schubert, and within a further four Chopin had completed his first book of studies, and Schumann his *Papillons* and the Toccata. The main stream of keyboard music becomes a delta.

And so the problem arises not so much of what to include as of *how* to include it. How do we segregate composers into chapters? Chronologically, geographically or stylistically? John Field, the Irishman, was fifteen years senior to Schubert: yet it seems logical to mention his nocturnes alongside Chopin's, while discussing Schubert's sonatas in relation to Beethoven's. It seemed natural to link Mendelssohn with his exact contemporaries, Chopin and Schumann, and yet to place Brahms (born 1833) in the present chapter. Some readers may jib at this, for was not Mendelssohn a craftsman in the classical tradition and Brahms a Romantic at heart? With this mild apologia the editor expects and accepts disagreement over the placing of this or that composer in one chapter instead of another. The highways and byways of the repertoire can be viewed from many angles. No one disputes Brahms's debt to Schumann, and an interesting comparison could be made between him and his direct contemporaries. The Brahms highway departed from the more spectacular scenic route favoured by the Liszt school. At the crossroads stood the towering personality of Beethoven, who influenced practically all his successors on no matter which side of the fence between 'romanticism' and 'classicism'. But the Brahms highway can be traced back beyond Beethoven to Bach, and by another route to the tradition of German song, hence to Schubert. If a further justification is required for the bracketing of these three composers, the city of Vienna provides the link; it was the birthplace of Schubert and the adopted home of

Beethoven and Brahms, as it had been of Haydn and Mozart. But Beethoven's contribution to the piano and to music in general – it goes without saying – was so significant and all-embracing that a new paragraph will not suffice. We must pause before embarking upon it.

BEETHOVEN (1770–1827)

On Beethoven's preliminary visit to Vienna in 1787 he is supposed to have excited Mozart's admiration through his powers of extemporization – 'Keep an eye on him, he will make a noise in the world' – and some idea of his daring flights of invention can be grasped from the grandest of his written-down cadenzas in the C major Concerto, op. 15, from the solo Fantasy, op. 77. and the long keyboard preamble to the Choral Fantasy, op. 80. Improvisation, as an adjunct to the more serious business of ordered composition, was an expected accomplishment in those days; and in the field of 'ordered composition' the young Beethoven accepted the piano as his main carrier of expression. By 1800, the year of the First Symphony and the op. 18 quartets, he had written the first eleven sonatas, copious chamber music with piano, and two piano concertos with a third on the stocks. His greatest legacy to the pianist was to be the thirty-two sonatas – in their variety, humanity and sheer intellectual power. Beethoven would not have minded the implication of the nickname 'the new testament of keyboard music'; he knew and respected Bach's *Forty-Eight* from his Bonn days. In Bonn he had already composed three youthful sonatas, interesting as stepping-stones, but he was twenty-six when he launched the mature series with op. 2. 'Mature' is not an overstatement. By now he was a master with a style and a will of his own, and it was inevitable that Haydn, who received the dedication, should have found him a recalcitrant pupil. The opening bars of op. 2, no. 1, with their personal use of dynamics (the leap from piano to fortissimo and the abrupt falling-away), proclaimed that Beethoven – though nurtured on the organ and the harpsichord – thought only in terms of the piano:

Yet the three op. 2 sonatas, published in 1796, were announced as 'pour le Clavecin ou Piano-forte'. So, for that matter, was the *Pathétique*! Not all prospective purchasers owned the latest instruments, and not until op. 14 does the alternative 'clavecin' (harpsichord) begin to drop out of the title-pages.

Beethoven's dramatic handling of dynamics was closely interwoven with tonality and structure (one good reason for deprecating editorial carelessness or interference with his markings). The nineteenth century brought a spate of unreliable, even impertinent, editions. Nowadays, thanks to Schenker, Schnabel, Tovey and others, we demand the Urtext – with editorial comments clearly differentiated from the original – and find that Beethoven almost invariably wrote precisely what he meant. It is the performer's, not the editor's, job to read between the lines of his occasional inconsistencies – Tovey's advice – and to adapt passages to fit larger keyboards can lead to dangerous anachronisms. Some early critics were, expectedly, bewildered by the turbulent aspect of Beethoven's music: the op. 12 violin and piano sonatas were found to contain 'clumsy, harsh modulations' and 'hostile entanglements'. In perspective it is easier to recognize his obvious debts to his forbears: his breadth and robust humour to Haydn (who was second to none in daring key-relations) and to Handel too (whom he worshipped); his sense of drama and pathos to Mozart (whose C minor Fantasy and Sonata had been published before Beethoven left Bonn). We even speak of Beethovenish passages in both Haydn and Mozart, which is putting the cart before the horse, unless we detect – as Marion Scott did – the imprint of his pupil in Haydn's last works.

It is traditional and convenient to divide up Beethoven's works into the three periods so often allocated to a creative artist's life. History resists such tidying-up: nevertheless the year 1800 is a useful landmark for Beethoven-lovers, for it is the date of the performance of the First Symphony and the completion of the op. 18 quartets. The symphony and the string quartet had become touchstones of a composer's worth, and six of the first eleven sonatas had adopted the four-movement plan associated with the larger forces: op. 2, nos. 1 to 3; op. 7; op. 10, no. 3; and op. 22. The 'extra' third movements, however, still sit on the fence between minuet and scherzo; op. 2, no. 3 is the only true scherzo, and op. 2, no. 2, though so called, is far less volatile than the 'minuet' of the First Symphony. The sketches for two other works – the op. 24 violin sonata and the *Eroica* – show us the speeding-up process at close quarters: a minuet in conception becomes a scherzo in realization. Nothing could better prove that Beethoven's most revolutionary gestures owe their strength to firm foundation. As for the early outpouring of piano sonatas, a form that seemed second nature to him, we should not underestimate them simply because they led to greater things. They already illustrate Beethoven's all-embracing quality.

Take op. 2, for example. The F minor, first in the book, is a terse drama played out in epigrams, and example 1 (above) gives an idea of its speed of action. On the surface the opening figure is no more than a cliché (compare the finale of Mozart's great G minor Symphony) but before two lines have passed the little decorative turn has detached itself and become a new starting-point. Its later use to summon back the recapitulation tellingly reverses the process. Even the adagio is compact and to scale, though spacious-sounding and lavishly ornamented (in Haydn's later manner, e.g. his *Genzinger* Sonata in E flat). In the tempestuous finale, where the key-conscious hearer may note premonitions of the *Appassionata* (also F minor), the unique feature is the long-breathed tune that stretches itself without change of pulse over the middle of the movement. But now compare op. 2, no. 2 in A major. Here the time-scale is luxurious, the harmonic progress leisurely; its humour ranges from the playful to the ferocious, with a few challenging outbursts of virtuosity that are offset by the surprisingly gentle ending of the final rondo. Op. 2, no.3, on the other hand, is a more obvious temptation to the virtuoso with its elementary flights of arpeggios and sixths and its C major brilliance. In reality it demands the utmost musical, as opposed to technical, precision – witness the string-quartet balance of the opening theme. The superb (dare one say romantic?) slow movement is in E major, a far remove that is suddenly 'related' when its theme is thundered out in C major towards the end.

Despite the vastness of the journey Beethoven was to undertake in the next thirty years these early sonatas are, in their own way, masterpieces. The ability to imbue an apparently simple, even trivial, figure with intense significance – this, knowing the Fifth Symphony, we may take for granted. But the thematic index to the sonatas is there to remind us. It is not sufficient to recognize Beethoven's remarkable craft in developing such figures into long paragraphs; we must add and admire his unfailing sense of the whole, of key-relations and continuity, so that seemingly disparate ideas unfold and link up with logic and dramatic purpose. The profundity of the 'early' slow movements? The next sonata, op. 7 in E flat (1797), has one of the best, a noble largo in which silence is as eloquent as

sound, until a moving bass fills in the spaces and marvellously enriches the harmony at the very end:

Ex. 2

Notice again the 'personalized' dynamics and the scoring
in the lower reaches of the keyboard. The whole of op. 7 is
on a grand scale: a brisk but proudly passionate first movement, warmth and tenderness in the quasi-minuet and the
rondo, with no danger of warmheartedness turning to
sentimentality – the strength of the well-placed minor-key
episodes sees to that. After op. 7, a lone and underrated
work, there comes another group of three sonatas, op. 10.
Of these the third, in D major, is the winner; its largo e
mesto was the first minor-key slow movement in the sonatas,
carrying through a mood of high tragedy and pathos to
the bitter end. For a parallel to such sustained tension, and
to the final disintegration of the theme through profound
emotion, we must look forward to the Funeral March of the
Eroica. The other sonatas of op. 10 (C minor and F major)
are inevitably overshadowed, and also by the fact that the
next in the series, the *Pathétique*, pursued Beethoven's C
minor daemon to greater lengths – and universal popularity.
The title is, for once, no nickname: it was Beethoven's own,
appropriate to a work of unashamed *Sturm und Drang*,
whose smouldering orchestral effects must have taxed the
pianos of the time. Yet its roots can be traced to Mozart's
stormy sonata in the same key, and there is even an uncanny foretaste of Beethoven's famous adagio halfway
through Mozart's. An unusual formal feature concerns the
introduction to the first movement that is, in fact, far more
than an introduction. It returns twice at climactic points, in

each case heralded by a pause. What then is the point of the
pause before the traditional exposition repeat? Obviously
the repeat, if made, should take in the introduction as well
as the allegro. Beethoven gave no contrary indication,
though most editors (even the best) have marked off the
allegro with its own reverse repeat-sign, thus unbalancing
this dual-tempo movement and making nonsense of the
'first time bar' pause.* But traditions, even spurious ones,
die hard – the writer was once accused of a lapse of memory
for obeying the original letter of the score! Rudolph Réti,
in his *Thematic Patterns in Sonatas of Beethoven*, analysed the
Pathétique down to the last quaver and revealed remarkable
features of structural unity that, consciously or subcons-
ciously, pervade the whole work. Réti's argument may be
laborious but it is convincing, and those interested might
begin by comparing bars 5 and 6 of the adagio with bars 5
and 6 of the rondo:

Ex. 3

Following the *Pathétique* there come two intimate sonatas,
op. 14, in E major and G major. They were probably
sketched much earlier, but Beethoven's interest in the
former led him to arrange it as a string quartet in F major –
not one of the accepted series. A transcription this way
round has far more significance than the common habit of
issuing *piano* arrangements of chamber and orchestral works,
for practical and study purposes. (One such arrangement, of
the String Trio, op. 3, was recently and extravagantly
claimed as a 'new' Beethoven piano sonata. But he did not
disdain increasing his sales in this way: the piano version of
the Violin Concerto and the four-hand one of the *Grosse
Fuge* are authentic. They are makeshifts nonetheless.) In
any case, a quartet texture often looks up from the pages of
Beethoven's piano music (see not only op. 14, no. 1 but op.

* Paul Badura-Skoda disagrees with me, citing the earliest editions.
Unfortunately the autograph has disappeared.

2, no. 3), even more so in the later works where counterpoint grows increasingly predominant (the opening of op.
110, variation two in the Arietta of op.111). Meanwhile, in
op. 14, no. 2, variations appear for the first time in the
sonatas: a miniature set on a march-like tune, placed
between a tenderly lyrical allegro (which inspired Schind-
ler to a rapturous account of Beethoven's free manner of
playing) and a scherzo-finale full of capricious cross-
rhythms. After this unorthodox behaviour the year 1800
produced a model sonata in op. 22 (B flat). It fulfils a four-
movement plan with splendid assurance and punctuality,
though its manner and moods are neutral – a work of
consolidation rather than adventure.

The next four sonatas, all completed around 1801,
continue to illustrate the variety among neighbours that
has been observed from the start. Whether we view them
as 'late early' or 'early middle' Beethoven is unimportant,
as it is more vital to note their flexibility of form in relation
to op. 22. The A flat Sonata, op. 26, begins with leisurely
variations – Mozart's K331 in A provides a time-honoured
precedent – and continues with a scherzo, a funeral march,
and a moto perpetuo finale. But this unconventional
sequence of events is capped by the two sonatas of op. 27,
each bearing the disarming label *quasi una fantasia*. The
first in E flat is strangely personal, almost childlike in
expression and a hit-or-miss for the performer; the second,
in C sharp minor, is invariably a hit, though the public-
wooing title of 'Moonlight' was not the composer's. The
veiled opening adagio makes its hypnotic effect through the
utmost restraint and shows, more than any previous music,
the sustained eloquence of the piano's singing tone at its
quietest levels. Here, unlike op. 27, no.1, 'fantasia' can
refer only to the unusual juxtaposition of moods: the
adagio is in sonata form, and so is the explosive finale,
whose urgent drama has no place for rondo returns. Neither
was the nickname 'Pastorale', given to op. 28 in D major,
Beethoven's. However, it fits its generally sunlit character
and the rustic nature of the drone-bass finale – perhaps, too,

the rumbustuous humour of the miniature scherzo. Beethoven's favourite movement, according to Czerny, was the melancholy andante with its quasi-pizzicato bass, a special keyboard effect he had used before in the slow movements of op. 2, no. 2 and op. 7.

Yet Beethoven expressed dissatisfaction with his piano music in general, and he proposed to 'strike out on a new road.' In addition his hearing had deteriorated, and his depths of personal suffering led to the brink of despair and the crisis of the Heiligenstadt Testament (1802). It has become unfashionable to relate a man's artistic achievements to his inner life, but it would be absurd to push this detachment too far. Maybe the unclouded Second Symphony, conceived in advance, emerged from the Heiligenstadt year; but so did the first stirrings of the *Eroica*, which can only be explained as an outcome of supreme mental effort. The great artist writes from his full experience of life (an idea well expressed in Deryck Cooke's *The Language of Music*) and suffering will deepen this experience in more than one direction. The *Eroica* had its repercussions in the piano sonatas, and no stronger emotional contrast could be found than that between the *Waldstein* and the *Appassionata*. This, again, is looking ahead. 1802 produced the three sonatas of op. 31, and of these only the second (D minor) betrays any subjective expression of impending tragedy. It is in fact, musically speaking, a tragic masterpiece, with a dramatic first movement haunted by a slow introductory arpeggio that later gives rise to those famous recitatives which, in Beethoven's words, should come 'like a voice from a tomb-vault':

Ex. 4

The importance of Beethoven's long-held pedal-marks cannot be over-emphasized – the rondo theme of the *Waldstein* is another case – as to remove the veil is to destroy the effect of mysterious suspense, even though we may admit some undetected half-pedalling on modern pianos. The adagio, too, is a test of the player's control, with its wide 'vocal' leaps and its left-hand drum-taps. The finale pursues an obsessed lonely path. So does the finale of Mozart's A minor Sonata (also written in a time of great personal distress): Mozart marks 'presto', Beethoven – performers please note – 'allegretto'. Op. 31, no. 1 in G major is seldom heard, though it contains some interesting Schubertian prophecies and has an unusual key-scheme for the first movement: B major in place of D for the second subject – a foretaste of the *Waldstein* but with none of its sweep or range. The E flat (no. 3) is more popular, with its informal opening and generally galant manner: a two–four scherzo of Mendelssohnian lightness, a melodious minuet, and a vigorous 'hunting' finale.

Courage and will-power triumphed at Heiligenstadt, and the new road that so astonishingly produced the *Eroica* soon produced sketches for the *Waldstein* Sonata, op. 53. Two intermediate works, op. 49, are a slight but delightful pair and date from an earlier period; the second borrowed the minuet theme from the Septet, or was it the other way round? But with the *Waldstein* a new vista opens up, and expansion of style was aided by expansion of resource, for in 1803 Beethoven had acquired an Erard piano with extended compass, upwards from F to C. The *Waldstein* (dedicated to Beethoven's early patron) was one of the first beneficiaries of this added brilliance. Accordingly, no work has suffered more from the onslaughts of 'virtuosi'. Its nobility and strength lie in its architecture. Marks and gradations are more vital than ever. All three movements evolve from pianissimo beginnings – a former nickname was 'L'Aurore' — and Beethoven's perception of the whole led him to reject the original slow movement (the Andante Favori, as it became) in favour of the profound Introduzione that makes such a perfect foil to the serene simplicity of the rondo theme. But 'simplicity' is a dangerous word to apply to great music, and the sketches show us the pains this theme cost Beethoven in the making. The obverse side of the medal is provided by op. 57 in F minor, the so-called *Appassionata*: its moods, alternately stormy and compassionate, have become almost synonymous with Beethovenism. Once again the sketches are revealing. We learn, for instance, that the first movement was conceived in common time until the incessant undercurrent of triplets, incorporating the famous 'fate' motif, persuaded it into twelve–eight. The andante, in straight variation form, again prompts the deceptive word 'simplicity'. Its theme is in fact alarmingly simple on paper, a rotation of basic harmony around tonic chords of D flat, with only one lightly-touched chromatic passing-chord to give it distinction. The variations subdivide the beat and engender a certain brilliance, but the harmonic inertia remains. Something akin happens in the slow move-ment of the Violin Concerto, at the end of which a modula-tion to the dominant has the effect of a world-shattering event. In the *Appassionata* a quiet diminished-seventh chord breaks the spell: it is taken up forcefully, and the finale wrenches us into the world of action. Between the *Wald-stein* and the *Appassionata* there hides a more modest neigh-bour, op. 54 in F. This two-movement sonata deserves hearing for its quizzical humour: a minuet beset by stormy octaves, and a moto perpetuo that runs the gauntlet of keys with irrepressible energy and effrontery. After the *Appass-ionata* Beethoven could afford to give the keyboard a rest, and he wrote no more piano sonatas for nearly five years.

In 1809, however, he produced three. They are the most heterogeneous collection imaginable: op. 78 in F sharp, a favourite of the composer's, intimate in manner and small-scale, but infinitely subtle in its pre-glimpses of 'late' Beethoven; op. 79 in G, deliberately modest and impersonal and sometimes called 'sonatina'; and op. 81a in E flat, which reverts to the grand manner and comes nearer to programme music than any of the sonatas. The three movements are labelled 'Farewell', 'Absence', and 'Reunion', supposedly inspired by the Archduke Rudolph's departure from Vienna during the Napoleonic invasion. Such emotions are universal, but the *Lebewohl* Sonata may be felt to suffer a little from the dictates of its programme – an enforced mixture of pathos and brilliance. Beethoven, in view of the circumstances, would hardly have welcomed the popular French title 'Les Adieux'. The two-movement op. 90 in E minor (1814) is also linked with an 'occasion' concerning an aristocratic patron, the marriage of Count Moritz von Lichnowsky. The music is self-sufficient: 'prose' and 'poetry' will sum up the contrast between the closely-argued first movement and the idyllic song that must, surely, have been admired by Schubert and Mendelssohn? The coda of this 'song without words' is rich in new developments, yet it closes into the most delicate and subtle of all sonata-endings:

It seems designed for domestic enjoyment, but – ironically – op. 90 was probably the only one of Beethoven's piano sonatas to receive a public performance during his life. And so to the last five sonatas, each highly important and none duplicating or even recalling any previous musical experience. 'Late Beethoven' is in fact approached with awe by hardened listeners and tested players; yet the composer, more and more isolated from the world by his deafness, pulled up no roots, and scorned no traditions in his innermost search for expression. The growth is still continuous, however immense the distance, however rarified the air into which the highest branches aspire. Time has passed since Tchaikovsky, who admired middle-period Beethoven, could find only 'glimmers and nothing more' in the late works. It was said that the deaf composer no longer considered instrumental (and vocal) limitations, but even accepting this debatable premise how much more rewarding that the spirit should transcend the letter than vice versa! The A major Sonata, op. 101, was finished in 1816 and dedicated to Baroness Dorothea von Ertmann, from all accounts an intimate rather than a brilliant player. In that case the 'reveries' of the first and third movements would have suited her manner more than the rigorous dotted rhythm of the alla marcia and the finale's strenuous fugal development. Counterpoint absorbed Beethoven increasingly as a distillation of musical thought where every note is an essential note. The last pages of Mozart's last symphony, and of Verdi's last opera, show that he was not alone in this desire to get 'back to Bach' or even, in his case, 'back to Palestrina'. In 1819 – note again the time-lapse – the *Hammerklavier* was ready, by far the largest and most challenging of all the sonatas. (The 'title' is simply German for 'pianoforte'). It enlarged the four-movement plan to an epic scale without resorting to the tempting 'romantic' cyclic devices – overt cross-quotations, retrospects – that had been hinted at in op. 81a and op. 101 (even in the finale of op. 27, no. 1). The *Hammerklavier* has its internal unities, among them the feature of a rising and falling third, and is all the stronger for not needing to advertise them. It is, however, fascinating to observe the mystique of key-association that led Beethoven's propensities for fugal writing into B flat major: the *Grosse Fuge*, the cadenza for the early B flat Concerto, the *Hammerklavier*. A few bars chosen at random will illustrate the mental and physical battle that rages and triumphs in the sonata's final fugue. They have a twentieth-century look about them – 'contemporary for ever', to borrow Stravinsky's phrase – and they show Beethoven's growing obsession with the trill as a 'personality':

Ex. 6

There was no need to conquer Everest twice, and in the last three sonatas of all (1820–22) Beethoven achieved a new conciseness, a new intimacy, a new warmth of heart. Opp. 109, 110 and 111 have been considered a trilogy, but it would be safer to call them complementary; they all turn traditional processes – sonata form, variations, fugue – to highly individual ends. The sonata-form compression in op. 109 (E major) is remarkable – the first movement runs its spacious course in four minutes, the second in two – and this throws the centre of gravity into the final variations on a heart-felt theme that comes round again, full circle, at the end. This andante completes the design; the addition of an orthodox finale could only shatter the effect of rapt

fulfilment. Op. 110 also reserves its full emotional depths
for the finale, unique in its juxtaposition and alternation of
recitative, aria, and fugue. How could Ernest Newman, in
The Unconscious Beethoven, patronize this as 'a recitative and
a short lament in song form'? No summary description can
convey the intense personal involvement that this music
commands and deserves. Even if we discount or mistrust
some of the stories that have been handed down, often on
slender evidence, of Beethoven's extra-musical inspirations,
it seems clear from the printed text alone that he regarded
the piano on the one hand and the quartet on the other as
the confidants of his most intimate thoughts. In op. 110 we
find subjective expression marks such as *ermattet* ('exhausted') and, at the advent of the inverted fugue subject,
wieder auflebend ('gaining new life'). All one might say
briefly of op. 111 in C minor is that it resolves the minor–
major conflict on the sublimest scale imaginable. An
introduction sets the scale, dynamically and tonally. As
Tovey might have put it, it views the solar system of keys
with awe before attending to the strife of earthly affairs and
passions. C minor had long been Beethoven's instinctive key
of *Sturm und Drang*, but the allegro of op. 111 is no mere
resurrection of former emotions. The context is new, for the
intellect and the spirit are more closely involved than ever
before. Technically the fugue and the sonata are integrated,
and the final clearing of the storm in the face of a quiet C
major chord expresses a very different triumph from the
jubilant finale of the Fifth Symphony: the less spectacular
but even greater triumph of inner peace. Two movements
say everything that has to be said, and with the serene C
major Arietta and variations of op. 111 Beethoven ended his
long association with the piano sonata.

Beethoven had watched the growing scope of the piano
and utilized its resources to the utmost – beyond the utmost
at times. Yet he can hardly be called a pioneer of piano
technique in the sense that Chopin, or even Clementi and
Czerny, were pioneers. The piano was a means to an end,
not to be wooed for its own sake but a vehicle for expression

– to be bullied, if necessary, into submission. There is scarcely a passage in Beethoven, early or late, that could be modified in the interests of technique, comfort, or 'effectiveness' without dissipation of the strength and will-power that made it. The artist thrives within limitations and even the much-worked Alberti bass and the routine range of arpeggio formulas served Beethoven well. Neither could Beethoven be called a harmonic innovator in the normal sense – in many instances Mozart was much more 'modern' in his use of dissonance – and his frequent reliance on tonic-and-dominant patterns, on Neapolitan sixths and diminished sevenths, has been ridiculed by those who obstinately refuse to see the wood for the trees. Wherein lies his extraordinary strength, then? The answer lies in Beethoven's unique mastery of tonality and key-relationships, the larger view of harmony; or, putting it another way, in the architectural sense that could find more resources in the deployment of ordinary structural bricks than less enduring, though more alluring, decorative ones. Only a shortsighted view can find a commonplace in the *Waldstein*. This is not to underrate Beethoven's gifts as a melodist, nor his ability to work in the smaller forms. Even the slenderest Bagatelle, like op. 33, no. 3 in F, bears his unmistakable fingerprints:

This might be written off as 'nursery music', but it contains the essence: the dramatic use of tonality, F major versus D major, and the dramatic use of dynamics, piano answered by pianissimo – a change of key demands a change of voice.

It was natural that the long gestation of most of Beethoven's large-scale works, coupled with his self-critical rejection of so many ideas, should have resulted in by-products. (The by-products might in their turn influence larger projects. I like to think, for example, that the F major–D major contrast in the above example so delighted Beethoven that he remembered it in the 'Peasants' Merrymaking' of the *Pastoral* Symphony.) There are, for instance, three sets of Bagatelles – and one or two random pieces may be included in this category as well. The Seven Bagatelles, op. 33, were published in 1803 but were probably collected from various dates. Op. 119 is an even more motley collection, some early, some late (judging from the upward compass of the writing), but their extreme brevity somehow unites them, and the eleventh in B flat is a little masterpiece (which Max Reger misguidedly inflated into a set of two-piano variations). Beethoven thought more highly of his last group of six, op. 126 (1823). They are more substantial, more related in their key scheme, and nearer in spirit and texture to the greater works of the period. But whereas the Bagatelles, in their grouping, seem to anticipate the Schumannesque cycles of miniatures, most of Beethoven's other piano-pieces have obvious precedents: rondos, minuets, dances, even the full-scale improvising Fantasy, op. 77, and the Polonaise, op. 89 (which begins with a cadenza before settling down to its main topic). The word 'fantasy' is disarming, but Mozart and Bach proved that a freely-roaming imagination could produce great music. But there is another type of improvisation: the absorption in the possibilities of a single theme, even a single figure. Haydn gave us a witty example in his entertaining Fantasia in C, and whether he knew it or not Beethoven emulated him in his *Rondo a Capriccio*, nicknamed 'The Rage over the Lost Penny' – an earlyish work served up posthumously and misleadingly as op. 129. A more definite by-product, through rejection, was the original *Waldstein* slow movement – too bland for such a context, maybe, but redeemed by some magic modulations – known popularly as the *Andante Favori*. There are also some four-hand duets, hardly comparable with Mozart's or Schubert's, but well worth attention: the Sonata in D, op. 6; the Marches, op. 45; and the exquisite variations, *Ich denke dein*. But mention of variations brings us back to a genre that produced at least three important works – and one great masterpiece.

Admittedly many of Beethoven's sets of variations are of no great weight; he exercised himself on various popular themes, even on 'God save the King' and 'Rule, Britannia'. Exercised is the word, for variation form was a challenge. It showed its influence on the sonata, too, sometimes taking over whole movements and affecting the behaviour of others – a theme might be repeated in a 'varied' form, a rondo might embellish the return of its subject. In general the classical variation set preserved the original key in order not to detract from the composer's sheer inventiveness. A change from major to minor, or vice versa, was accepted; anything further was liable to be disruptive – or spectacularly dramatic. The Six Variations on an original theme, op. 34, are unusual for their exploration of a whole circle of keys, falling by thirds from F major to C minor and thence, via C major, back home again. Moreover their manner is largely mild, decorative, and *un*spectacular. Despite their charm they have been dwarfed by another set of the same year (1802): the *Prometheus* Variations and Fugue, op. 35. Anyone hearing these for the first time is likely to exclaim 'But surely. . . .?' and with reason. The theme, taken from Beethoven's ballet music to *Prometheus*, was used again in the finale of the *Eroica*. Some of the procedures, too: the bass starts off with its own variations before the arrival of the theme proper and shows similar fugal aspirations, and there is a final apotheosis in slower time. Another middle-period set deserves mention: the Thirty-Two Variations in C minor. They have no opus-number and

Beethoven is said to have disowned them. Why, one Wonders? For they carry through the older passacaglia type of variations with conciseness, conviction, and sustained invention – in a line of succession midway between Bach's Chaconne and the finale of Brahms's Fourth Symphony.

The greatest, and longest, set had yet to come: the *Diabelli* Variations, op. 120 (1823). It was a lucky chance that the publisher Anton Diabelli should have invited the leading musicians in Austria to write a variation each on a waltz tune of his own, and good fortune that Beethoven took up the challenge by writing not one but thirty-three, thereby producing the most important and comprehensive work of its kind since Bach's *Goldberg* Variations. We should be grateful to, and not scornful of, Diabelli's 'cobbler's patch': its naïve simplicities provided an admirable starting-point for the increasing harmonic subtleties of the variations. Beethoven's very first variation established his seriousness of purpose, though by variation twenty-two he was not above throwing in a witty caricature (appropriate in the circumstances!) of Leporello's *Notte e giorno faticar* from *Don Giovanni*. Having probed the depths of the minor key in variations 29 to 31, he plunged into a vigorous double fugue in E flat, but allowed its final climax to 'evaporate' into the ethereal C major of the last 'tempo di menuetto' – the greatest stroke of all.

The rest of the scheme – the composite work Diabelli envisaged – was published separately and has been almost forgotten, though two contributions have more than historical interest: a fiery variation by a Hungarian prodigy named Franz Liszt which proved to be his first published composition; and a meltingly beautiful one by Schubert.

SCHUBERT (1797–1828)

Let us not bemoan the fact that Schubert's solitary Diabelli variation has been locked away among the commonplaces of the *Vaterländische Künstlerverein* without reflecting that vast areas of his piano music have suffered a similar neglect.

In this century Artur Schnabel was a pioneer, and nowadays at least half a dozen of the sonatas are assured of a
regular hearing. Yet recently Paul Badura-Skoda could
still speak of the 'unknown' Schubert who, according to
Deutsch's catalogue, wrote no less than twenty-two piano
sonatas, if we include incomplete and incompletely preserved works. Tovey, writing at the time of the 1927 Beethoven
centenary, told the following story:

> There is a curious English musical dictionary, published in
> 1827, which may sometimes be found in the four-penny box out-
> side a second-hand bookshop; and in this dictionary Beethoven is
> given one of the largest articles and treated as unquestionably the
> greatest composer of the day (though on the evidence only of his
> less dangerous works). Such was Beethoven's fame in the year of
> his death. Schubert died in the next year. There are five Schuberts
> in this dictionary, but Franz Schubert is not among them.

Tovey, or his publisher, made a slip in describing Schubert
as Beethoven's junior by seventeen years: he should have
said 'twenty-seven', which makes the situation more
understandable if not less regrettable. Had he lived for
another dozen years he would have heard his great C major
Symphony performed, thanks to the advocacy of Schumann
and Mendelssohn. Even then it was 'cut' – and he would
have had to travel to Leipzig.

No one needs reminding that of all instruments the piano
was Schubert's refuge. It is true that he played the violin,
early on, in family quartets; but as a domestic instrument
the piano was complete in itself – it could even if needs be,
stand in for an orchestra. Schubert never heard his greatest
symphonies played, but he could play (and hear) his four-
hand *Grand Duo* – a symphony in conception, probably in
intent – by inviting a friend round for the evening. Piano
duets are not strictly within the range of this book, but
Schubert's vast output of them must be mentioned. They
are treasures of domestic music-making and cover a wide
range of forms – variations, rondos, marches, divertissements
among them. The F minor Fantasy (D940) must be singled
out not only for its tragic beauty but for its compression of

a four-movement sonata scheme into a continuous whole and the drama of its key-relations: F *sharp* minor is used for the two middle sections. (Compare the shattering emotional effect of E major–F minor–E major in the slow movement of the String Quintet.) 'Compression' is a word seldom applied to Schubert. We speak more easily, albeit affectionately, of his 'heavenly length', thinking no doubt of the lavish time scale of his last three piano sonatas, the C major Symphony and the Quintet. Yet how dangerous to generalize! The 'little' A major Sonata (D664) could hardly be more compact, while the first movement of the A minor Sonata (D845) is one of the most closely-integrated sonata structures in existence. But here a confusion awaits the listener – or did, until Otto Deutsch took charge – for *this* A minor was published as 'op. 42' and two earlier ones in the same key appeared, also in reverse order, as 'op. 143' and 'op. 164'. Where Beethoven's opus-numbers are, with a few exceptions, a reasonable guide to the order of events, Schubert's are chaotic, due to the haphazard, often long-delayed, publication of his works. After years of research Deutsch did for Schubert what Köchel had done for Mozart – hence the 'D' numbers – and it may be helpful to list the piano sonatas as they appear in his catalogue (1951) alongside the opus-numbers that still linger in many editions and programmes:

Schubert's Piano Sonatas

Key	Year	D no.	Op. no.	Remarks
E major	1815	157		4th mvt missing
C major	1815	279		unfinished
E major	1816	459		publ. as '5 Klavierstücke'
A minor	1817	537	164	
A flat major	1817	557		'ends' in E flat
E minor	1817	566		4th mvt missing, perhaps D506?
D flat major	1817	567		first version of D568
E flat major	1817	568	122	
F sharp minor	1817	570–71		unfinished

B major	1817	575	147	
C major	1818	613		unfinished
F minor	1818	625		unfinished
C sharp minor	1819	655		sketch for 1st mvt only
A major	1819	664	120	
A minor	1823	784	143	
C major	1825	840		3rd and 4th mvts incomplete
A minor	1825	845	42	
D major	1825	850	53	
G major	1826	894	78	called 'Fantasia'
C minor	1828	958	'posth.'	
A major	1828	959	'posth.'	
B flat major	1828	960	'posth.'	

The romantic authors who wove stories around the unfinished B minor Symphony would have had their work cut out to account for the number of unfulfilled, incomplete, lost or partly lost Schubert manuscripts. Very little of his music was printed during his life, though he earned some immediate fame as a composer of songs. From the songs alone we should have admired Schubert's genius for the piano, and when Breitkopf turned down the *Erlkönig* in 1817 it was largely due to the unprecedented importance, and difficulty, of the accompaniment. In the songs the piano reigns as an equal partner, and many of the technical problems in the solo works arise from the pianist's need to be singer and accompanist in one. An example from the finale of the first 'complete' sonata, D459 in E, gives a foretaste of the new kind of textures that Schubert developed:

Ex. 8

The manuscript of D459 makes it clear that these so-called *Klavierstücke* were intended to form a sonata, perhaps with the omission of one or other of the two scherzos. Nevertheless the central adagio has appeared on its own in many a volume of favourite pieces.

The year 1817, as can be seen from the list above, was a prolific one for piano sonatas, and although the A minor (D537) inevitably pales in the light of its successors in that key, it has a fine drive and drama in its opening six–eight movement and, in curious compensation, a hesitant finale fraught with abrupt modulations. But Schubert's individual play with tonality, not only in the minor–major inflections that he made his own, would fill a book: it led to Tovey's masterly dissertation 'Tonality in Schubert' (1928), reprinted in his *Essays and Lectures on Music* (Oxford, 1949). Meanwhile the middle movement of D537 sounds a familiar note, a rondo with a fascinating key scheme, on a theme that Schubert perfected, eleven years later, in the finale of the last A major Sonata (D959). D537 has only three movements, whereas the other preserved sonatas of 1817, the E flat and the B major, complete their four-movement plans with a minuet and scherzo respectively. Here we might intervene and remark on the (generally) vast difference in character between Schubert's scherzos and Beethoven's. We are reminded that whereas Beethoven came to Vienna at a mature age from north, or at any rate north-west, Germany, Schubert was Viennese from the start. It is hard to pin-point, short of hearing it, the 'Viennese' quality that gives so much music from Mozart to Johann Strauss and beyond a special flavour, expressed by the German word *gemütlich*, and the coined expression *musizieren* ('to make music' for the love of it). These contribute, and so does the element of popular dance music, the Ländler and the waltz. Schubert was as likely to break into a three–four or three–eight dance rhythm in a sonata form movement as in a scherzo, and the scherzos themselves – even in the C major Symphony and the String Quintet – turn quite naturally to a carefree waltz or near-waltz rhythm, sometimes giving in their context an effect of tragic irony or pathos. This example is from the finale of the A major Sonata of 1819 (D664):

Not that D664 is in any sense a tragic work. It has its shadows, especially in the middle movement with its tender interplay between major and minor, phrase by phrase, but on the whole it is serene and warm-hearted, light-hearted in fact in the finale quoted above. The first movement is a song marvellously conceived in pianistic terms, and both in form and texture it is a model of economy – the shortest of the more familiar sonatas.

The second of the three A minor sonatas, D784, is another matter altogether; it has a Beethovenish obsession with tense short motifs, and an atmosphere of suspense. Never before had Schubert used dynamic changes with such dramatic and spine-chilling force as in the first movement, with its spare bleak unison opening and its fortissimo counter-statement – in which we can imagine the cavorting of Berliozian brass. In such surroundings the major-key second subject, in reality a metamorphosis of the first, appears like a benediction. The slow movement may be thought short for its context, but it is also strikingly original, with a *sotto voce* aside that later catches fire; and the finale, anticipating the flutes of Smetana's *Vltava*, extracts the extremes of contrast from its three–four time signature, fiercely exuberant and tenderly pathetic in turn – the dramatization of the dance *par excellence*. Schubert's orchestral treatment of the piano looks up again from the first page of the unfinished C major Sonata, D840, a work that promised to fill out the Olympian scale often associated with this key – from Mozart's C major Concerto K503 to Schubert's own C major masterpieces, including the *Grand Duo*. As in the *Duo* (and the sonata just discussed) the first and second subjects are closely related – two aspects of a single theme. The piano writing is uncompromising – a very different story from the grace of D664, or even the grimmer drama of D 784 – and, as Paul Badura-Skoda has rightly insisted, it demands a keen orchestral sense to bring it off. But despite the fully worked andante in C minor the remaining two movements are torsos, and the completed half of the sonata gives the feeling that, like the *Duo*, it is a symphony in disguise.

We must not complain too much, for the next sonata of 1825 – again in A minor – is in every respect a masterpiece (D845). Its first movement is also the perfect reply to the once-prevalent criticism of Schubert's handling of sonata form as naïve. The simple repetitions and transpositions in the *Trout* Quintet are not a fair target, for that delight-fully relaxed work was in its nature a divertimento. But D845, like the unfinished C major before it, binds form and content together in a wholly personal way. The opening subject ('dreamy' was Schumann's description) leads not to a counterstatement of itself but to a rhythmic *counterpart*. and the 'second subject', instead of producing new themes, reviews these two aspects of the first subject from the stance of the expected relative major (C major). Three brief quotations will illustrate this remarkable unity – the two A minor themes, and their fusion at the close of the exposition:

D845 being one of the few sonatas to appear in print during
Schubert's lifetime, it is interesting to read a Leipzig critic's
reaction: 'It moves so freely and originally within its confines, and sometimes so boldly and curiously, that it might
not unjustly have been called a Fantasy.' Then comes the
highest compliment: 'In that respect it can probably be
compared only with the greatest and freest of Beethoven's
sonatas.' (This favourable notice of 'a still quite young
artist' came in 1826, two years before Schubert's death –
alas, he was nevertheless 'still quite young'.) Free, like
simple, is a deceptive word: it seems unlikely that the critic
was thinking of the 'con alcune licenze' of the *Hammerklavier* fugue! The 'fantasy' notion presumably referred to
Schubert's flexible handling of sonata form in the first movement, far subtler than the wildest dreams of the text-books.
(Mozart's G minor Quintet, first movement, was another
example of the first and second subjects being, in Hans
Keller's phrase, 'split down the middle'.) The rest of D845:
an andante with variations (C major), a scherzo with a
Ländler-like trio, and a moto perpetuo finale largely subdued in tone but with vigorous (Slavonic?) outbursts –
compare Mozart's A minor and Beethoven's D minor
sonatas.

In the summer of 1825 Schubert, recuperating from a
long illness, went with friends into the Salzkammergut. He
wrote to his parents: 'I have been in Gmunden for six
weeks, the environs of which are truly heavenly and deeply
moved and benefited me, as did its inhabitants . . .' In this
mood the D major Sonata, K850, came into being, as happy
and courageous as the previous sonata had been tragic and

resolute. The scale and manner are grand, too, in all four movements – vigour in the first, with local colour in the yodelling second theme; a richly melodic and richly varied slow movement, modulating widely; a fully-fledged scherzo and trio; and the entrancing finale, filled with the flavour of popular dance and song (and irresistible as played by Schnabel and Clifford Curzon). Then, in 1826, the extremely personal G major Sonata, D894 – in this case *called* 'Fantasia', though not in Schubert's manuscript. It opens in an atmosphere of tender self-communion and returns repeatedly to this mood in spite of the strenuous developments that grow from its subtly flickering rhythmic 'germ'. This piece, with its leisurely tempo, takes the bloom off the slow movement proper, perhaps – a pleasant but more conventional andante; but the B minor minuet, with a B major trio marked *ppp*, is well known on its own, and the finale, outwardly innocent, shows a disregard for conventional phrase-lengths from the start.

A glance at Deutsch's catalogue justifies Britten's description of Schubert's last year, 1828, as a miracle, or words to that effect: the C major Symphony, the String Quintet, the *Schwanengesang*, the E flat Mass, some of the greatest four-hand duets, cantatas and songs, ending with *Der Hirt auf dem Felsen* – and, within September alone, the three last piano sonatas. Their contrasts and their contemporaneousness make the 'trilogy' parallel with Beethoven's opp. 109–111 and Mozart's last three symphonies tempting. Yet, as Philip Radcliffe remarks in his excellent monograph on the sonatas, they were for a long time underestimated, and therefore, in view of modern opinion, misunderstood. They share a heavenly length, as though Schubert defied the time that was so cruelly running out on him, but thereafter they differ, or should we once again say that they 'complement' one another? The C minor, D958, is the least often heard, partly because this key and its associated moods had been so fully explored by Beethoven: the terse opening invokes a direct comparison with the C minor piano variations Beethoven is said to have disowned. It is in the development's sinuous chromatics, rather than the rhetorical gestures, that the music is most eloquent, and the *pp* ending of the first movement looks back to the superb precedents of Mozart. But the adagio eschews convention in its daring play with tonality, and the final affirmation of its home key (A flat) with a cadence phrase previously played *pp* is striking indeed:

Ex. 11

The minuet, with its low-lying trio, is strangely brief and subdued; its livelier moves turn back, as if with foreboding, into the shadows of C minor. The finale, sublimely disproportionate, is a vast and obsessive adventure in keys, riding through them at a gentle gallop that, on account of the distances travelled, makes the movement a tour de force for the player. C major is among the keys visited, but the minor ending is irrefutable. This is not intended to patronize the C minor Sonata, but to expose its difficulties; it is wildly unlike any other Schubert sonata, and yet unmistakably typical – another aspect, disturbing but authentic. If the gallopings of its finale have been those of a dark horse, the blame must rest with the two remaining sonatas of September 1828; marvellously proportioned, they are not short on tonal adventure either.

D959 in A major, after a majestic opening, involves itself in a chain of fantastic modulations on its way to a 'simple' tender second theme and then resumes them before allowing this theme further hearing. The 'split down the middle' is not between first and second subjects but between the processes of exposition and development. But the slow movement has the greatest, most alarming, surprise of all: a plaintive song, harmonized in F sharp minor and A major respectively, is invaded by a cataclysmic passage of bravura recitative in which key as such ceases to exist. Even the scherzo, light and picturesquely scored, seems to recall this crisis in one abrupt wrench from C major to C sharp minor. The rondo finale recalls many things: thematically the slow movement of the early A minor Sonata of 1817, formally the rondo of Beethoven's op. 31, no. 1 in G (especially its coda), and in the last six bars the grand opening of D959 itself.

The B flat Sonata, D960, is not only the last but, arguably, the summit, and it has had staunch and eloquent advocates: Schnabel, Curzon, Kempff, Myra Hess. The story goes that Schnabel, who had the rare gift of 'holding' the slowest tempo, added ten minutes to his overall time when on form – and the first movement is neither allegro nor allegretto but 'molto moderato'. The music abounds in subtle masterstrokes, such as the deep mysterious trill that pervades the movement like a distant roll of thunder. Only once does it appear menacingly near, in the 'first time bars' at the end of the exposition – a good reason for insisting on the repeat in a movement already spacious, even by Schubertian standards. This spaciousness, and lyricism, is epitomized by the leisurely way the development finds its way back to the opening, with a magic interplay between B flat and D minor; and the calm of the coda makes the piece seem 'a work in itself'. In the slow movement (C sharp minor, turning to A major) we see cross-influences – the two cellos of the Quintet, just written, playing aloft in thirds, with an accompaniment reaching lightly across them. Philip Radcliffe aptly speaks of 'a brooding visionary quality'. To follow a slowish first movement with an andante sostenuto, and to bring it off, is remarkable; the remote key helps, and so does the splendidly generous 'consoling' theme of the middle section – the reverse type of emotional contrast from the alarms, at this point, in the previous sonata. D960 continues to expand its range, in the scherzo, light-footed but with a stubbornly syncopated minor-key trio, and in the finale, which exposes a whole chain of themes and makes a point of starting the first out of its proper key, on the dominant of C minor. (Compare the ultimate finale of Beethoven's op. 130 Quartet, also – be it noted – in B flat.) This strange twist gives an unusual orientation to the rondo-returns, and only 'corrects' itself on the last page. Once this is settled, all that is needed is the abrupt 'happy ending' that Schubert adds to this great, profoundly lovable, work.

As with Beethoven, it seemed simplest to deal with Schubert's sonatas before passing to the miscellaneous pieces. Taking a bird's-eye view in retrospect, as it were, it is worth noting that, in spite of his admiration for Beethoven, he made no attempt to follow the master in leanings towards cyclic form, i.e. links between movements. The subtler (subconscious?) unities are another thing, and functional analysis will yield dividends in the Schubert sonatas, maybe; but it was *outside* the sonata as such that he made deliberate unifying gestures – in the duet Fantasy in F minor mentioned earlier, and, more so, in the solo *Wanderer* Fantasy (D760) of 1822. (The violin and piano Fantasy in C, D934, is a further case and, like the *Wanderer*, it takes inspiration from a song, *Sei mir gegrüsst!*) Thematic unity in the various 'movements' of the *Wanderer* is illustrated very simply:

Ex. 12

It is strange that Schubert, who saw such drama in the settings of words, and in instrumental music too, should have remained aloof from the drama of the concerto – his pieces for violin and orchestra are early and small-scale – but it is far from strange that Liszt should choose the *Wanderer* to turn *into* a work for piano and orchestra, since it fitted, and may have helped to inspire, his own views on cyclic transformations. However time has shown that a successful concerto cannot be made out of a re-distribution of material otherwise conceived, and the *Wanderer*, despite its technical demands, is now most often heard in its original form.

At the other end of the scale are the numerous sequences of dances – waltzes, Ländler, minuets, écossaises – that still enhance a *Schubert-Abend* and reveal the Viennese quality many of us relish in Johann Strauss. For Schubert, in Otto Deutsch's words, 'felt at home in the circles of his friends, and there he was ready, though not a dancer himself, to accompany on the piano his friends' dancing for hours at a stretch.' The more serious and most popular of the piano pieces are the two sets of Impromptus, D899 and D935 ('op. 90' and 'op. 142'), and the six *Moments Musicaux*, D780.* Each set of Impromptus makes a satisfactory whole, though it is essential to play no. 3 of D899 in its original key of G flat major – thus linking it with the surprising E flat minor ending of no. 2 – instead of in the easier to read, though not easier to play, version in G major, a publisher's sop to the public! In no. 1 of D935 Schumann detected a 'sonata style', and this is borne out by the key scheme of the four: F minor, A flat, B flat (variations on a cousin of the B flat *Rosamunde* theme, also used in the A minor Quartet), and again F minor. The *Moments Musicaux*, like Beethoven's op. 33 and op. 119 Bagatelles, were collected from various years for their publication in 1828. The favourite here is the first F minor one, no. 3, but the pair in A flat (nos. 2 and 6) are touching pieces, sharing that tenderly ruminating

* The influence of the short piano pieces by the Bohemians Voříšek (1791–1825) and Tomašek (1774–1850) has often been noted.

character we noted at the opening of the G major *Fantasy* Sonata. Three *Klavierstücke* (also 1828) are less known, and therefore more rewarding still to the Schubert-lover: the first two in rondo form with widely contrasted episodes; the third more direct in feeling, though with an unawaited, albeit typical, change from C to D flat for the middle section. To quote Tovey: 'Schubert's tonality is as wonderful as star-clusters, and a verbal description of it as dull as a volume of astronomical tables.' Tables, however, are valuable as a means of location; wherein lies some excuse, it is to be hoped, for the fairly lengthy 'catalogue' approach of this chapter.

Postscript: scant attention has been given to the unfinished works, D840 excepted, as in their nature they are seldom likely to reach the concert-hall. The F minor and F sharp minor sonatas will continue to tantalize musicians, and to inspire some to 'finish' them, but the results – like Joachim's orchestration of the *Grand Duo* – can, at best, have only theoretical interest. There is plenty of 'finished' Schubert to rediscover, anyway.

BRAHMS (1833–1897)

From their output alone it is obvious that the classical sonata was 'a way of thought' to Beethoven and Schubert, and a parallel to the quartet and the symphony. Romanticism, however, was to find new outlets in the field of piano music, and it is no discredit to Schumann's and Chopin's sonatas to observe that the form was no longer as essential as it had been. Even Liszt's masterpiece, the B minor Sonata, was unique in his vast legacy; and neither Schubert nor Beethoven would have called it a sonata in the first place. But in 1853 Schumann was visited by the twenty-year-old Brahms, who arrived 'fully armed' with two sonatas finished and a third (the F minor) in his head. Brahms had probably written, and destroyed, many more. No one could have guessed that he would never compose another. Instead he turned to variation form and, much later, to groups of

short pieces – intermezzi and capriccios. Thus the piano
music shows us, neatly and chronologically, three facets of
Brahms's make-up: one, his admiration for Beethoven and
the desire to write in the grand manner (sonatas); two, his
growing self-criticism and his love of Bach (variations, with
plenty of strict counterpoint thrown in); and three, his
essential lyricism. The sonatas, remarkable as works of
youth, already reveal the tussle between heart and head.
(With them we can bracket the E flat minor Scherzo, op. 4.)
Significantly the first to be written – the F sharp minor, op.
2 – is also the most lavish in virtuosity and the most daringly
rhapsodic. From its opening onslaught of double octaves to
the cadenza-like close of the finale the Lisztians could, at
this stage, have claimed Brahms as a disciple, and the
transformation of the slow movement theme into the
scherzo was another point in his favour. The C major
Sonata, op. 1 and the F minor, op. 5 confirmed these
romantic leanings: the former adapted an old German
Minnelied for the andante, the latter prefaced its slow movement with lines from a love-poem by Sternau and recalled
its theme, now no longer idyllic but gloomily retrospective,
in an interlude between scherzo and finale. Brahms must
have been a considerable pianist, and the manner and
flavour of his music are, already, unmistakable. Yet he had
been nurtured on the classics by his teacher Marxsen, and
the C major Sonata proclaims the Beethoven influence
from the start – the rhythm of the *Hammerklavier*, and the
C–to–B flat plunge of the *Waldstein*. Contrapuntal devices –
canons, diminutions, and strettos – are called in repeatedly,
and even the most lyrical themes are examined for their
potential, sometimes with rather forced results:

Ex. 13

Schumann, romantic enough at heart but on the guard against extremism, recognized the strength and the aspirations and acclaimed them: 'This is he that should come.' Brahms became embroiled, unwillingly and unwittingly, in musical politics – on the 'classical' side of the fence. By the eighteen-fifties the scene was something of a battleground: on the one side was the Liszt–Wagner faction, hailing the music of the future; on the other the traditionalists, moderate if not sceptical. As early as 1830 Berlioz had fanned the flames of revolution with the *Symphonie Fantastique*, and within a year or two the young Liszt had transcribed it for piano solo. This was not pure virtuosity: in this form he could bring much new music to people who had no chance of hearing the original. But these were the avant-garde, and in due course Wagner carried the ultra-romantic flag to a summit in *Tristan* and *The Ring*. Perhaps the point of the hostility can be expressed and the gulf between 'absolute' and 'programme' music, intellect and emotion? This is only a half-truth, for there is plenty of emotion in Bach's fugues, plenty of intellect (and counterpoint) in Wagner. It depends on which we put first, on our attitude to the purpose of art: not so much on whether we respect tradition, but on whether we consider certain traditions played out. Now that the dust has settled, and we find ourselves in an infinitely more confusing age, we can look back and see that Mendelssohn and Berlioz, Brahms and Wagner, shared a common basic grammar – which is more than we can say of Sibelius and Schoenberg, or Boulez and the Beatles. There is an uncanny premonition of Hans Sachs in the coda of the F minor Sonata's slow movement, and although Brahms was rash enough to sign a manifesto dissociating himself from the 'New German' school he was objective enough to call himself 'the best of the Wagnerites'. His admiration of *Meistersinger* came from the heart.

Meanwhile Schumann never lived to see his prophecies fulfilled, for within months of his meeting with Brahms he succumbed to his final mental collapse. Brahms paid a tribute to his advocate in the *Schumann* Variations, op. 9 (on a theme from the *Bunte Blätter*), an intimate work incorporating ingenious canons. The lure and the discipline of variation form had begun. The four Ballades, op. 10, are an exception (1854) – a foretaste of the later groups, but also, as Peter Latham suggests, owing something to Schumann's *Phantasiestücke*. The first (D minor) betrays a literary influence, the grim Scottish ballad *Edward*, and it is appropriately bleak, with a fine dramatic climax in which we hear the 'big boots' of Beethoven – the Fifth Symphony rhythm that haunted the early sonatas and was to continue to haunt Brahms for years to come. ('Any fool can see that!' would have been his comment.) Another influence dates from his early concert tour with the violinist Reményi and permeates even his most serious works: the gipsy style, and in particular the fiddler's thirds and sixths with which Brahms loved to double a melodic line. They are to be expected in the Violin Concerto, written for Joachim; they colour the finale of the B flat Piano Concerto, second subject; even the song *Immer leiser*, even the Requiem. To return to variations, two seldom-heard sets soon followed, op. 21, the first on an original theme, the second on a Hungarian Song in an exotic three-plus-four rhythm. (The many Hungarian Dances, popular in all manner of arrangements, were originally written as piano duets. So were the Waltzes op. 39, and the four-hand Variations, op. 23 – not to be confused with op. 9 – on the moving theme Schumann believed to have been transmitted to him by the spirits of Schubert and Mendelssohn.) Brahms's approach to variations was classical in its adherence to the barring and structure of the theme. He aimed, with his eye on the symphony, at a greater refinement of technique than his youthful exuberance had achieved. Even contrapuntal devices, like canon and double counterpoint, had to be integrated within set bounds. The smoothness of variation 6 of the *Handel* set, op. 24, shows how well he succeeded. All padding and flamboyance has been stripped away:

Ex. 14

The *Handel* Variations (1861) are generally regarded as Brahms's 'classic' in the form, and the final fugue, with its inversions and augmentations, triumphantly proclaims the contrapuntist. The fugue subject, itself a variant of the start of Handel's theme, would suit organ pedals, and the shadow of Bach looms larger than ever in the impressive dominant wind-up near the end. When George Henschel visited Brahms he noticed that the *Forty-Eight* stood open on the piano desk; when an obsequious host offered the composer 'the very Brahms of wines' Brahms told him to 'take it away and bring some Bach!' – it was the age of the great Bach revival, and Brahms's name appeared in the list of subscribers to the Bachgesellschaft edition that, year by year, was bringing the vast corpus of Bach's music to light. With Brahms, strict counterpoint reconciled the head with a heart that expressed itself most naturally in romantic melody. Song-like ideas do not willingly lend themselves to dissection and discussion, but they may be blended and interwoven, and thus 'unified' in large-scale music.

Brahms's more solid textures, especially his fondness for doublings in octaves, thirds, and sixths, have baffled many traditionally brilliant pianists. He does not demand a great stretch as much as the ability to leap, and time and again he favoured the octave span instead of the extended position of the triad that Chopin developed. Two brief examples from the B flat Concerto:

One seldom finds unarpeggiated chords of the tenth in
Brahms, though the early sonatas abound in awkward
skips as though striving for an orchestral sonority. Yet his
piano style, like his orchestral style, suited his own music,
and if he turned away from exotic effects of colour – thereby
inviting criticisms of greyness, dullness and turgidity – it
was a symbol of integrity: a work must stand or fall on the
quality of its thought and not on its trimmings. Even the
fireworks of the *Paganini* Studies (1862–3) serve a musical
purpose: they too are 'classical' variations, and the use of
double counterpoint (e.g. Book 2, no. 1) also ensures their
value as studies by sharing muscular, as well as musical,
problems between the hands. The two sets are Brahms's
greatest challenge to the virtuoso (Clara Schumann found
them beyond her strength), and some virtuosos go one better
by playing both at a sitting. He further codified his technical
manner in a series of pure studies or exercises, the *Klavier-
übungen*; and made a few teasing transcriptions of well-
known classics (Bach, Weber, Chopin) that are infinitely
harder than they sound. One has only to compare the

sobriety of his left-hand version of Bach's Chaconne with Busoni's two-hand one to see why the former is seldom played in public!

The period of variation writing was followed by a lull in the output of solo piano works, though mention must be made of the two-piano version of the *Haydn* ('St. Antoni') Variations, better known in their orchestral form. In these, counterpoint runs more smoothly than ever, but could it be that Brahms's increased formal mastery in keyboard music had now served a double purpose and been channelled away? The First Symphony, having hung fire for twenty years, was at last ready in 1876, and the Second followed on its heels; the phase of large-scale orchestral works continued, culminating in the Double Concerto (1887). (Pianists can hardly complain, for the B flat Concerto was one of them.) But for the solo piano Brahms adopted, and continued to adopt, the smaller forms. The eight *Klavier-stücke*, op. 76, were completed in 1878 – the piano was no longer a conveyor of grand designs but a relaxation from Brahms's symphonic exploits. 'Have pity on my misery and send the longed-for Intermezzi' wrote Elisabet von Herzo-genberg over her cleverly-remembered quotation from op. 76, no. 7, which Brahms had tried out on his friends with others of the set. From now on 'intermezzo' is the favoured title for the short lyrical piece, and the simple ternary-form principle served Brahms well, with a gently contrasted middle section folding back to the opening. More vigorous, passionate pieces are called, deceptively, capriccios (nos. 1, 2, 5, and 8). Only the popular B minor, no. 2, is light-heartedly 'capricious', and nos. 1 and 5 are typical of the more gloomy introspection that tended to become a stereotyped emotion. Brahms's obsession with cross-rhythms, six–eight versus three–four, sometimes defeated its purpose as a compositional trick. Setting aside his Hungarian predi-lections as 'imports', the rhythmic element was less promi-nent in his make-up than the melodic. Even the springy iambic rhythm that injects so much vitality into the first movements of the Violin Concerto, the B flat Piano

Concerto and the Second Symphony became a habit and, it must be faced, lent a 'sameness' to the results.

The two Rhapsodies of op. 79 are more extended pieces and, as we have learnt to expect, far from rhapsodic in form. Both begin, however, in a spirit of development rather than exposition, with restlessly modulating sequences. The first and longer, in B minor, offers a 'second subject' (D minor) only to brush it aside for further development of the first, but the same idea offered in B major comes to stay – a musette-like trio, notable for its five-bar phrasing. The G minor is more obviously in sonata form, with a heroic ring at the start that gives way to a doggedly sombre march. Despite their minor keys there is enough contrast, formally and dramatically, to make the two pieces playable as a pair. Meanwhile the orchestra and large-scale chamber music occupied Brahms: the solo pianist had to wait another dozen years. It is relevant to his music as a whole to note that the finale of the Fourth Symphony (1885) is, or was, a latter-day passacaglia, sticking to its eight-bar text in a long series of 'ground bass' variations until the brief release of the coda. Brahms, however, had proved his point – the classical approach was still valid and fruitful – and, judging from the perennial popularity of the symphonies, posterity has largely endorsed it. Those not in sympathy could turn to the invective of Hugo Wolf in the Vienna *Salonblatt:* 'The art of composing without ideas has decidedly found its most worthy representative in Brahms.' But Wolf was a Wagnerite with a grudge. Arnold Schoenberg – an avant-garde composer if ever there was one – was soon to take the reverse view, and to maintain it. In 1947, fifty years after Brahms's death, he spoke of 'Brahms the Progressive':

It is important to realise that at a time when all believed in 'expression' Brahms, without renouncing beauty and emotion, proved to be a progressive in a field which had not been cultivated for half-a-century. He would have been a pioneer if he had simply returned to Mozart. But he did not live on inherited fortune: he made one of his own.

Late in life Brahms, through the playing of Richard Mühlfeld, rediscovered the lyrical qualities of the clarinet – in the Trio, the Quintet and the two sonatas. A parallel feeling of quiet maturity and resignation affects many of the last piano pieces too. Not entirely: the shade of Paganini hangs over the virtuoso Capriccio in D minor, op. 116, no. 1, and the E flat Rhapsody of op. 119 has a sense of triumphant resolution, not dispelled by its surprising minor-key ending. These last four groups – opp. 116 to 119 – date from 1891 to 1893. The seven pieces of op. 116 are called *Phantasien*, though the mixture of intermezzi and capriccios is as before. Op. 117 consists of three Intermezzi only. When Schnabel took them to his teacher Leschetizsky the latter asked how it was possible, in a virtuoso age, to group together three soberly-coloured andantes? In fact they are more often heard as individuals, especially the first in E flat (*Schlaf sanft, mein Kind*), and all three sound the note of earnest introspection that, later still, yielded the *Four Serious Songs*. The bare opening octaves of op. 117, no. 3 (C sharp minor) show a close spiritual and melodic kinship with the first of the songs:

The term 'capriccio' has vanished; in the six *Klavierstücke*, op. 118, we find instead a Ballade in G minor (no. 3) and a Romance in F (no. 4) – both introduce magic modulations for the middle sections. Op. 118, no. 6 in E flat minor is the most dramatic of all the Intermezzi, a forlorn theme developed to a great and tragic climax; but no. 2 in A is the perfect fusion of heart and head – we scarcely notice that (b) is a melodic inversion of (a). The effect is pure poetry in both cases:

Finally, op. 119: three more Intermezzi followed by the
Rhapsody in E flat. No. 1 in B minor, with its falling thirds,
was a favourite of Clara Schumann's, 'so sadly sweet in
spite of all its dissonances'. No 2 (E minor) turns the contours of an agitated theme into an idyllic middle section,
no. 3 (C major) is a capriccio in all but name, while two
brief quotations – one from the Rhapsody and one from the
F minor Sonata of forty years earlier – will show how little
Brahms's basic vocabulary had changed:

Those who insist on the 'progress of art' can remark that in 1893, the year of these last piano pieces, Debussy was writing *L'Après-midi*. But Brahms's aloofness from fashion paid its own dividends; Schoenberg called him a progressive, and his works are still firmly entrenched in the repertoire.

5

The Romantic Tradition

JOHN OGDON

*

THE BEGINNINGS OF ROMANTIC PIANO MUSIC

We can chart romantic piano music more easily than we can
chart romanticism in general. This is because the rise of
romanticism coincided exactly with the development of the
modern grand piano. The five octaves

of Mozart's time, a limited but marvellously expressive
range, become extended during Beethoven's last years to
six octaves. By the time Chopin and Liszt came to write for
the piano, a full seven octaves were available:

Mozart had explored the extreme registers of his keyboard; Beethoven, in his last sonatas, used the highest and
lowest octaves of the keyboard with extraordinary eloquence – this is indeed one of the colouristic features of the
piano writing of his last years. Chopin and Liszt carried this
usage further, pianistically if not musically; some of the
delicate filigree threads of sound woven by Chopin in his

Berceuse and by Liszt in *Ricordanza* are intimately bound up with the new range of sound available, and would have been impossible to realize on the instruments of a generation before. Also, as pianos changed, a new school of pianoforte playing emerged; the more sonorous sound which came naturally from the newly extended instrument called for a less exclusively digital technique from the performer, but rather for a combination of this traditional independence of the fingers with an increased muscular correlation with the wrists and forearms. These new developments of pianism were necessitated by the compound figurations of Chopin, the melodic use of the tenor register by Thalberg (1812–71), by Liszt's chordal writing, all of which were aspects of romantic piano writing destined to alter the way of playing the instrument. Such changes in pianistic technique did not of course happen overnight: when Chopin played in Glasgow and Edinburgh in 1848, his playing was described in ways which might remind us of Mozart's dictum that 'the passages should flow like oil': 'with what consummate sweetness and ease did he unravel the wonderful varieties and complexities of sound!. . . of the whirl of liquid notes he wove garlands of pearls';* 'his style blends in beautiful harmony and perfection the elegant, the picturesque, and the humorous;'† 'while all other pianistes (sic) strive to equalize the power of the fingers, M. Chopin aims to utilize them; and in accordance with this idea, are his treatment of the scale and the shake, as well as his mode of sliding with one and the same finger, from note to note, and of passing the third over the fourth finger.'‡ (Remembering the Victorian notation of the five fingers as +1234, we should probably understand the last remark to refer to passing the *fourth* over the *fifth* finger.) But playing such as this seems an evolutionary throwback when one reads of the leonine performances that Thalberg, Liszt and Brahms gave of their music. The imperfect but evocative grand

* Sir James Hedderwick
† The *Glasgow Courier*   quoted in Audrey Evelyn Bone's
‡ The *Edinburgh Advertiser*   '*Jane Wilhelmina Stirling*.'

piano had in any case great variety of texture; it was to prove ideal for that unravelling of imaginative sensuousness which is part of romanticism.

Tovey's 'interesting historical figures' must include many of the earliest romantic composers. J. B. Cramer (1771–1858) wrote many studies for piano – some of these are interesting and almost clear a path to Schumann's romantic expressiveness. Busoni edited eight of them some seventy years later, and delightful re-creations they are. There is no doubt that the best of them, e.g. the Study in B flat minor, are musically very convincing.

Even though they belong to another age, the *Biblical* Sonatas of Kuhnau (1660–1722) were ahead of their time in being sometimes explicitly influenced by extra-musical programmes, as was Clementi's Sonata in G minor, op. 50, no. 3 (*Didone Abbandonata*). This work, the last of his sixty-four piano sonatas, adopts a process of constantly transforming and varying a single theme throughout its course. This aspect of composition was to become known as 'thematic metamorphosis' and was widely employed by Liszt in his symphonic poems as well as by Schubert in his *Wanderer* Fantasy. (One of the more thorough-going of such compositions is Liszt's A major Concerto, which one witty critic labelled 'the travels and adventures of a theme'.) It is a method of creation which has something in common with Wagner's use of *Leitmotiv* and is an enforcement by the composer of those thematic resemblances and affinities which are often, on an unconscious level, present in any case.

Clementi (1752–1832) certainly possessed an original mind to perceive so early the possibilities inherent in this sort of musical thinking. His other sonatas include the brilliant F sharp minor (op. 25, no. 3), which used to be played by Horowitz, the Beethovenian two-movement Sonata in B minor (op. 40, no. 2), and the B flat (op. 47, no. 2) which he played to the Emperor Franz Joseph of Austria in 1788, in the presence of Mozart. Mozart was to carry its opening theme to greater heights in the *Magic*

Flute Overture. There are also many interesting if isolated movements in the less successful sonatas: the slow movement of the G major (op. 39, no. 2), the finale of the (different) B flat (op. 46), the second movement of the A major (op. 50, no. 1), and the Brahmsian finale of the D minor (op. 50, no. 2) – these would all merit performance played as separate movements. Clementi also wrote several sonatinas, and he was the architect of the still valuable *Gradus ad Parnassum*, a very fine course of keyboard exercises. He was a real craftsman, and has been variously claimed as the father of modern piano writing and of modern piano playing. His unexpected changes of harmony and daring use of the sustaining pedal are supposed to have influenced Beethoven. He did however live long enough to have been in his turn influenced *by* Beethoven. Clementi died at Evesham, in Worcestershire, in 1832, having for some years combined his composing activities with those of a music publisher and piano-maker.

Approximately contemporary with Clementi were Hummel (1778–1837) and Dussek (1760–1812). While they are less original than he, there are moments of adventurousness in their output. Dussek's E flat minor Sonata, for example, contains almost Schumannesque harmonic progressions. Hummel's main quality is perhaps the extraordinary ethos of his music, the world of arabesque it inhabits. Studded with melismata and fioriture, his sonatas and rondos contain an astonishing range and variety of ornamentation.* This use of filigree was to influence Chopin in his early works, before he found his own forms and intensely functional mode of decoration.

The most innately musical of all the harbingers of the romantic era was John Field (1782–1837). Born in Dublin, he lived for many years as an emigré in Russia, and, in the early nineteenth century, an Irishman in St Petersburg must have been a *rara avis* indeed. He invented the 'nocturne', a poetic mood-picture in sound, and brought to his

---

* Hummel's works for piano duet have a wider emotional range than his solo piano works.

invention formal poise, a chaste romanticism and an unerring keyboard aptitude. Nine nocturnes (there are at least
eighteen in all) were edited by Liszt, among them the
delightfully un-nocturnal rondo *Midi*, and the exquisite
ones in B flat major and E minor. John Field's other piano
works include a Sonata in B major, and two fantasies on
Russian folk-themes (in A minor and A major). In all his
music we see an original and cultivated sensibility, and his
influence, especially on Chopin and Liszt, was quite considerable. His music was published in his own lifetime, and
his B flat major Nocturne was quoted by Czerny in his
Treatise on Composition (published in 1848) as an example of
the form. The way in which Field influenced Chopin was
in the keyboard layout of the nocturne – the flowing left-
hand accompaniment contrasted with the singing melodic
line of the right hand – and in the balanced ternary structure.

Where did music stand at this time? Beethoven's structural intensifications, his dynamic power, his aural imagination, his disciplined freedom – these were all qualities which
could act as stumbling-blocks to later composers. Since we
even hear new works today which are influenced by
Beethoven's typical dynamic energy, we should not be
surprised that, in the nineteenth century, Spohr's Symphony in C minor and Hans Huber's Piano Concerto in C
minor, for example, imitated Beethoven's tonality and his
melodic and rhythmic figurations, while lacking his
marvellous sense of harmonic tension and relaxation.

CHOPIN

These harmonic tensions were dynamite, and it was
Chopin (1810–49) who re-fused them for romantic piano
music. His music was often misunderstood, since much of it
was created in the ambiance of the salons and ballrooms of
the aristocracy. His critics labelled him the 'poet of the
piano'. They were quite right: he combines Marlovian
grandeur with the formal control and humanity of a Virgil.
Like Mozart (and like Jane Austen and Henry James),

Chopin became a touchstone by which one evaluates all others. His development as a composer was astonishing; to compare the Rondo in C minor, op. 1, with the F minor Ballade is to acknowledge a spiritual development paralleling that between *Rienzi* and *Parsifal* and accomplished in half the time. When he left Poland for good at the age of twenty, he could say, like James Joyce after him, 'I go ... to forge in the smithy of my soul the uncreated conscience of my race', and, from the salons of Paris and in the solitude of Majorca, his unique artistic memory invested his work with a magnificently heroic Polish nationalism, the distillation of a nation's aspirations, refined through his own (partly French) sensibility.

Chopin's admiration for the music of Bach and Mozart must have helped him to obtain that marvellous clarity of line which is rarely obscured by even the most sophisticated harmonic progressions. His approach to compositional problems is so original that even when he appropriates existing forms as, for example, in the polonaises, studies, scherzos and nocturnes, they amount to new inventions.

His early works combine clarity of texture with an intensive use of the decorative patterns one would expect to find in the work of a gifted young early nineteenth-century composer well acquainted with the works of Hummel, Field, Rossini and Bellini (whose *bel canto* writing Chopin admired). These include the early G sharp minor Polonaise with its trio composed in homage to Rossini, the rondos (a popular form among the early romantic composers – there are examples by Weber, Mendelssohn, Hummel and Field), the (for Chopin) extravagantly flamboyant Variations on Mozart's *Là ci darem la mano*, and the Sonata in C minor, op. 4, with its exquisite larghetto in five–four time, possibly the first extended use of this metre and already showing the freedom and flexibility with which Chopin developed his melodies:

These works are already pianistically masterful, and beneath their cosmopolitan surface they show the emergence of Chopin's love of Polish dance forms, something which was to inspire him throughout his life. Another great influence upon Chopin at this time was the virtuosity of Paganini and Liszt. For a time Chopin and Liszt were close friends and the Twelve Studies, op. 10, are dedicated to Liszt.

This set and its successor, the Twelve Studies, op. 25 (dedicated to Marie d'Agoult), are technical and musical masterpieces. They enshrine the soul of the piano, and so unified are their form and content that it would be almost impossible to imagine them transcribed for any other instrument. Here is a brief résumé of the Chopin studies:

Op. 10, no. 1	C major	Compound arpeggios set in brilliant contrast to sustained bass notes. It has the harmonic sureness of a Bach prelude.
Op. 10, no. 2	A minor	The combination of a chromatic scale with chords in the right hand. The left hand accompanies, staccato.
Op. 10, no. 3	E major	A broad aria, with a quicker central section.
Op. 10, no. 4	C sharp minor	Basically a two-part invention involving considerable stretches in both hands.
Op. 10, no. 5	G flat major	The *Black Key* Study. All but one of the notes played by the right hand are black (D flat, E flat, G flat, A flat, B flat).

Op. 10, no. 6	E flat minor	A melody of restless melancholy, almost Tristanesque in its chromaticism and use of enharmonic modulations.
Op. 10, no. 7	C major	A toccata, featuring rapid alternations of the same note with the first finger and thumb of the right hand.
Op. 10, no. 8	F major	Right-hand arpeggios sweep down and away from a left hand which defines a strong, almost Scottish rhythm.
Op. 10, no. 9	F minor	The rhythmic pulse is defined in the left hand; against this, the right-hand melody makes an effect of apparent syncopation, owing to the initial absence of any melody note on the down-beat.
Op. 10, no. 10	A flat major	A study in cross-rhythms. Chopin's influence on Brahms may be clearly seen here.
Op. 10, no. 11	E flat major	Compound slow arpeggio chords, almost harp-like. One note is sometimes melodically sustained, while the arpeggios play around it. This is not easy to do if one holds the note with the finger, but the total effect is rich and orchestral.
Op. 10, no. 12	C minor	The so-called *Revolutionary* Study: a right-hand theme in octaves against complex figurations in the left hand.
Op. 25, no. 1	A flat major	Known as the *Aeolian Harp* because of the quiet arpeggios in both hands. The melody is brought out by the little finger of the right hand, and

		sometimes by the thumb of the left hand. A wonderfully translucent texture.
Op. 25, no. 2	F minor	Featuring cross-rhythms, and requiring little or no pedal. Melodically this piece is somewhat similar to the tenth of Liszt's *Transcendental* Studies (also in F minor).
Op. 25, no. 3	F major	A study in the precise rhythmic values of ornaments.
Op. 25, no. 4	A minor	A guitar-like timbre, with contrasts between legato and staccato. The left hand is a rhythmically constant background against which the right hand picks out and emphasizes the off-beat chords.
Op. 25, no. 5	E minor	Juxtaposes long and short grace notes. The middle section is almost Lisztian in its melodic use of the tenor register.
Op. 25, no. 6	G sharp minor	A dazzling study in right-hand thirds (known erroneously as 'double' thirds). The left hand provides a harmony of sometimes Wagnerian richness (cf. *Rheingold*).
Op. 25, no. 7	C sharp minor	Almost like a duet between solo cello and flute, a wonderful study in sustained lyricism.
Op. 25, no. 8	D flat major	A study in sixths.
Op. 25, no. 9	G flat major	The famous *Butterfly* Study whose splintered octaves bewitchingly contrast legato and staccato textures.
Op. 25, no. 10	B minor	Octaves in both hands: in

		the slower middle section octaves are used melodically, in the right hand alone.
Op. 25, no. 11	A minor	(*The Winter Wind*). Complex chromatic figurations in the right hand are contrasted with a strongly defined heroic theme in the left.
Op. 25, no. 12	C minor	Compound arpeggios in both hands. A return to the world of the first study of op. 10. Bachian in its richness and certainty of texture.

Though composed sporadically over several years, the studies are very convincing as sets. They cover a wide range of technical problems and the way these are woven into a highly poetic musical fabric has caused them to become part of the folk-heritage of the piano. Outwardly they do not differ so much from earlier sets of studies. Thus almost all of them deal with only one specific technical problem. The difference appears in Chopin's combining of the technical problem with a much more sophisticated harmonic and formal intensity than was the case in Czerny's or even Cramer's studies. Czerny's D minor Study, from op. 740, or Cramer's B flat minor Study deal adequately, and indeed on their own terms beautifully, with the problem that is set. Chopin goes much further in combining the problem with balancing and contrasting structural tensions in a way which had hitherto been regarded as the province of larger, weightier works. Each of his studies have the impact of a short sonata movement. Some of them (like the A minor, op. 10, no. 2) were composed at almost exactly the time of Chopin's departure from Poland, while in others, notably the two C minor ones, we see the first full emergence of that almost mystical identification with things Polish which was to remain a driving force throughout Chopin's life. This nationalism was to deepen, and nowhere is it more clearly seen than in the polonaises and mazurkas, which I should like now to examine in more detail.

Although the polonaise existed before Chopin's time – there are even examples by Bach and Beethoven – it was Chopin who invested this aristocratic dance form with a most personal and characteristic interplay of changing moods, and who really made the polonaise Polish, not cosmopolitan. His earlier ones already covered a wide range of emotion. I would cite, for example, the beautiful D flat section of the C sharp minor:

the drama of the E flat minor, immortalized in Paderewski's recording; and the tragic power of the C minor, perhaps influenced by Beethoven's *Appassionata* Sonata in its use of the flattened supertonic (D flat). The other early polonaises may be less profound – the popular A major, op. 40, no.1, known as the *Polonaise militaire*, and the early ones in D minor and B flat major – but they are delightful.

The later polonaises enlarge and expand the form in a way, thoroughgoing yet never pedantic, that one comes to recognize as characteristic. Three of them are very important. The first is the F sharp minor, op. 44, whose Goya-like intensity and almost inhumanly severe modulations imply a barbarism which becomes explicit in the atavistic passage (over a pedal A) that prepares its central section. This middle section is a mazurka, thus creating a remarkable coalescence of two different dances. The opening presages Franck's Symphony while its close calls to mind Bach's Chromatic Fantasy:

(c)
Bach

(d)
Chopin

These comparisons epitomize the attraction of this Janus-like work, which, while traditional, yet looks to the future.

The Polonaise in A flat, op. 53, known as the *Heroic*, (these titles are not generally Chopin's own) is even more famous. Similarly cast in ternary structure, it is a piece of resonant splendour, with a remarkable middle section heralded by bardic arpeggios:

Ex4

an example of the grandeur that Chopin was capable of. To play this middle section, which presents a noble horn-like theme over a rain of octaves, Liszt used to require of his pupils not speed, but 'the thunder of the Polish cavalry'. After this central episode, Chopin's return to the main section is a *tour de force*: few composers would have dared and achieved so apparently wayward and capricious a return in so grandiose a work. The masterful economy of the ending is also noteworthy – only the most concise reference to the middle section is needed to produce a complete sense of balance (cf. the end of the scherzo of Sibelius's Fourth Symphony).

The last of the three greatest polonaises is the Polonaise-Fantaisie, op. 61. Its freedom and mystery, its impressionistic shadowy half-remembrance of the dance must rank it as the *Kubla Khan* or, perhaps more accurately, the *Christabel* of piano literature. In both cases, one asks the meaning: it is a search for the inexpressible which puzzled and disconcerted even Liszt, whose experiments, great as they were, were not psychological depth-charges like this. Its intensely original chromaticism looks straight toward Kundry, in *Parsifal*. It is episodic in structure, very difficult to bring off in performance. Like the F sharp minor, it harks back to the past as well as forward to the future: if the impressionistic opening has a tinge of Debussy, nevertheless the remarkable passage of triple trills which precedes its reprise looks back to Beethoven for, like Beethoven, Chopin became increasingly fascinated in his later works by the expressive potential of trills (see, for example, the B major Nocturne, op. 62, no. 1). I have not spoken of its veiled splendours, its sudden outbreaks of heroism, its withdrawn lyricism. In the last resort, one can only listen to the music.

The mazurka was the other national dance form which inspired Chopin throughout his life. This is really not one dance form but several, all possessing similar rhythmic features. The main ones are the fiery *Mazur* (fast, with an accented second beat), the *Kujawiak* (slower and more languid, also with an accented second beat) and the *Obérék* (very fast, with accented first beats, not necessarily accented in every bar) – they are all in three–four time. A characteristic is that one beat is often longer in duration than the others, thus ♩. ♪♫ or ♩.♪♩ ♩ or ♫♪♫ ♩, and not for example ♫♪♫♪♫. Chopin wrote between fifty and sixty mazurkas (more are still occasionally discovered) and varied their outwardly similar structures considerably. Thus, the mazurka in Chopin's hands may be lyrical (B flat minor, op. 24, no.4), contrapuntal in texture (C sharp minor, op. 50, no. 3), dramatic (B minor, op. 33, no. 4), melancholic (E minor, op. 41, no. 2), inconsequential (C major, op. 7, no.5), hedonistic (D major, op. 33, no. 2), wistful (A minor, op. 68, no. 2), harmonically chromatic (F sharp minor, op. 59, no. 3), or modal (C minor, op. 56, no. 3); the pianistic colouring may even derive from the sound of another instrument (e.g. the bagpipe-like drone of the trio of the B flat Mazurka, op. 7, no. 1). They are all unified by Chopin's refined artistic sensibility, as he manipulates these varied forms and textures with the slightly sinister grace of a musical conjurer.

The nocturnes and preludes are more cosmopolitan and indeed, in a sense, more romantic, when one considers the number of legends which have grown up around them. There are twenty-six preludes in all: a recently-discovered one in A flat; the Prelude in C sharp minor, op. 45, which is an elegiac intermezzo tinged with Brahmsian melancholy, and the set of Twenty-four Preludes, op. 28, which traverse all the major and minor keys. The most remote keys occur in the middle of the set, and thus a complete performance gives a sense of contrasted tonality similar to that which we might expect to find in the first movement of a classical sonata. Thus, starting from C major, the first seven explore the simpler sharp tonalities (G, D, A and their relative minors); this corresponds with the straightforward balance of key-relationships in a first-movement exposition. The middle preludes (nos. 8–18) are in the remoter keys (e.g. F sharp, E flat minor), tonally parallel to the more distant modulations of a development section. The last six return through the simpler flat keys (E flat, B flat, F and their relative minors), just as a sonata recapitulation typically reverts to the simpler tonal contrasts of its exposition. The sequence of tonality through the preludes is thus one of progressive tension and relaxation. The simpler tonalities of the opening and closing preludes are balanced by simpler musical structures (e.g. the little A major Prelude). More complex forms, corresponding to the more remote tonalities, occur in the middle of the set (e.g. those in D flat, A flat and B flat minor). There are exceptions – for example, the D minor Prelude is a symphonic retrospect on the whole set – but generally Chopin's musical thinking appears to have adhered (probably unconsciously) to this ground plan.

Many of the preludes were composed in Majorca, where Chopin's fatal consumption declared itself. They contrast aggressive power with nostalgia to an unusually stark degree, and run through an immense variety of moods from the simple unforced lyricism of the A major and E flat major to the deep pessimism of the preludes in A minor and F minor. One of the most original in form is the D flat major, known as the *Raindrop* Prelude because of its constant regular reiteration of a single A flat around which both melody and accompaniment are woven, a feat which, in piano music, was not fully paralleled until Ravel wrote *Le Gibet* seventy-five years later. In the C sharp (= D flat) minor middle section the repeated A flats become notated enharmonically as G sharps. Here the harmony is reminiscent of Mussorgsky in its austerity – perhaps it was influenced by the sight of monks' religious processions in Valldemosa. Chopin did not encourage such programmatic interpretations, but the solemnity of such ceremonies inspired Mendelssohn and Berlioz, and must have been 'in the air' at the time.

The Preludes in E flat minor and B flat minor may have served as a sounding-board in Chopin's mind for the B flat minor Sonata which was to come later; the rhythms in particular foreshadow the Sonata. It is wonderful how original the preludes are in their aphoristic way, and how fully Chopin realizes the unique potential of whatever key he writing in: thus the F sharp minor and F minor are *Wilde Jagds*, short but sour, the G minor an amalgam of Beethoven and Rachmaninov, the B flat major Tchaikovskian in its melodic sweep (cf. the andante from Tchaikovsky's String Quartet in D), the E minor chromatic and, like Liszt's *Vallée d'Obermann*, filled with remorse, the F sharp major full of the unique sensuality of that key; while, on the other hand, the F major Prelude, with its irresolute cadence of crystal, is a perfect snapshot of green meadows, and the D minor ends the set in the shattering way appropriate to that key.

The nocturnes are larger works, but nevertheless terse

exploratory human dramas and mood-pictures that recall
the brevity and power of a great short-story writer. The
first, op. 9, no. 1 in B flat minor, opens with a rather Slavic
melody, which is repeated and varied; this is then followed
by a more impassioned middle section in the major, whose
unresolved sevenths already point a long way towards the
harmonic procedures of Satie and Debussy. The second
nocturne, op. 9, no. 2 in E flat, comes nearest of all to being
directly modelled upon John Field – it is a deservedly
popular apotheosis of salon romanticism, as are the F major
op. 15, no. 1 and the F sharp major op. 15, no. 2. The
Nocturne in G minor, op. 15, no. 3 was supposedly inspired
by *Hamlet*; Chopin neverthelesss did not make any literary
superscription to the music. We may look with more success
for poetic quotations on the title-pages of Brahms!

The two nocturnes, op. 27, are among the finest. The
first, in C sharp minor, contains a highly dramatic, almost
theatrical, middle section, and closes with that painful
bitterness unique to Chopin. The second, in D flat major, is
one of the most popular. Its sensitivity, its controlled lyricism and wonderfully pliant relationship between melody
and accompaniment are all things to marvel at. (It was
superbly recorded on 78s by Solomon.) The others may be
dealt with more briefly. The F minor Nocturne (op. 55,
no. 1) has a melodic affinity with Glinka's *L'Alouette* – with
delicacy it epitomizes Chopin's general structural approach
which was to contrast straightforward expository sections
with a more animated and contrasted central episode. The
G major (op. 37, no.2), with its haunting E major refrain in
six–eight time, is wonderful, almost a sketch for the F major
Ballade which carries the next opus number. The Nocturnes
in C minor (op. 48, no.1) and in E flat (op. 55, no. 2)
correspond respectively in their emotional ambiance to the
two of op. 27 – the one powerful, the other lyrical and
rhythmically sophisticated. The two last nocturnes, op. 62,
possess a uniquely heart-easing quality, and are almost
Beethoven-like in their nobly shaped melodies.

By contrast, Chopin's waltzes are mostly extroverted.

They are glittering *étincelles*, *feux d'artifice*, the brightest jewels in the greatest salons of the time. Here the key of A flat seemed to hold a special attraction for Chopin; those in this key have a courtliness and elegant aristocracy which matches the form perfectly. The A minor (op. 34, n. 2) has a melancholy which sets it apart from most of the others; we must again note Chopin's mastery in introducing a digression (in C major) two-thirds of the way through, without disturbing the waltz's structural balance.

The four impromptus combine something of both genres. The drama of the nocturnes and the felicity of the waltzes are both present in these colourful improvisations, finest of which are the Impromptu in F sharp major, and the popular Fantaisie-Impromptu.

I should like to turn now to the sonatas. All the major romantic piano composers eventually wrestled with the intricacies of classical sonata form. Chopin's solution to the problem was characteristically original, yet in a sense simple. He realized that his outlook on tonal relationships was now so far-reaching that an exact appropriation of the classical model (designed to meet the needs of a tonally more direct style) would not entirely work. Yet the schematic parabola of the sonata form was likely, as we have seen by the analogy of the Twenty-four Preludes, op. 28, to appeal to him. His masterstroke was that in neither of the two great sonatas is the first subject of the first movement recapitulated at the expected time. It is, so to speak, recapitulated while the development is still going on, which means that when the theoretical place of recapitulation arrives, all that needs to be re-stated is the second subject. This works perfectly; the movements are finely balanced, and yet the pedantry of a text-book recapitulation is avoided.

The B flat minor Sonata, op, 35, is in four movements. The first movement opens with an enharmonically notated introduction, marked *grave*:

which already implies the work's later refinements of chromatic modulation. The exposition and recapitulation of this movement follow classical precept in their tonalities. By contrast the development explores more than thirteen keys (some, more accurately, transitional modulations) before the tonic major is re-established in the recapitulation. This development is partly sequential, and leads to a powerful integration of the opening *grave* theme, prior to the recapitulation. In short, the first movement contrasts the straightforward tonal relationships of its outer sections with the maelstrom of tonal tensions generated in its development. The scherzo reverses this process – its central section (the trio) is tonally simple, but the main scherzo subject constantly generates new tonal centres (e.g. in the opening bars, E flat minor and F sharp minor). The Funeral March, originally composed as a separate piece, reverts to the simpler tonal relationships of the first movement's outer sections. Conversely, the finale pushes the intense chromaticism of the development to the point of atonality, in a musical prose-poem of haunted shadows. There are implicit thematic cross-references between the four movements, and the prevailing tonal relationships are made to work both in large structural perspectives and in small points of formal detail. The work is vengeful, lyrical and ghostly. The finest recording of it is still Rachmaninov's magnificent, unforgettable performance.

The Sonata in B minor, op. 58, is more lyrical: an affirmation of lyric heroism and unusual nobility. It presents the performer with many problems of tempo, phrasing and pedalling. The opening is unique in its certainty and majesty:

Although composed in 1844, at moments it seems a 'late' romantic work; the codetta of the first movement exposition

has a Delius-like nostalgia. The contrapuntal development section is a true heir to the quasi-fugal developments of the last Beethoven sonatas. The scherzo is the shortest of its kind in Chopin's output; it can sound too short if the difficult but important tempo relationship between the naturally quicker outer sections and the more relaxed trio is not found. The slow movement is a wonderfully evocative rhapsody, and the heroic finale shows how superbly Chopin could handle a traditional form such as the sonata-rondo. If this sonata seems more affirmative than the B flat minor, this is because the themes are broader, the cantilena more sustained, the use of the major key more prevalent, and the tonal relationships less involved, than in its predecessor. The recordings by Lipatti and Weissenberg are among the most convincing, in my view.

Chopin made many large-scale forms his own. In the first and third scherzos, he brought a new mordant irony to the already existing form. The first (B minor) opens with

dramatic chords which launch a large-scale ternary structure, highly passionate and rhetorical in detail. The central
section is in the major key, and more tranquil; here he
adopts a Polish folk-song in the style of a berceuse. The
recapitulation is, for him, relatively exact, and during its
course the opening chords of the introduction are repeated
and intensified with vehemence. The third scherzo, in C
sharp minor, develops this vein of drama still further. It
was dedicated to Chopin's pupil Gutmann, who had a
stretch capable of taking the opening left-hand chords
without spreading them. It opens almost atonally, and then
boldly contrasts clear-cut octaves with a decorated chorale.
The particularly brilliant coda has helped to make it a
great favourite with audiences all over the world. The
second scherzo, in B flat minor, is filled with a passion which
if hardly gentler, is more traditional. The E major (no. 4)
is the most feathery, the most scherzando: its ethereal
chords and rivulets of arpeggios have a Mendelssohnian
delicacy.

Other large-scale works include the F minor Fantasy.
Despite its title, its form is that of a very exact sonata first
movement, and in this sense it is structurally more traditional than the sonatas themselves, except for its ending in
the relative major (A flat). It opens with a long funereal
introduction, and its later drama has prompted some fanciful interpretations: one theory was that Chopin improvised
it when making up a quarrel with George Sand. In this
interpretation the opening two bars represent George Sand
knocking at the door, and the third and fourth bars Chopin's
reply, *Entrez!*. The dramatic course of the allegro then
presumably signified the to-and-fro of a passionate dialogue.

The Concert Allegro, op. 46, is likewise a work of strong
gesture and eloquent rhetoric. It is one of several lesser-
known works, such as the Bolero, op. 19, the Tarantella,
op. 43, and the Variations, op. 12; none of them has ever
been well enough known to acquire its meed of extra-
musical interpretation. It is in fact the quality of Chopin's
greatest works that, despite their poetry, they transcend

all concrete imaginings. The Berceuse and the Barcarolle
are good examples of this. How perfectly they are wrought,
and how clearly they show Chopin's ability to develop
and create to the very last bar of his music! The harmony
of the Barcarolle has a Wagnerian richness and eloquence,
particularly in its later sections. Chopin develops and
contrasts his material superbly. It is worth noting the
powerful digression (in C sharp major) which, as in the
A flat Polonaise and A minor Valse, precedes the return of
the main theme: one of the great moments of piano music.

Perhaps the finest and most original of all Chopin's works
are the four ballades. The first, in G minor, has a bold
originality which ranges from the famous delayed resolution of the minor ninth which ushers in the first theme,
through the impressionistic horn-like transition to the
second subject, through the glistening E flat major scherzando section, to the eventual dissonant figurations of the
fiery coda which enlarge still further upon this *idée fixe* of the
unresolved ninth. It is a work of great fire and beauty, and
an example of the truth and honesty with which Chopin
always faced the emotional implications of his thought.
The Second Ballade was supposed to have been inspired by
a reading of Mickiewicz, the nineteenth-century Polish poet.
The poem in question dealt with a lost city under the sea;
as an interpretation it is less fanciful than some, and has been
said to carry the authority of Schumann, to whom it was
dedicated. The ballade begins with a deceptively simple
theme in six–eight time which is later drawn into the vortex
of two passionate episodes, the first in A minor, and the
second starting in D minor. These episodic contrasts
eventually dominate the scene, and the work reaches an
unexpectedly violent climax in A minor, with just the
briefest memory of the opening theme to restore a sense of
formal balance. It is a lesson in the art of composition. The
Third Ballade, in A flat, shares with the others Chopin's
genius in re-charging tension three quarters of the way
through (in the C sharp minor development) where a
lesser composer would have gone over old ground again.

The Fourth Ballade, in F minor, is in my opinion the most exalted, intense and sublimely powerful of all Chopin's compositions. The pathos of the opening; the undulating waltz rhythm which gathers to itself the grandeurs of a Bach chorale and the passion of an operatic scena as it progresses; above all the uniquely sad and beautiful second theme (B flat major) – these all return, yet never twice in the same way, and invite us, like the heroine of Scott Fitzgerald's *Last Tycoon*, to a 'romantic communion of unbelievable intensity'. Its themes are the Platonic ideal of all similar themes; while its coda leads us to the marvellous limits of musical comprehension. It is unbelievable that it lasts only twelve minutes, for it contains the experience of a lifetime.

Chopin's 'wild Everest of art' is not the easiest point from which to embark in search of another composer, yet the great aspirations of Schumann (1810–56) are a worthy parallel to Chopin's achievement and, if Schumann's undertakings were not invariably successful, we should remember, especially today, Stravinsky's aphorism, 'nothing fails like success'.

SCHUMANN

Schumann's genius, which was by turns lyrical, fantastic and dramatic, usually expressed itself most perfectly in small forms. Most of his early works are for piano (he had at first studied to be a concert pianist). The tragic history of his later mental illness is well known, and it is not surprising that the later works are inhibited in comparison with the earlier, which are full of vitality and clear colouring. His opus 1, the *Abegg* Variations, already shows an interest in musical acrostics which later became obsessive. The theme is based on the letters A B E G G in musical notation (B being the German equivalent of our B flat). The work is now neglected, but used to be popular and was played, for example, by Busoni. It belongs to the same genre as the early sets of variations by Chopin, and is likewise influenced by Field and Hummel.

The *Papillons*, op. 2, sound a more personal note. They are a set of fantastic miniatures and, like *Carnaval*, op. 9, and *Faschingsschwank aus Wien* were inspired by the associations of a carnival. Schumann concealed his personality behind two *noms de plume*, the passionate Florestan and the poetic Eusebius. Perhaps the idea of a carnival, with its masked guests, enabled him to project his personality more vividly, as if behind a mask. Certainly, in these carnival-inspired works he released an energic tide of unconscious imagery which he did not admit in his absolute works, sometimes to their loss. *Papillons* ends with the 'grandfather song' later used in *Carnaval* (where the first of *Papillons* is hinted at again).

Carnaval, op. 9, subtitled '*Scènes mignonnes sur quatre notes*' is one of Schumann's most vividly original works. The notes in question derived from Asch, the birthplace of Ernestine von Fricken, which can be rendered in German notation either as A, Es, C, H or As, C, H – or, anagrammatically, Es (S), C, H, A, which are the 'musical' letters of Schumann's name. The four notes are whirled through many transformations in a bewildering array of movements which, as character-portraits, remain unparalleled. The tributes to Chopin and Paganini are superb, while the Brahmsian portrayals of Ernestine von Fricken and Clara Wieck (later Clara Schumann) are wonderfully convincing – their names in the carnival are Estrella and Chiarina. In *Aveu* Schumann shows his essential spiritual simplicity. The final march (in three–four time) takes its strange title from the fact that Schumann had founded a group known as the Davidsbund, which set out to oppose philistine tendencies in music. To blend these diverse elements into a unified work was difficult, and Schumann extended the piano's resources considerably, notably in the cross-rhythms of the toccata-like *Pantalon et Colombine* and the final march.

Paganini's virtuosity made a strong impression on Schumann and the results can be seen not only in *Carnaval* but also in the two sets of studies (op. 3 and op. 10) which were based on Paganini's *Caprices*. These are fairly exact transcriptions, lacking Liszt's flair for re-creating their essence in another medium. Much more successful, both technically and musically, are the powerful *Études symphoniques*, op. 13, which are a set of variations on a theme by Clara Wieck's father. This work has deservedly held a steady place in the repertoire. The prestissimo chordal variation is among the most hazardous in piano literature:

The lengthy and brilliant finale is based on a theme by Marschner, and generates a cumulative excitement through Schumann's characteristic use of an obsessively repeated dotted rhythm ♪♪ ♪♪ ♪♪ ♪♪.

Other early works include the *Davidsbündlertänze*, op.6, based on dance forms (another commemoration of the Davidsbund) and the Toccata, op. 7, a masterly composition showing the depth and seriousness of Schumann's study of piano technique. Like the Chopin Fantasy it is in classical sonata form. Its development features octave technique, while the return of the recapitulation over a dominant pedal-point

may have influenced a similar passage in Wagner's *Meister-singer* Prelude. Its technical procedures recall both Chopin's *Winter Wind* Study and Liszt's *Feux follets*: all three works possess common denominators of virtuoso pianism, though the beautiful quiet close is uniquely Schumannesque. The Toccata is of great difficulty and in my opinion Josef Lhévinne's recording remains the definitive performance.

A later work, in which Schumann returns to the spirit of *Carnaval*, is *Faschingsschwank aus Wien* (*Carnival Jest from Vienna*), op. 26. This is in five movements, combining the formal aspects of sonata (in the finale) and suite. The jest lies in Schumann's quoting the *Marseillaise*, at a time (1830) when the anthem was banned from performance in Vienna because of the recent revolutionary uprisings in France. The first movement is a tremendous farrago, while the middle scherzino is delightfully witty, with its allusion to fairground trombones. The second and fourth movements, entitled Romanze and Intermezzo, contrast the reflective and passionate elements, Eusebius and Florestan, of Schumann's nature, and the sonata-form finale ends the work brilliantly.

Among Schumann's many smaller works, the *Scenes from Childhood*, op. 15, stand out for their simple fresh beauty. In them is discernible a process of transformation of the opening theme which is achieved with an art that conceals art. The set includes the very popular *Traümerei* and closes with the magical *The Poet Speaks*. By comparison, the *Album for the Young*, op. 68, is a more didactic work.

The Three Romances, op. 28, include the once popular F sharp major, which makes use of Thalberg's invention, the effect *a tre mani*, i.e. the theme is divided between the

thumbs of each hand, and the accompaniment woven above
and below it. Finest of all the shorter works is the *Arabesque*,
op. 18, a wonderful parallel in musical terms to the beauty
of Lamb's *Dream Children*. Its coda is unforgettable:

Ex.10

Even in this work we note Schumann's respect for tradition
– it is in rondo form.

Among these smaller works are the many fantasy pieces
Schumann wrote throughout his life. Mysticism, nature,
the inner recesses of the mind, an innocent questing; these
are the qualities which lie at the core of the varied works
which include the lovely *Fantasiestücke*, op. 12, the *Waldsce-
nen*, op. 82, the *Oriental Scenes*, op, 66, and the *Fantasiestücke*,
op. 111. Throughout the op. 12 set, which includes *Des
Abends* (*In the Evening*), *Aufschwung* (*Soaring*) and *Warum?*,
we find some of the most perfect examples of Schumann's
mastery of small forms, of his characteristic personal
mysticism combined with an objective awareness of natural
beauty.

Among the larger works the eight *Noveletten*, op. 21, hold
strong place. Using the traditional forms of march, toccata, waltz and polonaise, they have an immediacy
which suggests another carnival in progress. At least, one
certainly hears the village fiddler tuning down in fifths at
the end of the sixth Novelette. The first, in F major, is
march-like, and carries through a superb, almost Lisztian,
scheme of tonal relationships based on the succession
centres F–A–D flat–F. The second, in D major, is an
extensive toccata which used to be played by Busoni. The
sixth in A and the seventh in E are charming folk-scenes.
The fifth, in D, is a *polonaise en rondeau*, whose ceremony

gives way to feeling in its beautiful closing pages. The eighth, in F sharp minor and D major, is an extended two-part work: the first part is a rondo (without the final recapitulation), and the second part a fantastic dance of progressively accelerated and retarded speed. The two parts are linked by a hushed intermezzo, one of Schumann's finest pages. The motoric speed-changes of the second part may well have influenced Bartók, and as a whole the work echoes the aspirations, insight, and tragic incompletion of Schumann's life.

Schumann's life-long devotion to the tradition of the classical symphony caused him to produce three piano sonatas, the F sharp minor, op. 11, the F minor (*Concert sans Orchestre*), op. 14, and the G minor, op. 22, though he showed less aptitude than Chopin for making existing forms work in a new way. Yet all three sonatas are shot through with moments of great beauty, notably the introduction and slow movement of the F sharp minor, the slow movement of the G minor, and the scherzo of the F minor. Generally we note a penchant for moto perpetuo figurations, and for rhythmic patterns which are driven very hard without achieving Brahms's synthesis into nodal points of tension. The piano sonatas do not unlock the secrets of Schumann's mind – strange, since the Piano Concerto and the third and fourth symphonies, also essays in absolute musical forms, are splendid works. Three large and important works remain for consideration: *Kreisleriana*, op. 16, *Humoreske*, op. 20, and the Fantasy, op. 17. *Kreisleriana* is another gallery of fantastic inventions, inspired in this case by the creations of the Gothic novelist (and composer) E. T. A. Hoffmann. The work centres obsessively around the tonalities of G minor and B flat, and is the most drenched in fantasy of all Schumann's piano works. The effect is as of a hypnotic, haunted dream. The *Humoreske* is less successful; although deeply poetic in the hands of a Richter, it perhaps contains too much temperamental contrast to be a unified whole.

The C major Fantasy is of a different overall calibre, and

is the most intensely human of Schumann's piano works. It was dedicated to Liszt, who in turn dedicated his B minor Sonata to Schumann. The work is in three movements, which were originally entitled 'Struggle; Triumph; Palms'. A quotation from Beethoven's *An die ferne Geliebte* appears towards the end of the first movement. The score carries the motto 'Through all the world's wild vibrating sounds, one still note can sound to him who listens'. The tonality of C major is used throughout the outer movements as a symbolic haven of simplicity to which Schumann returns time and again after the modulatory stresses of his developments. This is very apparent in the beautiful pages which close the first and third movements. In its masterly piano writing, its sustained flights of lyricism and its juxtaposition of powerfully contrasted types of expression, the Fantasy reveals the best of Schumann. Technically it contains a good many difficulties, especially in the second movement: this is a triumphal march in E flat whose tonal and structural relationship to the outer movements presents an interpretative problem apart from its own intrinsic technical demands. In the end, however, the listener comes back to the simplicity and beauty of the Fantasy, not to its difficulties, and it is with simplicity and beauty that it ends:

Ex. 11

Schumann's later piano works are less immediately compelling. As he became more haunted by illness, he tended to take refuge in a style which maintained his hard-won mastery of counterpoint and harmony, but flickered only intermittently into the wide-ranging zeal and fantasy which had earlier possessed him. His interest in counterpoint bore an unexpected fruit in the Studies for Pedal Piano, op. 58, which are masterly in their use of canon. Other works, such as the *Albumblätter*, op. 99 (which contain the theme on which Brahms was to base his *Schumann* Variations, op.9), and the fine *Fantasiestücke*, op. 111, which are Beethovenian in tonal contour, have fallen into a sometimes undeserved neglect.

This phrase 'undeserved neglect' is likely to recur in considering the romantic era, partly because many twentieth-century artists have appropriated the ideal of a new classicism in their work. This 'classicism' may refer to a relatively recent past, as in the case of the Second Viennese School in music, or to a remote past, e.g. the drama and poetry of ancient Greece, and it may even refer to works which in their own time were considered romantic or outré. It has shaped such works as Stravinsky's *Oedipus Rex* and *Persephone*, the late sonatas of Debussy, Eliot's *Cocktail Party*, Joyce's *Ulysses* and Birtwistle's *Tragoedia*. It has elicited a somewhat undesirable critical reaction to the music and art of the romantic era, delaying for instance, the recognition of the true significance of Chopin, Wagner and Herman Melville for generations, and is still thwarting full recognition of other artists of scarcely lesser insights (e.g. Liszt, Le Fanu, Alkan).

Weber (1786–1826) and Mendelssohn (1809–47) are two composers whose piano music has fallen into this undeserved neglect, partly due, doubtless, to the sheer quantity of the romantic repertoire, which can make it difficult to see the wood for the trees. (The fact, too, that lesser-known piano works go out of print aggravates the problem.)

Weber's four sonatas are strikingly bold in concept and execution. The second, in A flat, used to be the most popular, and was played by Schnabel. More recently the third (D minor) and the fourth (E minor) have been revived by Gilels and Richter respectively. However, the best of the four is probably the first, in C major, whose four movements form an impressive unity; this holds true even though its finale, a moto perpetuo, was once popular as a separate concert piece. The slow movements of the sonatas especially repay close study, and show the skill and care with which Weber has used traditional forms. As a whole the sonatas are remarkable for the way in which, without losing their originality, they blend strength with wistfulness and Mendelssohnian delicacy. They add up to a unique experience, which we should indeed expect from the composer of the beautifully original *Invitation to the Waltz* and the coruscating *Rondo brillante*.

While Mendelssohn usually showed a more wholehearted commitment to the classical tradition, his sonatas are, surprisingly, more experimental in form than Weber's: the finale of the E major, for example, is preceded by an extended free recitative passage, while the B flat major contains a ghostly scherzo, which is re-introduced in the finale to quite extraordinary effect. The Sonata in G minor which Mendelssohn composed when he was twelve is more traditional in form, though the harmony of its slow movement is yet another proof of his fantastic precocity. The Preludes and Fugues are remarkably natural in their easy contrapuntal and harmonic mastery, and have a seriousness and grandeur which is not fully recognized.

Mendelssohn's other piano works include the famous forty-eight *Songs without Words*; these originally appeared as eight sets of six pieces, and include such small masterpieces as the A minor *Volktanz*, the B flat minor (in six–sixteen time, a typical Mendelssohn scherzo), the passionate F sharp minor, and the E major. The seven *Characteristic Pieces*, op. 7, the two sets of three Fantasies, op. 16 and op. 28, the evergreen Andante and Rondo Capriccioso, op. 14, and the *Variations sérieuses*, op. 54, also reveal his elegance, his balanced formal sense, his melodic directness, his textual legerdemain. His piano works encompass a remarkable, almost Scarlattian, technique of rapid chord repetition, and a complete understanding of the concept of leggiero. An example of the remarkably varied, and underestimated, emotional range of his best music must be the beautiful *Album Leaf* in E minor unhappily now probably out of print. His command of variation technique and, a point of detail, his frequent use of suspensions, influenced both Brahms and Alkan. He has long been criticized for being, in the pejorative sense, a 'Victorian' composer. Remembering that the Victoriana of today become the valuable acquisitions of tomorrow, we may yet see a reversal of opinion. I hope so.

Mendelssohn's influence on the course of romantic piano music was not, however, a great one. The stylistic departures of the later romantics can nearly always be traced back to Chopin, Schumann and Liszt. I should like now to consider Chopin's influence, to which is owed so much of Wagner's harmony, Debussy's refinement and Rachmaninov's technical figurations. The elegance of early Scriabin, the passion of Szymanowski (1882–1937) and the heroic style of Paderewski (1860–1941) all owed much also to the example of Chopin's subtle mind.

The most directly influenced was Scriabin (1872–1915). His early works include many waltzes, mazurkas, preludes, studies and nocturnes, and his skill as a pianist (his sensitive pedalling was especially remarked) must have helped him to breathe new life into the forms one would have thought Chopin had totally exhausted. Among Scriabin's early works are the twelve Studies, op. 8 (including the famous D sharp minor), and the Prelude and Nocturne for left hand alone, op. 9, which he composed when he temporarily injured his right hand while practising Balakirev's *Islamey*. Later he turned to larger forms, composing ten remarkable piano sonatas (eleven if one includes a little-known unnumbered sonata, based on themes from his Third Symphony, and published by Jurgenson) and large-scale works such as the fine Fantasy in B minor, op. 28 (very much inspired by the form of Chopin's Fantasy), the *Tragic Poem*, op. 34, and the *Satanic Poem*, op. 36.

Scriabin eventually evolved a personal philosophy of pantheistic mysticism which found musical expression in a 'mystic' hexachord (C–F sharp–B flat–E–A–D, reading upwards) which loosely underpins many of his later works.

These pieces have less in common with Chopin, being futuristic in sound; the most successful are the fifth, seventh, ninth and tenth sonatas, the poem *Vers la flamme* and five Preludes, op. 74, where for the first time he uses chords of superimposed thirds instead of fourths, which lends to these pieces, almost alone in Scriabin's output, a Bartókian timbre. Many of his best works were written during his period of transition from Chopin-influenced romanticism to modernity, e.g. the third and fourth sonatas and the Eight Studies, op. 42. In these pieces his later harmonic tensions are tempered by his widespread use of the emollient major second and perfect fourth.

Generally, Scriabin has been considerably underrated, since his compositions combine aural sensitivity with a remarkably original pianistic layout. The way he floods the keyboard with sound (as, for example, in the seventh sonata) presents a remarkable if idiosyncratic solution to the piano's limitations as a sustaining instrument. His exotic trills and figurations should not in my view be criticized as excesses but rather understood as an attempt to make the piano sing.

Karol Szymanowski's musical development was somewhat similar, since he was also strongly influenced by Chopin in his early works (e.g. the Preludes, op. 1, the four Studies, op. 4, and the variations, op. 3 and op. 10) and yet eventually found a heady alchemy of Oriental languor and Western formalism which mark his music as a parallel to the poetry of Elroy Flecker. His finest piano works include the three *Métopes*, op. 29, the Studies, op. 33 (dedicated to Cortot), the three *Masques*, op. 34 (the last dedicated to Artur Rubinstein), and the third sonata, op. 36, as well as many smaller pieces, notably mazurkas. His mature work emits an aura of extreme *fin de siècle* opulence. An occasional lack of clarity in texture, however, stops these interesting pieces from ranking with the masterpieces of Debussy and Ravel. Szymanowski was interested in classical and medieval mythology, as his choice of titles shows; the three *Métopes*, for instance, are named *L'île de Sirènes*,

Calypso and *Nausicaa*, and the three *Masques* are, respectively, *Schéhérezade*, *Tantris the Buffoon* (an anagram of Tristan), and *Sérénade de Don Juan*.

The inspiration of Chopin was evidently both functional and decorative to this later gifted Polish composer; functional is his extension of Chopin's original attitude to large-scale forms – in his sonatas Szymanowski combines Chopin's formal freedom with an attempt to continue that fusion of sonata, fugue and variation which is so important in the late Beethoven sonatas; decorative, on the other hand, are Szymanowski's intense chromaticism, and his languorous melodies, in both of which he travels further along the paths cleared by Chopin.

Paderewski was inspired more by the external and nationalist aspects of Chopin. His use of Polish dance forms, and his continuation of Chopinesque variation form (which however had interested Chopin only in his early years) had convincing results in the Variations and Fugue in A minor, and the Variations in A major. However, his most famous composition is the neo-classical Minuet in G. As a composer, Paderewski was essentially a miniaturist, and the technical demands his music makes are far less than, say, Scriabin's or Szymanowski's – strange, when one remembers his uniquely heroic piano playing.

It is not possible to consider the influences of Chopin, Schumann and Liszt as being in three watertight compartments. Most late romantic composers for the piano were strongly influenced by them all, in different ways. Rachmaninov (1873–1943) is an example, yet he developed on strongly original lines. As a young man he suffered a nervous breakdown as a result of the savage reception his First Symphony received at the hands of the St Petersburg critics. Later, however, with the help of a course of psychoanalytic hypnotism from a Dr Dahl, to whom he dedicated his Second Concerto, he developed anew his inexhaustibly thoughtful art, and all his mature work bears the unmistakable imprint of his granitic personality. Chief among his solo piano works are twenty-four preludes (including the famous ones in C sharp minor and G minor), six *Moments musicaux*, two sets of *Études-Tableaux*, and two piano sonatas, as well as many shorter compositions and transcriptions (of Bach, Kreisler, and Mendelssohn, among others). The sonatas are unaccountably neglected, considering that their development sections especially are as beautifully organized as those of the famous concertos. Some of the preludes, like the C minor, recall Chopin in their craftsmanship, and occasionally a Schumannesque lyrical sense is evident, as in the slow movement of the D minor Sonata. However, the breadth of his thought and his sweeps of melancholy grandeur are typically Russian, a quality that was never to leave his music, even though he lived for many years in America. (It is perhaps significant that he took American nationality only in the last year of his life.) His music, like his playing, carries an almost physical impact. On the technical side he got away once and for all from later equivalents of the Alberti bass, and his left-hand parts are a wonder of fluidity and grace. His massive chordal and octave writing sometimes shows Liszt's influence. He remains a master of inspired genius, both in small and large forms.

Rachmaninov's great friend Medtner (1880–1951), was once known as the 'Russian Brahms', on account of his interest in intricate rhythms. Unlike Rachmaninov, Medtner was influenced more by Schumann than by Tchaikovsky: his many piano works include twelve sonatas (some of which carry titles, e.g. *Sonate romantique*, *Sonata-Ballade*, *Sonate orageuse*), three sets of *Forgotten Melodies*, and many *Fairy Tales* and *Dances* in which his Schumannesque sense of fantasy is given full rein. The sonatas are somewhat portentous, although the G minor and E minor merit revival. Among his best works are the two *Contes*, op. 20 (the first Rachmaninovian, the second a sombre *Campanella* in the middle register of the piano), and the two *Elegies*, op. 59, philosophizings in sound which explore the tri-tonal relationship of A–E flat in a quietly original way.

LISZT

Scriabin, Szymanowski, Rachmaninov, Paderewski and Medtner; would any of these composers have written quite the same music if Liszt (1811–86) had not lived? Certainly not – some indication of his immense power and influence. Liszt's genius, enthusiasm and altruism helped indeed to change the course of musical history. The impact of his personality and playing has been well described by Hanslick: 'His playing was free, poetic, replete with imaginative shadings, and, at the same time, characterized by noble, artistic repose. . . . What a remarkable man! . . . His head, thrown back, still suggests something of Jupiter. Sometimes the eyes flash beneath the prominent brows; sometimes the characteristically upturned corners of the mouth are raised even higher in a gentle smile . . . The audience applauded, shouted, cheered, rose to its feet, recalled the master again and again, indefatigably. . . . A darling of the gods indeed!'

Aaron Copland in his *Music and Imagination* generalizes thus about Liszt: 'Think of what Liszt did for the piano. No other composer before him – not even Chopin – better understood how to manipulate the keyboard of the piano so as to produce the most satisfying sound textures ranging from the comparative simplicity of a beautifully spaced accompanimental figure to the shimmering of a delicate cascade of chords. . . . Liszt quite simply transformed the piano, bringing out not only its own inherent qualities, but its evocative nature as well: the piano as orchestra, the piano as harp, the piano as cembalum, the piano as organ, as brass choir, even the percussive piano as we know it may be traced to Liszt's incomparable handling of the instrument.'

As a melodist Liszt had much in common with Chopin, despite a liking for more ornate melodic inflections, while as a contrapuntist he shared with Berlioz a brilliantly external application of classical counterpoint, since both delighted in combining seemingly intractable themes in the various fugati which stud their works; harmonically, Liszt was

profoundly original – his unresolved cadences (*Nuages Gris*),
daring chordal writing (First *Mephisto* Waltz) and chords of
superimposed thirds and fourths (Third *Mephisto* Waltz)
lead straight to the procedures of Debussy, Scriabin and
Bartók.

As a young man he was deeply impressed, like Berlioz,
Chopin and Schumann, by the virtuosity of Paganini.
Thus, in his early years (1830–48) he wrote many brilliant
Studies, operatic fantasies and transcriptions which vie
with Paganini's in virtuosity. Prominent among them are
the extraordinary Fantasy on Paganini's *La Clochette* (the
same theme as *La Campanella*, but here much more extensively developed) and the six *Paganini* Studies of which five
were based on the violin caprices, the odd one out being the
popular *La Campanella*. Liszt's skill at recreating the music
in terms of the piano (and, in the case of the final version
of the fourth Study, with the minimum of alteration to the
violin's original text) is nowhere better shown. Few works*
defeated his amazing powers as a transcriber, and his
transcriptions of the Beethoven Symphonies and of Berlioz's *Fantastique* played an invaluable part in getting these
works more widely known.

The greatest of Liszt's early compositions are the twelve
Transcendental Studies. Like the *Paganini* Studies, these exist
in two versions† (three if we count the *Douze Études en forme
d'Exercises*, op. 1 which Liszt wrote when he was fifteen, and
which contain the germ of the later work). The Studies are
dedicated to Czerny, and have affinities with Paganini's
Caprices and Chopin's Studies. They may be briefly
characterized as follows:

---

* One of them apparently was the Mozart G minor Symphony K.550,
which Mendelssohn claimed was impossible to re-create in terms of the
pianoforte. After trying the opening, Liszt is supposed to have agreed
with him.

† The first version was published in 1839, the second in 1852.

1. *Preludio,* in C	An introductory improvisation.
2. A minor	In the manner of a Paganini caprice, with the pianistic equivalent of saltando bowing and double-stopping.
3. *Paysage,* in F	A charming pastoral mood picture, growing more passionate. Distant bells toll in its closing bars.
4. *Mazeppa,* in D minor	Inspired by the poems of Byron and Victor Hugo, which tell the legend of the Cossack leader who was sentenced to death by being bound to a wild horse, and who survived the ordeal to become the eventual ruler of his tribe.
5. *Feux follets,* in B flat	*Will-o'-the-wisps,* an Allegretto, which combines Mendelssohn's delicacy with the thoroughgoing technical demands of Schumann's Toccata.
6. *Vision,* in G minor	Of Berliozian splendour, its theme seemingly referring to the *Dies Irae.* Compound arpeggios of evocative power.
7. *Eroica,* in E flat	A heroic march, also rather Berliozian.
8. *Wilde Jagd,* in C minor	A wild hunt which introduces almost Stravinskian syncopation. The unexpected juxtaposition of contrasted difficulties makes this one of the hardest studies. Its lyrical sections look forward already to Wagner and Franck.
9. *Ricordanza,* in A flat	As Busoni said 'a bundle of yellowed love-letters'. The chordal second theme is in wonderful contrast to the Chopinesque cadenzas of the rest.
10. F minor	An agitated drama, having melodic affinities with the Chopin F minor Study op. 25, no. 2. Emotionally it is akin to the *Appassionata* Sonata of Beethoven, and the F minor Ballade of Chopin; significantly all three works are in the same key.

11. *Harmonies du soir,* in D flat	Looks forward to the evanescent textures of Debussy and the massive chordal writing of Rachmaninov. Highly sustained, almost ecstatic in its lyricism.
12. *Chasse-neige,* in B flat minor	A study in tremolo, a world of half-colours and shafts of brilliance. The most profound Study of the set.

These twelve Studies are one of the pinnacles of romantic piano music. Lina Ramann rightly calls them 'an unparalleled, gigantic work of spiritual technique', and it is surely of them that Busoni must have been thinking when he said 'Bach is the foundation of piano playing, Liszt the summit. The two make Beethoven possible.' Indeed, if the Forty-Eight and the thirty-two Beethoven Sonatas are the Old and New Testaments of piano literature, the Studies of Chopin and Liszt should be the Apocrypha. Liszt goes much farther than Chopin in the freedom with which he tests the idea of the study. The first three are recognizably in the line of descent from Czerny and Cramer, each of them concentrating upon one technical problem; the later studies of the set are much longer, and some of them are more truly symphonic poems for piano rather than studies in the traditional sense. In the 1839 version no titles are given to any of the studies, although it would be surprising if he did not already have the titles at least in his mind, in view of the music's extremely descriptive character.

Among Liszt's innumerable operatic transcriptions and fantasies should be mentioned the Tarantella on Auber's *Muette de Portici,* a *tour de force* of fantastic pianism; several fantasies based on Meyerbeer's operas, notably *Prophète, Robert le Diable* and *Les Huguenots,* and the fine transcriptions of Weber's overtures to *Oberon* and *Der Freischütz*; he also made many transcriptions of Verdi and Wagner, notably the paraphrases on themes from *Ernani, Rigoletto* and *Simone Boccanegra,* and the transcription of the overture to *Tannhaüser* and the Liebestod from *Tristan* (drawing from the keyboard a Messiaen-like range of sonority). There is

also the *Hexameron*, a *piéce d'occasion* written for the salons
of the Princess Belgiojoso; Liszt edited and rounded off a
group of variations by various composers, including
Chopin, Thalberg, Pixis and Herz. His catholic taste also
reached to the classical and pre-classical eras; there are, for
example, transcriptions of works by Arcadelt, of Bach's
organ music, of songs by Schubert and Schumann (notably
Erlkönig, *Ave Maria* and *Widmung*), and the interesting
Fantasias on Beethoven's *Adelaide* and *The Ruins of Athens*.

This account though not exhaustive, gives some idea of
the energy and devotion Liszt poured into his musical life.
The finest of the operatic fantasies are probably the two
based on Mozart's operas – the unfinished *Figaro* Fantasy,
completed by Busoni, and the extraordinary *Réminiscences
de Don Juan*. This *Don Giovanni* Fantasy is based mainly on
the duet *Là ci darem la mano*, preceded by the Commenda-
tore's theme and followed by the *Champagne* aria. The whole
work is remarkably symphonic in organization considering
its character, and there is real excitement in the virtuosity
with which Liszt develops, varies, contrasts and combines
the various themes. Its extraordinary textures are worth
quotation (it is interesting to compare it with Chopin's
variations on *Là ci darem la mano*):

Ex.12

Liszt's flamboyance aroused some disapproval, notably
from Chopin and Mendelssohn: in this early period he was
in fact already sketching many of the compositions which
appear in their final form in the Weimar period (1848–60),
notably the first versions of the piano concertos and the
Années de pèlerinage. He was in fact always conscious of
tradition (as a pupil of Czerny he was, after all, a grand-
pupil of Beethoven) and at Weimar he became more so.
Wagner's development of 'the music of the future' and his
search for the ideal of authentic and accurate performance
(in his famous essay 'On Conducting', for example) undoubtedly influenced Liszt, who became, at this time, more
absorbed in composing, less interested in playing, and
deeply conscious of musical and national traditions. The
result was a clearer formal logic, that 'unerring instinct for
form' of which Constant Lambert wrote. In the *Années de
pèlerinage* I admire both the happy miniatures, the *Eclogue,
Pastorale, Au Bord d'une source* and *Le Mal du pays,* as well as
the large-scale conceptual breadth of *Vallée d'Obermann* and
Après une lecture de Dante. The *Années* fall into four books as
follows:

I *Suisse*	1. *Chapelle de Guillaume Tell*	A bold opening, with Phrygian modal harmony, leads to a grandiose theme: its middle section makes use of 'echo' effects.
	2. *Au Lac de Wallenstadt*	A murmuring water-minia-ture. The key of A flat is usually associated with calm in Liszt's music.
	3. *Pastorale*	A sprightly miniature, in binary form.
	4. *Au Bord d'une source*	Another water-picture, also in A flat. Its sparkling effect partly derives from a roman-tic re-creation of Scarlattian textures, e.g. much use of crossed hands.

5. *Orage*	Remarkable in its musical onomatopoeia. Technically a good key to many of Liszt's characteristic bravura passages.
6. *Vallée d'Ober- mann*	A beautiful, rather Weberian opening paragraph, is developed extensively; it then gives way to a dramatic recitative, and a final section in the tonic major closes the work. Unity is achieved by the varied but consistent use of a descending scalic figure.
7. *Eclogue*	A pastoral, in A flat.
8. *Le Mal du pays*	A Grieg-like evocation of nostalgia.
9. *Les Cloches de Genève*	A broad, programmatic canvas.

II. *Italie*

1. *Spozalizio*	A beautifully composed piece in which two themes are stated and then combined with rare mastery.
2. *Il Penseroso*	Technically, a study in chromatic harmony and suspensions. The date of its first version was 1838, an indication of Liszt's harmonic daring.
3. *Canzonetta del' Salvator Rosa*	A robust *chanson*.
4. }*Three* 5. }*sonnets of* 6. }*Petrarca*	Also existing as songs, these are Liszt's equivalent to the poetic drama and passion of the Chopin nocturnes. Their lyricism and pianism rank them high among his shorter works.
7. *Après une lecture de Dante*	Also known as the *Dante Sonata*, this fine fantasy shows Liszt's pervasive use of thematic metamorphosis:

It is strikingly original in its savage rhythms and whole-tone harmony. A fresco of livid colour, Liszt's effortless command of stunning keyboard effect is here shown at its strongest. As a sonata movement, it follows Chopin's example in omitting the recapitulation of the first subject.

III. *Venezia e Napoli*	1. *Gondoliera*	A barcarolle, quieter and gentler in mood than Chopin's.
	2. *Canzona*	Based on an aria by Rossini — much use of tremolo.
	3 *Tarantella*	Particularly brilliant and effective, with a lyrical middle section. This probably influenced the tarantella of Busoni's Piano Concerto.
IV. (*Rome, 1873*)	1. *Angelus*	Simple and affecting.
	2. & 3. *Threnodies at the Cypresses of the Villa d'Este.*	The second is very Wagnerian, the first more stark.
	4. *Jeux d'eau à la Villa d'Este*	A masterly exercise in tone-colours which looks forward to the impressionism of Debussy and Ravel.
	5. *Sunt Lachrymae Rerum* ⎫ 6. *Marche funèbre* ⎭	Evidence of Liszt's growing interest in his last years in the authentic bases of Hungarian folk music.

7. *Sursum Corda*	A coda to the set. The whole-tone harmony of the middle section is striking, as is the way the piece works up to a great climax over a reiterated pedal E.

The work as a whole is an astonishing achievement and intermittently occupied Liszt from youth to old age. In it we see the extent to which he derived his inspiration from an extra-musical programme, and how he was influenced by the national characteristics of the countries he visited. Yet the works are conscientiously wrought musically, and, indeed whether Liszt wrote *Hungarian* (there are nineteen), *Spanish* or *Rumanian* (there are one of each) Rhapsodies, German *Liebestraüme*, or Italian sonnets, he remained first and foremost a cosmopolitan musician of genius, rather than a nationalist (except possibly in his last years).

The *Harmonies poétiques et religieuses* continued and refined the style of the *Années de pèlerinage*. They include the *Bénédiction de Dieu dans la solitude* (whose association of the tonality of F sharp with religious devotion foreshadows Messiaen's *Vingt Regards sur l'Enfant Jésus*) and *Funérailles*. This powerful composition builds up three large sections, the first heroic (F minor), the second lyrical (A flat), the third heroic (D flat); which are then recapitulated in a quarter of the time, a procedure of composition, macrocosm followed by microcosm, far ahead of its time. *Funérailles* was dedicated to the memory of Chopin, whose death in 1849 was commemorated by Liszt with several works in Chopinesque forms composed in the Weimar period, notably the two ballades (the second, in B Minor, is Franckian and Sibelian) and the two hypnotic polonaises. Later works cast in a heroic mould are the two *Legends, St Francis preaching to the birds*, and *St Francis walking on the waves*, in which delicacy and power are merged most movingly.

Finest of all Liszt's piano works is probably the Sonata in B minor, composed in 1854. It was described by Wagner as 'beyond all conception beautiful, great, noble; sublime even as thyself'. Its thirty minutes develop four themes

with a naturalness and mastery which proved to be inimit-able. Like the last sonatas of Beethoven, Liszt's combines in its vast structure the musical elements of fugue, recitative, fantasia and variation. Its success stems from the simplicity and directness of its basic patterns, themes and motifs. In this work Liszt showed an instinctive genius in counter-balancing his ornate pianism with a simple cellular motivic structure. The sonata is obscurely tragic, Faustian in concept, its fugue (more accurately a fugato) Mephisto-phelean, and its opening and closing pages are of haunting beauty. It codifies the stresses and exaltations of one of the most gifted romantic composers. It is an epochal work, both for the piano, for its documentary importance as a chronicle of the romantic age, and for its revealing insights into the heroism and anxieties of Liszt's generous character.

There are other worthwhile compositions from the Weimar period – the neglected Berceuse, the three Concert Studies (including *La Leggierezza* and *Un Sospiro*), the two Studies entitled *Waldesrauschen* and *Gnomenreigen* and the *Consolations*, should be mentioned – but the Sonata, in its perfect balance of form and content, stands apart. His later works (1861–86) tend to fragment the style he had so painstakingly built up. Personal disappointments (the failure to obtain a legal dispensation to marry Princess von Sayn-Wittgenstein) and professional disappointments (his failure to establish a permanent musical centre in Weimar) may partly account for this. The old fire burns brightly as ever in the Variations on Bach's cantata *Weinen, Klagen* and in the highly original Fantasy and Fugue on BACH. Generally, however, the once-ornate decoration is cut to a minimum, melody is more austere, often with a more genuinely Hungarian inflection than hitherto, counterpoint becomes implicit rather than explicit, and the rhythmic structure ever more fluid and experimental.

Among the late works are the Third *Mephisto* Waltz, with its Scriabinesque motif of superimposed fourths,

Ex. 15

La Gondola lugubre, inspired by Venetian funeral processions, the *Csàrdas macabre* with its remarkable chain of consecutive fifths, the *Csàrdas obstiné*, the charming *Christmas Tree* Suite, several short mood-poems such as *Nuages gris* (so admired by Debussy and Stravinsky), *En Rêve* and *Farewell*, evocative dance-remembrances such as the four *Valses oubliées*, the five Hungarian Folk-songs and the Hungarian *Historical Portraits*.

In these late works Liszt is a seer, bequeathing his visions to posterity and seeking no immediate reward from the world around him. He would have had his reward had he known the great influence his music was to have on Debussy, Scriabin, Bartók and Sibelius. Others included Grieg, Saint-Saëns, Borodin and Richard Strauss (1864–1949), whose Lisztian (and Brahmsian) Sonata in B minor, op. 5, does not however contain the lyric individuality of his Piano Pieces, op. 7.

Among the composers of Liszt's own time, Litolff (1818–91) is largely forgotten, except for the once-popular Scherzo from his *Concerto Symphonique*, for piano and orchestra. Liapunov (1859–1924) is rarely played. His F minor Sonata is one of several – including those by Reubke (1834–58) and Benjamin Dale (1885–1943) – directly inspired by the form of Liszt's masterpiece. Both this and his twelve *Transcendental* Studies (which include the brilliant *Lezghinka*, evidently a sibling of *Islamey*) are well worth revival.

A more interesting and more profoundly gifted composer for the piano was Alkan (1813–88). He was an almost exact contemporary of Liszt, and had the misfortune to die in a very bizarre way, when a bookcase, from which he was taking a copy of the Talmud, fell on top of him and crushed him to death. His life was scarcely less bizarre: he lived as a recluse, and never played his own major works in public. Yet his command of the piano was such that he was supposed to be the only person before whom Liszt was nervous of playing. Alkan's music has a totally original melodic tincture, a harmonic sense which may alternately be very simple or extremely complex, and it is underpinned by a rather sinister liking for obsessive rhythms. His major works include two sets of Studies in all the major keys (op. 35) and all the minor keys (op. 39). This latter set includes the Symphony and the magnificent Concerto for solo piano, and the Variations *Le Festin d'Esope*, which interpret unspecified fables by Aesop in a miraculously incisive way. These are the best known works by Alkan, but the autobiographical *Grande Sonate* (which includes the resplendent *Quasi-Faust*), the Sonatina in A minor, the tone poems *Le Chemin de fer*, and *Le Tambour bat aux champs*, and the three Studies, op. 76 (composed respectively for left hand, right hand, and for the two hands in perpetual and similar motion) are all worthy of serious consideration and study, and must one day achieve their deserved place in the repertoire. Some of Alkan's music has been edited and recorded (splendidly!) by Raymond Lewenthal, to whose pioneering efforts much of the revival of interest is due. Among the later romantic composers, Moszkowski (1854–1925) is now somewhat forgotten. His best music has something of Liszt's technical ease, and his Studies (e.g. *En Automne*), his Barcarolle in G, and Valse in E all have great charm. Tausig (1841–71), a pupil of Liszt, combined charm with dazzling virtuosity and some emotional depth in his best works, which include many studies and a Hungarian Rhapsody, *Ungarische Zigeunerweisen*, which stylistically lies somewhere between Liszt, Wagner* and Balakirev.

It was however, Busoni (1866–1924) who as a composer most directly followed Liszt's example as composer, transcriber and editor. He shared Liszt's interest in musical philosophy, and left a body of piano music which ranges stylistically from neo-Brahmsian (e.g., the early preludes, op. 37) to highly experimental (e.g. the *Sonatina Seconda*). Busoni's music makes much of an almost Britten-like ambiguous tonality (compare, for example, the arpeggios of superimposed thirds in the *Fantasia Contrappuntistica* with the first *Sea Interlude* from *Peter Grimes*), and runs a Stravinskian gamut of stylistic change, from neo-classical to semi-atonal, from romantic to neo-classical. He attempted to etch his music with an Italianate clarity and adumbrated a 'young classicism' similar to Stravinsky's neo-classicism. His most important piano works are the six sonatinas (which include one composed on Christmas Day 1917, one composed *ad usum Infantis*, and another based on themes from Bizet's *Carmen*), the Elegies (subdued mood-pictures, of which only *All'Italia!* has remained at all popular), the charming *Indian Diary* (based on Red Indian folksongs), the powerfully morbid Toccata of 1920, and the *Fantasia Contrappuntistica*, a completion of Bach's *Art of Fugue* which marked the zenith of Busoni's interest in large-scale 'architectonic' structures (the two-piano version is actually

---

*Nor indeed should Wagner's (1813–1883) piano music be totally forgotten. His output included two sonatas and some interesting 'genre' pieces, such as the early F sharp minor Fantasy.

prefaced by a drawing of the Palace of the Popes at Avignon).

Besides this considerable output of original works, Busoni made many transcriptions for piano, notably of Bach's C major and D minor organ toccatas, the Bach violin Chaconne, and the Liszt Fantasy and Fugue *Ad Nos, ad Salutarem Undam*. Stylistically, he always moved towards the future, experimenting with new scale and chord formations, and even envisaging the existence of electronic music. His influence has been widely felt: such works as Casella's *E Notte Alta*, Ronald Stevenson's masterly *Passacaglia on DSCH*, and Dallapiccola's *Sonatina Canonica* and *Quaderno Musicale per Annalibera* all follow, in different ways, Busoni's precepts of structure and sonority. Less easy to assimilate is the sometimes mordant and ironic capriciousness of Busoni's best music. In this aspect, and in his many-sided gifts, it is Prokofiev (1891–1953) who is most similar to Busoni.

Prokofiev's style, like Busoni's, also changed considerably at different times, possibly partly owing to a lengthy period of living in France in the nineteen-twenties, and then returning to Russia for the latter part of his life, changes of environment which must have shaped his thought in unexpected ways. His piano music frequently seems to dispose the hands in a new and totally original way:

Ex. 16

and his piano writing has influenced both Russian and American composers, notably Samuel Barber (in his fine Piano Sonata), Kabalevsky, Shostakovitch, Peter Mennin and Benjamin Lees. Prokofiev's pianistic figurations derived in their turn from Liszt, Mussorgsky and Rachmaninov, but the blend is new and original. His major piano works include nine sonatas which encompass all periods of his life: the first is an interesting student work (like Scriabin's first, it is in F minor); the second is a large-scale work in his more romantic vein; the third a brilliant one-movement work, using earlier sketches, which also provide the basis of the fourth, a profoundly evocative masterpiece in its combination of languor and energy; the fifth is somewhat more subdued; the sixth, seventh and eighth form a triptych, since they were all composed during the Second World War – in them Prokofiev's pianistic art reaches its zenith, especially in the astonishing toccata-like finale to the seventh: and the ninth is a contemplative work, somewhat Wagnerian in its first movement development, and rather underrated. Elsewhere he revealed more strongly his Busonian taste for the grotesque, especially in the *Sarcasms*, op. 17, the *Suggestion Diabolique*, op. 4, and the *Visions Fugitives*, op. 22. His range is greater than this, however: the Sonatinas, op. 59 are almost Ravel-like in their pastoral delicacy, while the *Contes de la vieille grand'mère* are truly Russian fairy-tales; nor should one forget that the Toccata, op. 11, is one of the finest modern examples of this form.

The anti-romantic elements in Prokofiev's music mark a certain point in the long move which the late romantic piano composers made away from the nineteenth-century Germanic musical hegemony. It is thus in stark contrast to the traditionalist Max Reger (1873–1916). While some of Reger's works are remarkable for their mastery of counterpoint (especially the *Telemann* and the *Bach* Variations), their fullness of texture convinces one of the rightness of the contemporary innovations of Schoenberg and Bartók, which really closed the era of romantic piano music.

The romantic era was not a tidy one, in music any more than in literature, nor in piano music any more than in music generally. Weber and Schumann had continued the Beethovenian tradition, while Chopin and Mendelssohn were temperamentally closer to the aesthetic of Bach and Mozart; Liszt stood apart, and yet produced music of classical structural balance. Behind this surface diversity of approach, the progress of musical thought remained constant and the results eventually may be seen to have been inevitable.

6

The Growth of National Schools

JAMES GIBB

*

T HE piano became *par excellence* the focal instrument of the Romantic Ego, thanks to its self-sufficiency and its incomparable powers of assimilation and evocation. These were put to their greatest test in the nineteenth century. But the romantic age was also the era of growing national consciousness, and the rise of distinctly natiónal schools of composers is the subject of this chapter. A sense of nationalism is a comparatively recent development, even in the most powerful countries. Germany was not united until the eighteen-seventies, Italy only shortly before; Belgium won independence in 1830, Norway only in 1905 – a year before Grieg's death. Ironically, war brought unity. The Napoleonic Wars had drawn together the vast spread, and different races, of the Russian Empire. It was the conscious aim of the Russian nationalist composers to give them an inspiring sense of unity, and in their turn the Russians' suppression of the Polish insurrection of 1830 fired the national fervour of Chopin's mazurkas and polonaises. The defeat of the Austrians by the Italians in 1859 gave the Czechs an opportunity for founding their own national theatre and opera-house, soon to be presided over by Smetana. While Prussians were marching through the streets of Paris in 1871, the thirty-six-year-old Saint-Saëns and his patriotic colleagues were founding the Société Nationale de Musique.

These countries, and many more, re-explored their own heritages. Most of them had strongly entrenched alien cultures, not by any means necessarily deriving from their political enemies. Folk music played its part in the reawakening: in some countries folk traditions were fast dying. In Norway, for instance, serious folk-song collection began only in the eighteen-forties, about the time of Grieg's birth. In Great Britain, too, due to rapid industrialization, the art was vanishing, to be saved by later pioneers like Cecil Sharp and Vaughan Williams. The researches into Hungarian and Rumanian folk music by Bartók and Kodály came later still. Research was less necessary for the Russian nationalists: they could hear their folk-songs at all times, as could the Czechs. Perhaps the most musically vital of all the folk traditions was to be found in Spain, where tyrannical attempts to centralize government had only served to accentuate the differences between the provinces. Two of these, the Basque and the Catalan, had their own separate languages. Spanish folk-song in itself embodied several foreign influences – the Moors, the Jewish synagogue and the itinerant gypsies. Spain appealed powerfully to romantics even in the most distant countries: Glinka, for instance, made the arduous journey from Russia and cut his musical teeth on Spanish folk-song. The spread of railways was to facilitate such cross-influences. V. Stassov described the impact of Liszt's and Berlioz's visits on Russian musicians and, in turn, the appearance of Rimsky-Korsakov and others in Paris in 1889 had crucial effects on the course of French music. The most noted Spanish composers were saved from atrophy by the train to Paris, where Debussy's vision stimulated their own, and where French painters and writers had long before this been influenced by Spain.

Germany became the lure of music students, but gains in craftsmanship were offset by rigid dogmatism. In the end, Scandinavians, Czechs, British and Russians had to develop their own national characteristics. The French were less consciously national in their aims, less dependent on native folk-song, yet no music could be more identifiable than theirs. Even the tidal wave of Wagnerism failed to drown them. On the contrary, the Bayreuth pilgrimages of French poets, painters and musicians led to a unique confluence of ideas. The Impressionist composers owed even more to the Symbolist poets (many of them ardent contributors to the *Revue Wagnérienne*) than to the painters. The eclectic, sophisticated French survived the slough of nationalism without replacing one dogma with another.

FRANCE

Couperin and Rameau, these are truly French .... French music is all clearness, elegance; simple natural declamation. The aim of French music is before all, to please .... The musical genius of France may be described as a fantasy of the senses ...

Debussy.

You may loudly proclaim that the fundamentals of the art of my father and myself are anti-Rameau.   C.P.E. Bach.

Time has not narrowed the gap between French and German music. One has only to compare, say, Hindemith's *Ludus Tonalis* with Messiaen's *Vingt Regards sur l'Enfant Jésus*, written within a year of each other, to realize that it has become a great chasm. Prejudices crackle, and to speak of music as an international language sounds like empty piety. Yet the nineteenth century witnessed the danger of French subjugation to Wagnerism, and the escape from the Wagner aura had original and highly productive results.

The refined sensitivity of French poetry produced a melodic sense wholly tuned to the character of the language – one can almost hear the words that hover behind the melody of a Fauré nocturne.

Yet the first great figure in French piano music owed more to German tradition. César Franck (1822–90) was in fact a Belgian born in Liège. His mother was German, and his father, ambitious and tyrannical, took out French naturalization papers in 1835 so that his two sons could enter the Paris Conservatoire. César Franck's first piano works were superficial trifles designed to display his youthful dexterity and obey the imperious dictates of his father. His heart was never in a virtuoso career, and his creative gifts only found their true soil from the time of his appointment as organist in the church of Sainte-Clotilde. Here he developed his gifts as an extemporizer and found a haven in which he could integrate his intense religious belief with a humble attempt to emulate, for him, the highest ideals of the art as represented by the late works of Beethoven.

The current fashions in opera and the theatre held no attraction for Franck, and even the swamping impact of Wagner came to him more at second hand through his great admiration for Liszt. Nevertheless, through the association of friends and pupils he was to acquire a peculiarly French melodic voice, mainly by way of Gounod, who shared his religious beliefs and, through an original lyrical gift, was himself freeing French opera from its Italian and German models. Franck had the capacity of absorbing foreign musical influences without allowing them to dominate him. His increasing chromaticism was perhaps Wagnerian; but the overt eroticism of *Tristan* was sublimated into the wilting submission of Catholic humility, producing a harmonic language immediately recognizable as his and his only. He turned the harmony of *appoggiatura* to his own purpose and in the Prelude, Choral and Fugue, his masterpiece for the piano, he adapted the formal disciplines of late Beethoven and Liszt's cyclic form to a seemingly improvisatory language. The thematic links between the opening theme and the fugue of Beethoven's op. 110 sonata are not lost on Franck – nor is the ecstatic, pianistic loosening of contrapuntal shackles on its last page. The simple-minded Franck had no kind of contact with Mephistopheles, and the two cells from which the Prelude, Choral and Fugue grows are never transmuted in the Lisztian sense: they simply grow to more and more passionate affirmations of faith.

After a quiet introduction the appoggiatura idea is stated

Ex.1

from which the Fugue is later derived. The other dominating theme is the Choral, significantly rounded off with humble drooping phrases. The pianistic language combines his skill as an improvisator on the organ with a Lisztian mastery of clearing simultaneous lines. There is real genius in the climax of the fugue, when its subject is introduced as a middle voice between a canon based on the Choral, the whole interwoven with the Prelude's opening arpeggios:

A highly charged emotional impulse is contained by a unique sense of overall shape.

The same kind of success cannot be claimed for the only other important work Franck wrote for solo piano, the

Prelude, Aria and Finale. Here the emotion is more self-conscious and the craftsmanship more obvious. The overworked sequences, modulating predictably upwards, eventually have no more dramatic importance than the hitching up of one's trousers. Fluent skill is no compensation for the lurking sentimentalities of pious prostration. Nevertheless Franck's seriousness of purpose was an important legacy.

'Art has the right to go down into the depths, to insinuate itself into the hidden secrets of dark and desolate souls. This right is not a duty.' These were the words of Camille Saint-Saëns (1835–1921) and it comes as no surprise to find his solo piano works uncommitted. They are full of elegance and intelligence – qualities highly prized by the French, yet none has gained a permanent place in the repertoire. Even his fugues, for all their ingenuity, lack tension. Saint-Saëns was the captive of his own precocious gifts: at eight he played Field and Mozart concertos by heart and at ten he knew all the Beethoven sonatas. Yet absence of passion was a mark of his playing as well as his compositions, despite his wide enthusiasms: first Mozart, and then Bach, Liszt, Wagner and Schumann. Two of his concertos maintain their place, and also the excellently written *Variations on a Theme of Beethoven* for two pianos. Ironically he forbade publication in his lifetime of his most popular work, *Le Carnaval des Animaux* for two pianos and orchestra. He had a great gift for frivolity and a still greater fear of being accused of it. After his last unsuccessful attempt at the Prix de Rome, Berlioz, his one supporter, came out saying, 'He knows everything, but he lacks inexperience.'

His friend Bizet (1838–75) was also a gifted pianist with an outstanding ability to reproduce any music once heard. Yet he only wrote one major work for piano solo, the *Variations Chromatiques de Concert*, which reveals his admiration for Beethoven's C minor Variations without sharing that work's superb aptitude for the instrument. It looks more like an orchestral reduction, unlike the original piano-duet version of his deservedly popular *Jeux d'enfants*. Ravel remarked that the opening night of Chabrier's opera *Le Roi malgré lui* changed the whole orientation of French harmony, and Poulenc declared that the *Dix Pièces pittoresques* (1880) were as important for French music as the preludes of Debussy. In fact these marvellous though uneven pieces make one wonder at his avowed Wagnerism. Chabrier (1841–94) was a notorious piano-pounder, yet he produced music of the most tender sensitivity, as in no. 2 of this set, *Mélancolie*, with its delicate changes of texture and gentle Schumannesque canons. Rhythmical surprises and abrupt changes of key were typical: the *Danse villageoise* starts off boldly in eleven-bar phrases and the *Menuet pompeux*, which Ravel orchestrated, contains delicious incongruities. Exuberance, the fresh and unexpected, the naïve and the suave, flow through the two-piano *Trois Valses romantiques* with ironic bonhomie and charm. The raucous music-hall laugh and the tenderest entreaties are interwoven with subtle craftsmanship. (Debussy's two-piano *En blanc et noir* owes much to Chabrier.) His last important solo piece, the *Bourrée fantasque*, has an irresistible *joie de vivre* and an honest vulgarity. By now Chabrier had overcome his early hesitations of technique: although the piece is in C minor, note the subtle ambiguity of the suspended F sharp that introduces the seductive second theme.

The finest works of Gabriel Fauré (1845–1924) still require special pleading in this country. Like Schubert, he was modest and prolific, freely acknowledging his debt to Saint-Saëns. In his piano music he favoured Chopinesque genres – the nocturne, the barcarolle (he wrote thirteen of each), the impromptu and so on. He eschewed pictorial titles and exhibitionism (only three of these pieces end loudly and one of them, the Sixth Impromptu, was originally written for the harp). Fauré's pianistic style derived from Chopin, Schumann, and Mendelssohn, though he did not acquire Mendelssohn's penchant for staccato. The music flows on with deceptive ease but melody and harmony are, from the start, splendidly individual, with constantly arresting and expressive modulations. His returns to base are made with natural grace and insouciance – like a

cat, as many have said, but one without claws. There is no
demon in him; we look in vain for the romantic frenzy of a
Chopin ballade or for any sign of virtuoso demagogy. Yet,
as in the best of Mendelssohn, there is eloquent lyricism in
Fauré: most touching of all, perhaps, in the songs and in
the chamber music, but it invests many of his piano works
with the glow and conviction of a real master.

Fauré's personality is clearly identifiable even in his
earliest pieces, with their overt models. The First Nocturne
in E flat minor for instance, begins like a Chopin prelude,
and later emulates one of Chabrier's *Pièces pittoresques* in its
parallel writing for treble and bass. Yet already the
harmonic slant, the gentle lyricism and the subtle pianistic
timbres are Fauré's own. The First Impromptu and Barcarolle, too, quietly invest traditional formulas with sinuous
variation. The Second Impromptu is a Chopinesque tarantella, and the popular Third Nocturne flirts suavely with
sentimentality – a vein turned by Poulenc to a self-mocking
irony. Only when approaching his fiftieth year did Fauré
reveal the full depth of his pianistic genius: in the Sixth
Nocturne in D flat and the Fifth Barcarolle in F sharp minor.
The Nocturne opens with reflective tenderness:

Later the same phrase modulates with increasing agitation, rising, for the first time in Fauré's piano works, to heights of rhetorical passion.

The Fifth Barcarolle also pivots on an exuberant transmutation of its quiet opening phrase, but is still more adventurous in its tortuous harmonies and the commanding breadth of its climax, perhaps the only one to aspire to the passion of Chopin's precedent.

Variation form demands concentration in a fundamentally ruminative composer, but Fauré's *Theme and Variations* are somewhat awe-struck by the grandeur of their model, Schumann's *Études symphoniques*. The homage is genuine, but only in the fourth, and particularly the lyrical ninth, variations does his personal eloquence and harmonic felicity shine through. Charles Koechlin, his pupil and friend, emphasized Fauré's debt to Gregorian plainsong: and Norman Suckling, in his perceptive book on Fauré, saw a modal influence in the 'Hellenic serenity, and luminosity' of the later works. Here musical thought is pared down to essentials; like Liszt in his old age Fauré is most surprising when he speaks quietly and with the fewest words. Fauré had already demonstrated his new eloquence in 1910, the year of Debussy's first book of preludes: the Ninth Barcarolle in A minor, has a supple ease which disguises its sure sense of direction. Canonic imitation amid arpeggios is managed with a nonchalance that would have been the envy of Thalberg, the inventor of the 'three-handed' trick. Like many before him, Fauré had often lighted on the whole tone scale, an early stock-in-trade of the avant-garde Impressionists, and its equally natural concomitant of augmented-triad harmony. He never elevated it into a dogma, any more than Debussy did, but in his Fifth Impromptu (a kind of *perpetuum mobile*), also dated 1910, he made prodigal use of it, to the extent of a *jeu d'esprit*. Harmonic weapons are also sharpened in the highly concentrated but uneven Preludes, op. 103. This final economy of style is not without its dangers; the fewer notes are occasionally over-weighted with enharmonic double-meaning, and a faltering in impulse sometimes leaves a rather arid landscape. But the Eleventh and Twelfth Nocturnes are superbly satisfying – in particular the latter, with its melancholy, nostalgic passion rising to a magnificent climax of disturbing parallel triads:

This nocturne and the Tenth Barcarolle represent the peak of Fauré's achievement in his favourite piano genres. Both end hesitantly hovering between major and minor chords: both settle for the melancholy, solemn and resigned minor.

While most of the disturbing novelties of French piano music were tucked away in modest short solo pieces at the beginning of this century, two works stand out like defiant monuments: the sonatas of Paul Dukas (1865–1935) and Vincent d'Indy (1851–1931). The former, in E flat minor, appeared in 1900 and was acclaimed by Debussy, the composer whose work was tugging most powerfully in the opposite direction. The grandeur and piano style owe much to Franck, but there is a more pleasing clarity of texture, and the sequences neither cloy nor meander. Alas, the ghosts of Franck's Symphony and Liszt's Sonata haunt the last movement out of its wits: self-inducement to high sentiments proved too much of a strain.

Dukas's only other large work for piano, the *Variations, interlude et finale sur un thème de Rameau*, is altogether more successful. From the tender four-part writing of the first variation to the finale, which combines folk-dance with academic devices, it embodies a Beethovenish surety of design. Was the last page's lingering farewell to the whole-tone scale an affectionate dig at his old friend Debussy?

From 1910 onwards Dukas's dedication to teaching seemed to dry up the wells of invention: he wrote little to pass his own highly self-critical censorship. Vincent d'Indy was also a dedicated teacher. Discipline, intellectual and moral, had been visited upon him from an early age by his maternal grandmother, his mother having died in child-birth. Even after she had gone blind she used an alarm clock to insist on the disciplinary schedule, producing a child prodigy of the piano, a precocious composer, and later, a devoted but dogmatic teacher. After serving in the Franco-Prussian War d'Indy was among the first founders of the Société Nationale de Musique, though César Franck in fact schooled him in the craft of the German masters. Like Franck he came under the spell of Wagner by way of Liszt. His dedication to 'cyclic form' amounted to dogma: he even claimed Dukas's Sonata as a perfect example without itemizing any evidence. However his own Sonata, written six or seven years later, left no doubt about his principles. Blanche Selva, its remarkable first performer, wrote a detailed account of d'Indy's intentions. In shape it is a kind of tryptych: not only the outer variation-movements but the long five–four scherzo embodies the thematic cells of the whole work ingeniously, even wittily. But the piano writing lacks the natural finesse of Dukas: for all its deftness, a Franckian odour of sanctity pervades the work. D'Indy's last work for piano, the relaxed *Fantaisie sur un vieil air de ronde française* is far more endearing to play, harking back to the unbuttoned high spirits of Chabrier, and a relish for French folk-music. D'Indy's influence on French music had been immense. He was self-consciously patriotic despite his German-influenced craftsmanship. D'Indy and Debussy remained good friends even though their music had declared war.

After a heady brew came the cooling draught. The music of Erik Satie (1866–1925), one of the most original characters in musical history, came in like the voice of a child, saying outrageous things with complete, honest calm. What he had to say came from a profound instinct: the core of an astonishing number of future developments in French music can be found in Satie's seemingly naïve miniatures. His Three Sarabandes appeared in 1887, the same year as Chabrier's *Le Roi malgré lui*. Like that work they employed chains of consecutive ninths but in a completely different way. There is nothing voluptuous in Satie's harmony; the chords impart a cool statuesque immobility to the melodic line:

Many of his works were written in groups of three, each giving a different aspect of the same material, like a sculpture seen from other angles. The *Gymnopédies* again have a disarming simplicity; but unlike the sarabandes, their charm derives from a sinuous melodic line over a mostly irregular juxtaposition of gently dissonant chords.

The music never develops in the classical sense: its elegance is wholly French. When Satie first met Debussy, possibly at the 'Chat Noir' where they had both earned money playing for the cabaret, he spoke of the need for a Frenchman 'to free himself from the Wagnerian adventure, which in no way corresponded to our national aspirations. And I told him that I was not anti-Wagner in any way, but that we ought to have our own music – if possible without Sauerkraut.' Satie's own path, in any case, lay in

precisely the opposite direction. The egomaniacal proportions of Wagnerism were answered with a modest whisper.
The piano works demand delicate sensibility but hardly
any technical prowess – indeed the composer had little to
offer as a pianist. Ravel took on the task of performing the
Gymnopédies for the first time: his own enthusiasm for Satie
is reflected in 'Beauty and the Beast' from the *Mother Goose*
Suite. In Satie's next set, the *Trois Gnossiennes*, he abandons
bar-lines and introduces characteristic instructions for the
performer: '*Ouvrez la tête*', '*De manière à obtenir un creux*',
'*Enfuissez le son*' – quite a mild foretaste however.

Medieval church music haunted his first piano pieces, the
four *Ogives*, and he became the official composer of the
bizarre sect of Rosicrucians. The preludes he wrote for
Peladon's play *Le Fils des étoiles* (*Wagnerie Kaldéenne*) experimented prophetically with chords built upon fourths.

The impersonal, aloof quality hardly applies to the music
he wrote after severing relations with the Rosicrucians. The
Pièces froides are anything but cold and the first set *Airs à
faire fuir* do anything but succeed in their stated purpose:
without bar-lines, they are fluently pianistic and conceal
their harmonic skill behind a bland nonchalant face. (The
Trois Morceaux en forme de poire for piano duet, not three but
seven pieces, apparently written in answer to criticisms of
his formlessness, turn a satirical private joke to delightful
ends.)

Already noted for his nonsensical titles, Satie went to
wild lengths in the endearingly lunatic instructions that
came thicker and faster on the page, and which he insisted
should never be read aloud at performance. Works like *Les
Trois Valses distinguées du Précieux Dégoûté* and the *Chapitres
tournés en tous sens* contain ideas followed up by Poulenc,
Milhaud and others, though it is a pity that the audience
cannot share the performer's delight that Mademoiselle
machine marries a man who is as dry as a cuckoo. Television might legitimately enhance our enjoyment of *Sports
et divertissements* (1914), which was published in fascimile
with Satie's own exquisite script alongside the drawings of

Charles Martin, or the *Sonatine bureaucratique*, a brilliant
essay in neo-classical pastiche, founded on a Clementi
sonatina and anticipating Stravinsky's method in his
Pergolesi ballet. No jokes accompany the late Five Nocturnes
(1919). They underline the gravity and wisdom of the clown
with a suave elegance that comes near to the late works of
Fauré. Satie's cool detachment, however has an elegant
beauty of its own, entirely lacking in nostalgia.

Debussy (1862–1918) was ten when he went to the Paris
Conservatoire as a piano student with a state scholarship.
He had been prepared by a reputed pupil of Chopin,
Mme Mauté, mother-in-law of Verlaine. Everything
pointed to the likelihood of a virtuoso's career; at twelve he
was playing Chopin's F minor Piano Concerto, and
Chopin's music really set the seal on his own approach to
piano writing. Mme Mauté's advice on Chopin's pedalling
as a 'kind of breathing' influenced his own quest for the
new sonorities and colours. The same approach struck him
when, at the age of twenty-three, he heard Liszt play. In
all Debussy's piano music one looks in vain for explicit
pedalling instructions, except for the occasional tie extended
beyond the time value. Yet *implicit* in his fastidious sonorities is a completely personal attitude to the pedals too
subtle to be indicated, but without which his ideal of an
instrument 'without hammers' would be unthinkable.

His early experiences of piano music could not have been
more varied. When he was eighteen he was engaged by
Nadezhda von Meck, Tchaikovsky's patroness, as tutor to
her children and resident pianist to the household, in the
summer vacation in Switzerland and Italy, and the following year in Russia. His duties included playing duets with
his employer, who introduced him to arrangements of the
latest orchestral works of Tchaikovsky, and Tchaikovsky
himself received from Mme von Meck one of Debussy's
first piano compositions, the *Danse Bohémienne* (of which he
did not think very highly). At this time Debussy also became
acquainted with music of Glinka, Borodin and Rimsky-

Korsakov. Although he had seen the score of *Boris Godunov* which Saint-Saëns brought back from Russia in 1889, it was not until 1896 that he whole-heartedly recognized Mussorgsky's genius. The Franco-Russian alliance was not only a political but a musical antidote to German domination. Mussorgsky's suites of songs, *Sunless* and *The Nursery*, also made a profound impression on Debussy: 'never was refined sensibility interpreted by such simple means', which might well describe the achievements of Debussy's own maturity, the two sets of *Images* and Preludes. Mussorgsky's bold originality in starkly few notes answered the longing in his own mind. Even as a student Debussy questioned accepted practices of harmony: 'il faut noyer le ton'. However, the early *Two Arabesques*, like the Ballade and the Nocturne, are still within the bounds of exquisite salon-music with nothing to shock its most popular purveyor, Cécile Chaminade (1857–1944), the toast of our grandmothers. Not until the *Suite Bergamasque* do we find confident signs of a growing personal style; here above all *Clair de Lune* introduces us for the first time to Debussy's particular dream-world with his widely spaced pianissimo sonorities. In the ten years that separated the *Suite Bergamasque* from his next piano works Debussy absorbed and transmuted a host of influences. He went through his Wagner fever, and visits to Bayreuth produced the liberating effect of simultaneous attraction and repulsion. His own individual mastery of orchestral colour in *L'Après-midi d'un faune* (1894) established him at once as the most original genius in France.

The Suite *Pour le Piano* (1901) finds him embarking on the methods which were to free him. In the prelude his growing obsession with augmented triads spills over into long engagements with the whole-tone scale. Here we have a step-wise descent a whole tone at a time with defiant ecstatic chords:

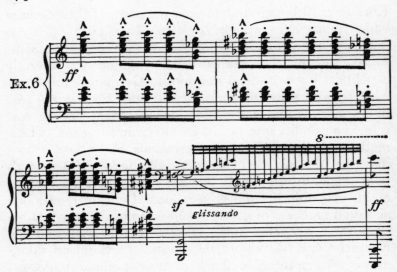

Later the subversive implications of these chords are explored in a limbo of keylessness. Yet in no sense was Debussy a mere sensationalist. The harmony was not in itself *outré*, even though its context was new. The sarabande in *Pour le Piano* is strongly reminiscent of Satie, with its parallel chords and strong modal influence. The concluding toccata is a hedonistic extension of *perpetuum mobile*, maybe without the technical originality of Ravel's later example. Already in the year of *Pour le Piano*, Ravel had produced a work whose originality Debussy responded to: *Jeux d'eau*. It was new, and not only in its pianism. The sensuous effects of pedalled arpeggios, already explored by Liszt, were here extended and given equal importance with the melodic material. Ravel's simultaneous sounding of alien arpeggios in the cadenza (F sharp major and C major) was recalled in Debussy's much later prelude *Ondine* (D major and F sharp major), but the very affinities of the two composers reveal their differences. Even the mutual attractions of Spanish folk-music had different origins and very different results; Ravel's mother was Basque and sang Spanish folk-songs to him from his infancy. Debussy had no need of direct experience (though he spent one afternoon at a bull-fight in San Sebastian); he was already infatuated with Spanish music when he asked to borrow the score of Ravel's *Habañera*. *La Soirée dans Grenade* from the *Estampes* was Debussy's first essay in the Spanish idiom. As Falla pointed out 'not a bar is directly borrowed from Spanish folk-lore yet the entire piece down to the smallest detail makes one feel the character of Spain'.

His other Spanish pieces show the same unerring touch. The prelude *La Sérénade interrompue* is a model of ironic compression: a nocturnal serenader with his guitar, amorously pleading in three–eight, is put off stroke by another in two-four, while the pained conventions of flamenco are sympathetically parodied. Another prelude, *La Puerta del Vino*, inspired by a picture post-card, returns to the *Habañera* rhythm, but with still sharper contrasts of sentiment and harmonic acerbity. The erotic and fatalistic elements of Spanish song are side by side: there are no novel chords, but an entirely original manner of placing and combining the familiar.

If Debussy owed a debt to Ravel's *Habañera* in *La Soirée dans Grenade* (and the unjustly neglected *Lindaraja* for two pianos) he owed another to *Jeux d'eau* in the increasing pianistic flexibility of *Jardins sous la pluie*. Here he makes use of two French nursery tunes, *Do-do l'enfant do* and *Nous n'irons plus au bois*: in the course of the gathering storm they are bathed in whole-tone washes of colour. The release of new powers is linked with an exultant joy in natural phenomena, carried further in *L'Île Joyeuse*, where the pianistic brilliance suggests the kaleidoscopic colouring of his contemporaneous orchestral works. It was inspired by Watteau's painting *The Embarkment for Cythera*, and though originally intended for inclusion in the *Suite Bergamasque* one can see how disastrously it would have outweighed its neighbours.

In all these works, colour plays an increasingly important role. Debussy consciously aimed to reproduce, in music, the effects of his favourite Impressionist painters. The fusion demanded no less than a new language to express itself and it would never have released such floods of change had it been born of a superficial desire to be novel.

A new phase opened with the first book of *Images* (1905), of which Debussy wrote, 'I think I may say, without undue pride, that I believe that these three pieces will live and will take their place in piano literature, either to the left of Schumann or to the right of Chopin.' This self-confidence is reflected in the unerring effect of *Reflets dans l'eau*, where the blurring of key merges into a background of peaceful, established tonality. It has the certainty and justness of Rameau and Couperin. Yet even in his *Hommage à Rameau* it is impossible to trace any direct allusions. Though couched as a sarabande, with modal and pentatonic tributes to tradition, its contemporary harmonies create their own ritual beauty. They contain the serene satisfaction of logic, but with no definable laws; Debussy's harmonic secrets defied imitators, and even Ravel's debt in *Le Gibet*, unconscious maybe, only served to emphasize the individuality of both composers. In spanning the years from archaic to modern times, Debussy himself owed much to Satie, that 'gentle medieval musician lost in our century', as Ravel called him.

Debussy strongly disliked having the restrictive label 'impressionism' attached to his music, but if there is an area where painter and musician can share territory, it is surely in the pictorially titled *Images*. There the whole-tone scale came into its own. In the equal relationship of all the intervals there was no 'pull' in any direction, and he was able to sustain an unruffled, static, mood of contemplation; it also allowed different levels of colour to be maintained, without the simultaneous use of both pedals disturbing the euphonius glow of sound, as in *Cloches à travers les feuilles*, where the overtones released by pedal both soften and enrich the mildly dissonant seconds. Debussy hardly ever allowed the whole-tone scale to dominate a whole piece. (The prelude *Voiles* is an exception, and even that has a pentatonic outburst.) Though a useful and necessary challenge to the tyranny of tonality, Debussy never completely abandoned that tyranny – even the late Studies maintain, however, tenuously, key-signatures. The different elements of his language were used side by side without incongruity or artifice. The exotic shades of the pentatonic gamelan orchestra are suggested in *La lune descend* alongside the solemnity of parallel chords. There is even a dream-like inconsequential quality in the elusive flash of the fish in *Poissons d'or*; or the abstracted bustle of *Mouvement* with its wild descending shouts of joy, that are surely reborn in Stravinsky's *Petrushka*.

Fauré's *Dolly* Suite for piano duet contains some of the most enchanting music ever written for a child, actually the daughter of Emma Bardac, who later became Debussy's second wife. In 1905 Dolly acquired a half-sister in Chou-Chou, Debussy's own daughter, for whom he wrote the *Children's Corner* Suite, giving the pieces English titles: the three-year old Chou-Chou had an English governess. There is an affectionate irony in the paternal glance. In *Doctor Gradus ad Parnassum* he parodies Clementi, and the ragtime of the *Golliwog's Cake-walk* pokes irreverent fun at the opening of *Tristan*:

To underline that the music was more important than the source of his inspiration, Debussy had the titles of each of his Preludes printed at the end in brackets and with hesitant dots. These short intimate works contain the essence of his thought and feeling. We do not really *need* to know that the first prelude is called (. . . . . *Danseuses de Delphes*) and was inspired by a sculpture at the top of a pillar in the Louvre, showing three Bacchantes in dance posture. Just as pertinent is Nadia Boulanger's observation that it shares its three-section key-sequence with many of Bach's preludes. We can still marvel at the dignified grace of the pianissimo chords and the spacious beauty of different sonorities moving in opposite directions.

The most original explorations that Debussy made in writing for the piano were in the hushed resonances of pianissimo textures. His ideal of an instrument 'without hammers' is recalled with the frequent admonition 'loin-tain'. But any idea that vague outlines can be faithfully obtained with vague control is doomed: the composer's delicate placing of every note demands the highest qualities of technique and sensibility from the performer. The sustaining pedal, so often the camouflage of the floppy-fingered pianist, must be allied to an exact and nervously sensuous command of every tonal nuance the instrument is capable of. The delicate play of wind on a boat's sails in *Voiles* and the unpredictable puffs and gusts in *Le Vent dans la plaine* require a subtle combination of both pedals. Likewise the voluptuous Baudelairean *Les sons et les parfums tournent dans l'air du soir* with its floating textures and final far-away sound of horns. Debussy's pianism rarely calls for the sharp percussive edge. Even the Gregorian chant that roars out of *La Cathédrale engloutie* is marked 'sonorous without hardness', and the hushed effects he more often requires need a characteristically malleable touch, obtained more easily, some have said, by an oblique stroking of the keys than by vertical pressure.

For Debussy as critic, the exhibitionistic virtuoso was an enjoyable sitting target. His own calls on virtuoso powers always sprang from a poetic idea and have their own special character and difficulty. The tumultuous seas in *Ce qu'a vu le vent d'Ouest* demand an orchestral palette and a menacing physical strength: the threatening use of the lower register of the instrument suggests Liszt, but the waters St Francis walked upon were tame compared with these. Another kind of brilliance is called for in the fierce gymnastics of *Feux*

d'artifice, but for all its virtuosity it has the detached effect
of a vivid dream. By the time Debussy embarked on his six
sonatas for various instruments (only three of which were
completed) and his last piano works, he was a sick man with
a strong presentiment of death upon him. In alternating
fits of depression and confidence he himself expressed
contradictory opinions about his work.

Performances of the Twelve Studies (1915) are still
absurdly rare, and perhaps for this reason acknowledgement
of their importance has been tardy and half-hearted. He
wrote them in the short space of seven weeks in a cottage on
the Normandy coast near Dieppe: 'I write like a madman,
or like one who is condemned to die the next morning.' Far
from debilitating his gifts, the disease had fired him to the
most visionary concentration in the short time left to him.
They are dedicated to Chopin, a complete edition of whose
works Debussy had recently edited for Durand. Like
Chopin's studies, each one is devoted to a particular
technical difficulty – the playing of thirds, sixths, octaves,
repeated notes and so on. But Debussy shared Chopin's
impatience with mechanical drudgery, and his studies
exercise the imagination of the player as strenuously as his
fingers. Not for him the noble persistence of Liszt who, in
old age, claimed that he still practised Czerny for half-an-
hour each day. Debussy's first study *Pour les cinq doigts*
(*d'après Monsieur Czerny*), begins with a solemn application
to a five-finger exercise, mischievously interrupted by
foreign notes and tempting changes of rhythm (and with
chords that have since become jazz clichés):

The virtuosity that Debussy demands is not the sort to win
easy plaudits from the gallery. It is more real than apparent:

no. 7, *Pour les degrés chromatiques*, is more treacherous than Liszt's *La Leggierezza*, but Debussy's swift and elusive chromatic runs have a burden of melancholy to carry. Melancholy, too, haunts the ambiguous tonality of the superb no. 9, *Pour les notes répétées*. By dot, dash and line Debussy demands that the length of the staccato notes is to be varied and coloured according to a constantly changing musical context. Like the second movement of his Violin Sonata its wry humour somehow contains a regretful disillusionment with romanticism. The distant calls to jollity that were heard in the prelude *Les Collines d'Anacapri* are recalled in the middle section of no. 10, *Pour les sonorités opposées*, but here they have a hollow pathos. A hypnotic G sharp pedal-note haunts the piece almost as much as the B flats of Ravel's *Le Gibet*.

Debussy told his publisher that in *Pour les quartes* 'there are effects that you have never heard before': it is the most original of the set, and seems to grow spontaneously from a constant renewal of small cells, baffling logical analysis, but triumphing in practice. Later manifestations of athematic music are said to have taken their cue from these last works of Debussy, but few contemporaries can match the sheer memorability of his ideas, or his instinct for structure. While looking forward to the future the Studies also reveal a maturer tapping of old devices, shorn at last of Impressionist haze. Even when he would appear to be obsessed with a purely technical problem as in no. 6, *Pour les huit doigts*, written so as to make any use of the thumbs an inconvenience, the timbres fall into a satisfying dramatic pattern. The rich sensuality of *Pour les agréments*, the athletic joy in the fragmentary kaleidoscope of *Pour les octaves* and the bold leaping confidence of *Pour les accords* are the measure of Debussy's triumph, the triumph of an agnostic creative genius over death.

The pianist Alfred Cortot has described the student Ravel as 'a deliberately sarcastic, argumentative and aloof young man who used to read Mallarmé and visit Erik Satie'.

Behind the mask the individual stylist was already formed. Compared with Debussy, whose style was slow to grow, Ravel (1875–1937) burst out of the egg almost fully-fledged, if not quite ready for flight.

His first published piano composition, the *Menuet antique* ('this somewhat retrograde work', as he called it) looks back at an archaic formula and adds modern artifice to the old; astringent harmonic surprises, athletic juggling of lines, and occasional modal reflections, with a predilection for ninths and secondary sevenths inherited from Chabrier. Four years earlier, Ravel and a fellow-student, the pianist Ricardo Viñes, both sixteen, had studied the *Trois Valses romantiques* of Chabrier and played them to the composer who gave them characteristically ebullient and contradictory advice. Now, in the same year as the *Menuet antique*, Ravel's *Sites auriculaires* appeared: two pieces for two pianos, the unpublished *Entre cloches*, and the famous *Habañera*, (later transcribed intact in the orchestral *Rapsodie espagnole*). 'I consider that in embryo the latter work embodies many of the elements which were to dominate my later compositions, and which through Chabrier's influence (his *Chanson pour Jeanne* for instance) I have been able to crystallize.' We have already seen what effect this work had on Debussy, but Ravel's retrospective observations about it are easily substantiated in a host of examples. Most obvious of all is the persistent seventh chord with the cross-grained pedal-point, which occurs in *Alborada del Gracioso* and in the second bar of *Scarbo*:

Dance forms, whether folk or courtly, are a dominant feature of Ravel's music. The *Pavane pour une Infante défunte* has enjoyed a popularity which the composer regretted. Overshadowed by Fauré's *Pavane*, over-influenced, as he confessed, by Chabrier, the melodic line nevertheless has, already, Ravel's characteristically cool poignancy. It is curious to note the oblique way in which his originality appeared. In setting himself a conscious challenge, usually of an imitative or purely technical nature, his imagination pushed him off course into entirely new channels. His own initial lack of confidence in his most far-reaching innovations is a symptom of shock. The publisher Demets had to wrest the manuscript of *Jeux d'eau* forcibly from Ravel's hands. Headed by a quotation from his friend, the poet Henri de Régnier – 'A river-god laughing out of the waters as they caress him. . . .' – Ravel had written it as an exploratory creative exercise, with the aim of extending Liszt's evocative use of the upper register of the piano. Although it is based, as Ravel said, 'on two themes like the first movement of a classical sonata, without being entirely subjected to the classical scheme of tonality', the opening arpeggios are not so much a theme as a decorative effect. A tenuous harmonic impression is made to serve a structural purpose. This was the strikingly original idea that inspired Debussy in his search for a means of reconciling a Symbolist dream-world with new formal disciplines, though much water was to flow under the bridges before he achieved the Study in fourths and the ballet *Jeux*. (Water was a deeply significant psychological visitant in the dream-world of the Symbolists.) Meanwhile Ravel pursued different paths. His next piano work, the *Sonatine*, turned away from purely sensuous washes of sound and rediscovered economic textures and the stricter shapes of sonata form. The falling fourth of the opening (suggested perhaps by Bach's prelude in the same key, F sharp minor, in the second book of the *Well-Tempered Clavier*?) pervades not only the first movement, but also, in one guise or another, the other two. The second movement, a minuet, opens with its counterpart, a rising fifth, and the second subject of the finale is no less than a five–four version of the first movement's opening. At no point is tradition seriously undermined. The tremulous romantic feeling of the first movement, the exquisite grace of the second and the sensual energy and nostalgic sighs of the last – all are perfectly framed in the accepted disciplines of the classical era. French sensibility, economy, intelligence and charm are distilled in this characteristic little masterpiece.

Whereas the *Sonatine* demonstrated a line totally divergent from Debussy, Ravel's next piano work, the *Miroirs*, (which also appeared in 1905) explored some of the close affinities. Sharing many of the literary tastes of Debussy (Poe, Baudelaire and Mallarmé) he ventured to the edge of the Symbolist dream-world, but his clarity of thought and classical purity of line shed too much direct light to indulge the half-shades of the Symbolists. *La Vallée des cloches*, despite its static bell-like overtones, has a central section of pure explicit Ravelian melody. Debussy's haze-like dream is only the decorative surround for Ravel. *Noctuelles* extends the natural pianism of *Jeux d'eau* but is more complex in texture, while *Une barque sur l'océan*, for all its incidental beauties, seems over-written and less mature. By far the most successful are *Oiseaux tristes* and *Alborada del Gracioso*. The former was the first of the *Miroirs* to be written and suggests a recent communion with the Debussy *Images*; but the picture painted is far more direct and objective. The Hispanism of the *Alborada* has a more biting and immediate presence than Debussy's *La Soirée dans Grenade*. The discordant notes added to simple chords for rhythmic emphasis look back to the audacities of Scarlatti in his Spanish vein, and recall similar processes in the *Iberia* Suite of Albéniz, which began to appear a year later in 1906. Ravel was born in Ciboure, near the Spanish frontier, and Spanish folk songs became part of his fundamental musical thinking. André Suares has written, 'I recognize Spain in every part of Ravel – in what he is and in what he does. This little man is so dry, so sensitive, at once frail and resistant, caressing and inflexible, supple as tempered steel . . . .' As the man, no less the music, and in particular the *Alborada del Gracioso* (*Dawn Song of the Jester*). Pianistically it is the most virtuosic piece to date, gathering hints from the repeated-note technique of Liszt's *Hungarian* Rhapsodies and Balakirev's *Islamey*, but extending them with glee and a certain cruelty.

Cruelty and fear are the theme of *Gaspard de la nuit* (1908), Ravel's virtuoso masterpiece, inspired by the highly-charged romantic prose-poems of Aloysius Bertrand. Again his inspiration took an oblique course. Musically, his expressed aim was to surpass the complexities of *Islamey*; but the sworn hater of romantic effusiveness was spurred to fearless heights of poetic truth by the melodramatic extravagance of the poems. He sub-titled the pieces *Trois Poèmes pour piano* with justification. In *Ondine* the melancholy song of the river-goddess is surrounded by luscious, seductive waves of arpeggio; in *Le Gibet* the cruelty is cold and static with a Debussian pedal-note sounding through the piece; in *Scarbo* the macabre terrors of a harrying goblin hurtle the composer beyond the diabolic extremes of virtuosity in Liszt and Balakirev. All laughter in *Gaspard de la nuit* is sardonic and cruel. In this sense *Scarbo* is the most Spanish of all his piano works. Even its silences are frightening and the vicious elusiveness of the goblin is expressed in startling harmonies. *Scarbo* is a unique masterpiece in the literature of piano virtuosity: Ravel never attempted anything like it again, nor, wisely, has anyone else.

Ravel's next important piano work was first presented anonymously at a concert of the Société Musicale Indépendante in 1911, the audience being invited to guess the authorship. The guesses ranged from Kodály to Satie, but a small majority correctly ascribed it to Ravel. Here his model was Schubert, but again the impetus was oblique and the sum total pure Ravel – in fact, a purification and concentration of the harmonic complexities of *Gaspard de la Nuit*. The *Valses nobles et sentimentales* are prefaced with a quotation from Henri de Régnier: 'le plaisir délicieux et toujours nouveau d'une occupation inutile'. In the following year Ravel orchestrated them for a ballet, *Adélaide ou le langage des fleurs*. That *Gaspard* was an end, rather than a gateway to further discovery, is still further underlined by his final work for solo piano, *Le Tombeau de Couperin*. 'In reality', he said in a biographical sketch, 'it is a tribute not so much to Couperin himself as to eighteenth-century music in general.' Each piece was dedicated to a friend killed in the war. Many critics have turned a cold shoulder to the delicate beauty of the Fugue, but no one can deny the poignant melodic beauty of the *Forlane* with its gentle, stinging harmonies or the stylish vigour of the *Rigaudon*. The natural fusion of simplicity and artifice in the Minuet is as remarkable as the virtuoso audacity of the Toccata, surely the finest *moto perpetuo* ever written for the piano. From its first tingling repeated notes to its final flurry of alternating chords, it forms a magnificent apotheosis of Ravel's piano-writing.

Debussy, speaking of his own Studies said, 'I am still not sufficiently dead to be safe from comparisons.' Debussy referred to Chopin, but, in fact, had nothing to fear. Nor had Ravel, although until recently the shadow of Debussy has denied him his due place. Their rivalry seems more and more irrelevant as time goes on. For all their undeniable mutual debts the less alike they appear to be. Even on common ground, their impressionistic piano pieces demand a different approach, a different kind of touch. The dream-like washes of sound from Debussy's instrument 'without hammers' require a more malleable finger action than the crystalline shimmer of Ravel's watery effects. The invidious comparisons once applied between Mozart and Haydn are now dead as the dodo, so let us wish the Debussy–Ravel affair an equally final burial.

Satie was the musical godfather of the brilliant group of composers for a time tenuously associated with the nickname, 'Les Six': Poulenc, Milhaud, Durey, Auric, Tailleferre and Honegger. The sheer impudence of the manifesto that Cocteau wrote to announce their aims commands respect. Away with Teutonic profundity, away with the precious, esoteric harmonies of the Debussyites; let the pretty, jolly tunes of the circus and music-hall take over; life is short, nothing's durable; have a good laugh! It looked as if half a dozen Grand Masters of Chess had elected to play draughts. But not all desired to keep up the relentless levity that was expected of them. It was not long before Milhaud and Honegger slipped under the awning and got away.

Darius Milhaud (born 1892) dedicated his first piano work, the Suite of 1913, to Jean Wiener, one of France's first and most skilled enthusiasts of Negro jazz. Some of the hectic gaiety of early jazz appears in Milhaud's formidable first piano sonata, in which academic contrapuntal skill rubs shoulders with gloriously banal tunes. Some of his earliest essays in bitonality occur in this work: he regarded polytonality as a logical development for the Latin mind. (Bitonality had first been suggested to him in studying a two-part canon of Bach.) Milhaud's use of bitonality, however, was not merely cerebral. Married to the lazy rhythms of Brazilian popular melody in his *Saudades do Brasil* it has remarkably poignant beauty.

The character of Brazilian folklore had attracted Milhaud while he was acting as secretary to the poet and dramatist Paul Claudel in 1917–18. Claudel was then French Ambassador in Rio de Janeiro but, though accurately in the style, all the tunes in the *Saudades* are Milhaud's own. The spectacular popularity of his two-piano suite *Scaramouche* has distracted attention from some of the solo piano works that deserve a better fate, most notably the suite *Automne* with its exquisite final *Adieu* which has the touching simplicity of his idol, Satie. However, the second sonata, despite its impressive ingenuity, falls victim to its own effortless volubility. In this it resembles the sonata of Georges Auric (born 1899) whose astonishing fecundity is hardly matched by compelling ideas.

Arthur Honegger (1892–1955), a Swiss by birth, never showed much sympathy for the insolent levity of Cocteau's propaganda. His early *Trois Pièces* are respectively terse, lyrical and sharply vigorous. The *Sept Pièces brèves* reveal the influence of Satie and Milhaud and are masterly in their concentration. In the arioso of the *Prélude, Arioso et Fughetta sur le nom de Bach*, over a continuous slow *ostinato* based on the four notes of Bach's name, he achieved a genuinely individual lyricism, while the fughetta has a brilliantly gawky wit. The one composer who consistently maintained the roguish spirit of Les Six was Francis Poulenc (1899–1963) who from the start played recklessly with his outstanding gifts of mimicry. No one's style was sacred or safe from him. Each piece of pastiche is carried off with a knowing wink and outrageous charm. There is semi-parody of sentimentally pretty tunes, or is it ironic self-mockery in the enjoyment of them? He has the swagger of a modish intellectual clown in top hat and tails, yet behind the party dress there is a warm and unmistakably individual personality fully-formed already in the earliest *Mouvements perpetuels*. 'Sans traîner' is a favourite injunction in his works, and indeed any romantic lingering would tip some of his music straight into the Chaminade camp. Some of the nocturnes thumb their nose at their Polish model and go fast and flippant. The surprise ending of his second nocturne epitomizes absolutely his mock-serious, lyrical teasing. The improvisatory *Soirées Nazelles* has a brash, Prokofievian sweep, and the later Intermezzo in A flat contains a mock-sentimental tune of great charm in Lisztian textures.

There was certainly no trace of sentimentality, mock or otherwise, in Charles Koechlin (1867–1951), Poulenc's teacher. He himself had been a pupil of Fauré, whose melodic fluency he inherited, but with Koechlin suave arpeggio accompaniment is replaced by equally suave and graceful counterpoint. The *Sonatines* which he wrote for his children (nos. 4 and 5 are particularly fine) combine ingenuity with ingenuousness, and the Preludes, op. 209, are gems of form with a modesty of feeling that amounts to diffidence.

Modest charm is also the hallmark of minor figures such as Paul Ladmirault (1877–1944) a Breton, and Gabriel Grovlez (1879–1944), both pupils of Fauré. Their miniatures are valued additions to the repertoire of works of 'moderate difficulty'. There is a provincial, unpretentious elegance in the Suites of Deodat de Sévérac (1873–1921), *En Vacances* and *Languedoc*. Jacques Ibert (1890–1962) has a talent for the picturesque, his ubiquitous *Little White Donkey* dominating a modest landscape of pianistic elegance.

Of much greater importance are the piano works of Albert Roussel (1869–1937). A late starter, having embarked at first on a naval career, and certainly no virtuoso at the piano, he was nevertheless able to devise a long crescendo of frightening effect in the first movement of his Suite, op. 14, owing something to Debussy, but charged with his own more astringent harmonies. The Sonatina, op. 16, contains a novel experiment in form which he never repeated: its two movements are in fact four, the opening *modéré* leading without a development section into a scherzo, which later uses material from the opening. The *très lent* in five–eight time which follows eventually gathers speed imperceptibly to lead into a fast rondo which again recalls the opening material. Though looking somewhat opaque on paper, Roussel's textures are lucid in performance, and his unsentimental harmony and rhythmic vitality combine, selectively, elements of the Saint-Saëns tradition with Debussy, in prophetic style.

Lucidity and precision are also the hallmarks of Jean Françaix (born 1912) a brilliantly urbane pupil of Nadia Boulanger. In his witty *Danse des Trois Arlequins* the texture is spare to the point of parsimony, and the two-piano *Huit Danses exotiques* have a rhythmic and harmonic piquancy that rivals Milhaud. At the other end of the scale the piano scores of Florent Schmitt (1870–1958) reflect his belief that the instrument is no more than a convenient and defective substitute for the orchestra, though *Stèle* is a poignant elegy to Dukas and *La Tragique Chevauchée* a frightening representation of the Mazeppa legend.

The laughter of Les Six, which had a refreshing irrelevancy when first heard during the horrors of the First World War, sounded rather hollow in the nineteen-thirties. The resilient turn which French music took owes most to Olivier Messiaen, the first to extend the prophetic probing of Debussy's last works. Whereas Messiaen's quest for deeper spirituality was centred on a mystical form of Catholicism, that of André Jolivet (born 1905) turned towards the primitive religions. His suite *Mana* is concerned with the magical properties of various inanimate objects made of straw or wire, given to the composer by Varèse: from this sprang a style of extraordinarily evocative suggestion in a language of extreme dissonance and rhythmic complexity. Evidence of this strongly individual personality, of intuitive foresight and spontaneous vitality appears in both of his piano sonatas. The influences of Fauré and Ravel were formative for the early work of the Swiss Frank Martin (born 1890) who, like his compatriot Honegger, was able to make fruitful use of German method. His attraction to Schönberg has as much a background of revulsion as did Debussy's to Wagner, as can be seen in the superbly terse and rhythmically vital Eight Preludes written in 1948 for Dinu Lipatti.

Born in Geneva, like Martin (there any resemblance emphatically ends), Ernest Bloch (1880–1959) performed the remarkable feat of arriving at a specifically Jewish idiom, recognizably inspired by the spirit of the Old Testament prophets and owing as little to his place of birth as to the work of other composers. The dramatic confrontation of formal ritualistic chant and individual rhapsodic energy brings an impressive fire to the first movement of his Piano Sonata. Its spacious plan is matched by a genuine grandeur of spirit also evident in the short pieces, *Visions and Prophecies*.

SPAIN

The musician who did more than any other to garner the past tradition of Spanish classical music and the living folk culture was a Catalan. Felipe Pedrell (1841–1922) rescued the works of Cabezón and Victoria from obscurity and made the most important collection of Spanish folk-songs. The latter were the mainspring of his country's revived musical life, and in no field more than in piano music, which was dominated by a magnificent triumvirate – Albéniz, Granados and Falla.

Isaac Albéniz (1860–1909) also a Catalan, was for a time a pupil of Pedrell. After a sensational start as a prodigy, followed by studies with Marmontel in Paris, he rebelled against parental exploitation and embarked without a penny for Costa Rica, thence to Cuba and the U.S.A., where he earned enough to return for study in Leipzig, and, later still, with Liszt. In the period 1880–89, after great success as a travelling virtuoso, he lived in Spain, studied composition with Pedrell, and dedicated his creative life to the development of specifically Spanish music. He only rarely used his native Catalan folk-music, and was much more attracted by the 'exotic' scales and rhythms of Andalusia. The guitar influenced all keyboard music emanating from Spain, from Scarlatti onwards. Albéniz based his instrumental style on imitation of the subtle colours, harmonies and rhythms that he heard from the guitars of his skilled compatriots, and on the plangent melody of *Cante Jondo*.

Many of his early pieces for piano, produced at a staggering rate, were facile transplantations amounting to little more than mimicry. But even from this period *Seguidillas*, *Sevillanas*, the world-famous *Tango* (better known in Godowsky's sugared version), and particularly *Cordoba* have won a permanent place in the repertoire. Yet none gives more than a hazy clue of the riches to come in the *Iberia* Suite. His maturity came in fact with unprecedented suddenness, summer without a spring.

Albéniz's first serious studies in composition were with d'Indy and Dukas in Paris, when he was already thirty. After a spell in London, with a remunerative but uninspiring commission to write operas on Arthurian legends, he settled in Paris in 1893. It was the French who deepened his craftsmanship and liberated his imagination. For this he owed most to Debussy; he even listened to his beloved guitar with new ears.

The *Iberia* Suite (1906–9) consists of twelve pieces, in four volumes, mostly evocative of particular scenes or areas of Spain, each exploiting a characteristic rhythm. Usually in ternary form, they contain central episodes of vocal character, almost invariably in Andalusian style; nearly all the title-places are in or near Andalusia, as musically strange to the Catalan Albéniz as the Hebrides to a Welshman. Although he hardly ever used an actual folk-song, Albéniz's mastery of the idiom was complete. *Evocacion*, which opens the set, inhabits the same country as Debussy's *La Soirée dans Grenade;* a remarkable example of cross-influence. The enriched harmonic language, the subtly extended melodic line, and the sonorities of different registers are exploited with the discrimination of a master, and matched with almost absurdly punctilious expression marks.

In *El Polo* one is instructed to play '*toujours dans l'esprit du sanglot*' and in *Jerez* one must play '*brusquement*' in the right hand while making the left '*bien expressif*'. These instructions may seem absurd on first sight but are richly justified in their musical context, as are the extraordinary lengths to which Albéniz will go to pick out individual notes in a chord by making the fingers of one hand intrude between the fingers of the other, so that a performance of *Lavapies*, for instance, is for the onlooker rather like a mortal combat between two giant spiders.

El Puerto (the port of Santa Maria on the river Guadalete) exploits the abrupt contrasts of harshness and sensual langour already familiar in Debussy's *La Puerta del Vino*, emphasised by the use of three different Andalusian dance-rhythms, the *polo*, the *bulerías*, and the *seguiría gitana* (a gypsy variant of the *seguidillas*). *Fête-Dieu à Seville* was Albéniz's first extended work, and the first to reap the full harvest of his Lisztian studies. In form it resembles a Liszt Hungarian Rhapsody, with a programmatic pattern to follow; a religious procession celebrating Corpus Christi. Warmth and exuberance are the dramatic features of Albéniz's Andalusia; pathos too, but not the cruel fatalism that Falla found so vividly in their intense religious ritual.

The two pieces which begin the second book, *Rondeña* and *Almería*, exploit the gypsy alternation of six–eight and three–four rhythm, and add harmonic 'visitors' to give a sharper edge to the rhythm (much as Domenico Scarlatti did with his discordant chord-clusters), as in this example from *Rondeña*:

The middle section of this piece shows specially subtle choice of harmony and skill in placing notes which suggest a vocal line with guitar accompaniment: although the voice part is played in the middle register of the piano it sounds as if the singer is straining in the upper range of his voice. Here the art of mimicry is transcended and we have a truly creative and individual contribution to piano writing. Blanche Selva, to whom Book 2 was dedicated, declared it impossible to play. A first glance at *Triana* is certainly daunting, with its Lisztian intricacy of figuration around the vocal refrain of the central section.

An extended introduction on solo guitar is a familiar characteristic of Andalusian folk music. In *El Albaicín* the simple 'plucked' notes move from a dignified melancholy to bitter anguish, a far remove from the innocence of the early and popular *Rumores de la Caleta* with its lulling repetitiveness. The song, when it comes, is in the familiar Phrygian mode of *Cante Jondo* and the reflective coda expresses a deeply personal, bitter resignation; Debussy particularly admired this piece. *El Polo* (the name of yet another Andalusian song and dance) has not the same formal discipline, with its over-persistent sobbing. The nonchalant gaiety of *Lavapies* (a popular quarter of Madrid) demands high virtuosity and a reckless spirit. In Book 4, *Jerez* has a unique stately beauty: it is imbued with the very soul of the guitar. Of *Eritaña* Debussy wrote that it was 'the joy of morning, the happy discovery of a tavern where the wine is cool'. There remains the formidable *Navarra*; left unfinished, but completed by de Sévérac. The extremes of Spanish masculine pride and grandiloquence, almost toppling into self-parody, are presented with Lisztian brilliance and spaciousness.

Enrique Granados (1867–1916) had many things in common with Albéniz; a Catalan, an outstanding pianist, a composition pupil of Pedrell's who also went to Paris. After this the resemblances are few. He did not share Albéniz's preference for Andalusian music, despite his famous *Spanish Dance No. 5*: his style was more poised, pianistically more Chopinesque, its inspiration more nostalgic, even sentimental. Obsessed with the bygone Madrid of Goya's days, his most important piano work *Goyescas* (six pieces subtitled *The Majas in Love*) was in fact a homage to the paintings he revered. There is a flexible grace, dignity and pride in the set, occasionally marred by erratic formal organization. The first, *Los Requiebros* (*Compliments*) is based on a melody from a popular stage *Tonadilla* of the early nineteenth century by Blas de Laserna. The second, *Coloquio en la Reja*, is a love-duet, and the third, *El Fandango de Candil*, a stately dance in which guitar, castanet and voice are beautifully interwoven, though it rambles at great length. The fourth, *Quejos ó la Maja y el Ruiseñor* (*The Maiden and the Nightingale*), is an exquisite lyrical master-piece, perfect in form and quintessentially Spanish (the opening so reminiscent of Scarlatti's B minor Sonata L33). The two pieces of the second part, *El Amor y la Muerte* (*Love and Death*) and the epilogue *Serenata del espectro* (*The Ghost's Serenade*) are genuinely poetic, incorporating quotations from each piece in the first part, but the discursive length of all except the *Maja y el Ruiseñor* makes a convincing unity impossible. Out of this important piano work Granados created his opera *Goyescas*, which was produced with great success in New York (1916). Returning from these perform-ances Granados and his wife were drowned when their ship was torpedoed by a German submarine in the English Channel.

Granados's predilection for Goya's Spain was fed by a selective and highly romantic imagination. The Catalan Albéniz's passion for Andalusian music was in part vicarious. The Spanishness of Manuel de Falla (1876–1946) is in-escapable in every note he writes. His mother was a Catalan and a good pianist. His father was Andalusian. Three years of study with Pedrell at the Madrid Conservatoire decided the national orientation of his own music. In 1907 he set off for a seven-day trip to Paris and stayed for seven years. The greatest fruits of his friendship with Debussy, Dukas and Ravel are to be found in his orchestral and stage works, but there are treasures in the solo piano works too. The *Quatre Pièces Espagnoles* (1909) are worthy to stand beside the *Goyescas* and the *Iberia* Suite and in some ways they excel them in their economy of means. The opening *Aragonesa* derives entirely from a single vigorous tune:

Ex. 11

Its second bar provides the seed for a calmer theme, which (after a climax on a Debussian augmented triad) later goes with the first. Though sparing of notes the texture is more intricate than anything from the other members of the triumvirate. The *Cubana*, with its gentle alternations of three-four and six-eight and its easy natural modulation, is as poetic as the *Montañesa*, which inhabits a Debussian world of suspended animation and heady excitement. The final *Andaluza* has all the harsh energy of rasping guitar, and a violent sense of tragedy in the Phrygian wailing melismata of Andalusian *Cante Jondo*. Falla's *Fantasia Baetica* was written in 1919 for Artur Rubinstein who had his first great success in Spain and, in return, became the first great international advocate of Spanish piano music, introducing many countries to the *Goyescas*, the *Iberia* Suite and *Nights in the Gardens of Spain*. The *Fantasia*, Falla's only extended solo piece, strives at times for the additional orchestral colour of the *Nights*, but abounds in arresting details of harmonic and rhythmic freedom in spite of its untypical lack of concision. To reproduce the vocal inflections of Andalusian song would require one of Haba's quarter-tone pianos, but Falla suggests them in his clashing grace-notes.

Falla's virtual silence throughout the last twenty years of

his life has been accounted for in various ways: disillusionment brought about by the political stagnation of his
country; withdrawal into religious mysticism (never
seriously substantiated); and a realization that his particular nationalism had no more to say; this last a curious
argument in view of the fertile new ground of the Harpsichord Concerto. The mystery remains, but so does Falla's
superiority over his successors.

Joaquín Turina (1882–1949) has described his first
meeting with Albéniz in 1907, accompanied by Falla, in a
Paris café: 'then I realized that music should be an art and
not a diversion for the frivolity of women and the dissipation of men'. Alas, in Turina's case the sound craftsmanship of the d'Indy training and the folk traditions of his
own country never achieved a creative synthesis. Only his
Rapsodia Sinfonica for piano and strings has enjoyed a short-
lived popularity in this country. The solo piano works, for
all their fluency (he was a pupil of Moszkowski in Paris),
make a muted impact. After the burning authenticity of
Falla, Turina's national dress looks tawdry, touristic and
sentimental. Less ambitious but more convincing are the
few piano works of the Cuban-born Joaquín Nin (1879–
1949). He also studied in the Schola Cantorum and with
Moszkowski. Nin became a noted musicologist, championing the early harpsichordists like Soler and Scarlatti (whom
he claimed as a Spanish composer). The *Danza Iberica* has
Scarlatti's lithe, athletic sparseness and a simple panache
of refreshing individuality. His *Message à Debussy* has a
touchingly capricious charm and bears the following
inscription: '*Lorsque les yeux de Debussy se fermèrent à jamais,
sur la nuit de la mort, une soudaine angoisse vint répandre au coeur
des musiciens d'Espagne une inapaisible nostalgie!*'

Among the minor figures to emerge from the Paris scene
is Federico Mompou (born 1893), one of the few Catalan-
born composers who have not turned to other parts of Spain
for inspiration. Mainly self-taught, his aim is to re-create the
ideals of the Catalan primitives of the fifteenth century. He
has been compared to Satie, and he has also experimented

with the abandonment of bar-lines, though Satie would hardly have aspired to the widely-ranging pianism of his enchanting *Dialogues*. Although most of his pieces have a simplicity that only the recluse can achieve, no one can deny the poignancy of the *Trois Variations* or the static delights of *Charmes* which can mesmerize us as compulsively as a Debussy prelude.

The archetypal romantic is always a traveller, at least in his mind. With the rapid rise of industrialism and the squalor of the large cities he yearns nostalgically for the rustic simplicity of the past. For the musical traveller Spain always exerted the most powerful attraction. So pungent and picturesque was its popular music that many composers, like Bizet and Debussy, did not need to go there to absorb it at first hand. Ironically, as we have seen, it was the Spaniard himself who had to travel to further his art. Meanwhile Iberian traditions had crossed the Atlantic; the voluble and improvisatory works of the Brazilian Villa-Lobos (1887–1959) and the Argentinian Alberto Ginastera (born 1916) have both added new colour to the pianist's repertoire.

SCANDINAVIA

While Handel was writing *Judas Maccabaeus* to celebrate the Duke of Cumberland's victory over the Highland clans at Culloden Moor in 1746, terror and economic attrition drove many Scots from their native land, among them Alexander Greig (sic), great-grandfather of the composer. Having settled in Bergen, he became in turn successful lobster-exporter and British consul, handing down the post to son and grandson. Edvard Grieg (1843–1907) derived his musical gifts from his mother, however. She had trained as a pianist in Hamburg, and in due course Grieg was sent to Leipzig. Confidence in his own creative gifts flourished on the manure of contempt for his composition lessons, but his piano teacher, E. F. Wenzel, who had been an intimate friend of Schumann, became a dominant influence. He also gained much from piano lessons with Moscheles, while resenting his abuse of Schumann and Chopin. (Wagner was another strong attraction that Grieg thought fit to keep quiet about). Already his dream-world, as he put it, was in the realm of harmony, and here his idiom remained original and unmistakable. As a boy he had been strongly affected by the impassioned chromatic harmony of Mozart, a selective influence that later produced one of the most misguided acts of homage in the history of music: Grieg's additions of second-piano parts to some of Mozart's solo sonatas, in which he cushions the texture with a deep velvet opulence. Such perversions, however, should not distract attention from Grieg's own lyrical gifts, which were given impetus by the consciously nationalistic ideals of Scandinavian romanticism. For four centuries Norway and Denmark had been united. In Copenhagen Grieg had a casual brush with the composer Niels Gade (1817–90) but he fell completely under the spell of the much younger Rikard Nordraak (1842–66) whose obsession with Norwegian folksong and literature released a latent affinity in Grieg's nature.

Grieg's first characteristic piano works, the *Humoresques*, op. 6, show at once his natural integration of vital folk-rhythms and his own personal harmonic idiom. His first assault on the larger forms, however, revealed life-long limitations. The Sonata in E minor, op. 7, dedicated to Gade, shows no heart or stamina for alien disciplines. The opening has some kinship with Schumann's G minor Sonata, but lacks its impulse and pianistic resourcefulness. Grieg's two-bar sequences nag away conscientiously but never cohere. The slow movement and the minuet, on the other hand, are welcome miniatures, but in the wrong setting. Wisely, Grieg never attempted another piano sonata. The more convincing Ballade, op. 24, is, in fact, a set of continuous variations on a folk-like melody. The simple, diatonic theme is at first clothed in rich, descending chromatic harmonies that anticipate Delius, abandoned for simpler ones in the less ruminative variations. Memories of Schumann crowd in but never submerge the individual personality and the grand design.

As a miniaturist, Grieg was a master. The ten volumes of *Lyric Pieces*, beginning with the delicate Arietta (1867) and ending with a curiously insipid waltz version of the same piece (1901) delighted public and publisher alike, and assured the composer a comfortable old age. Folk convention may excuse the ubiquitous bare fifths in the bass, and maybe the persistent chains of archly varied two-bar phrases deserve Debussy's famous remark 'a pink sweet filled with snow'. At their best, however, the pieces achieve a concentrated lyricism and charm unique among salon miniatures.

Popularity and the swing of fashion have not succeeded in killing *The Butterfly, Wedding Day*, or the *Norwegian Dances*. Even the delicately palpitating *To Spring* is worthier than the once-famed *Rustle of Spring* of Grieg's compatriot Christian Sinding (1856–1941). Fashion can hardly affect Grieg's exquisite *Notturno* from op. 54: its original use of unprepared ninths reminds one of Ravel's rash remark that he had never written anything uninfluenced by Grieg, and even the young Debussy was not immune. Nevertheless Grieg's most original piano works remain the most neglected, though in one sense the Norwegian *Slåttar* are not original: they are transcriptions of dances taken down from a Hardanger fiddler in Telemark. The notes the peasant fiddler actually played were printed beside Grieg's piano realization in the first edition. As re-creations they have been hailed as worthy precursors of Bartók's folk-arrangements, as this stark example from no. 3 demonstrates:

Ex.12

The *Slåttar* were published a year after Norway's independence, the year before Grieg's death.

Sibelius (1865–1957), whose symphonies brought universal fame to Finnish music, was much less eloquent than Grieg in his own early sonata, and the grander aspirations of the three lyric pieces *Kyllikki* (inspired by the Kalevala legends) were inhibited by his uneasy keyboard style. The three Sonatinas, op. 67, are less ambitious and more ingratiating. The first, in F sharp minor (incorrectly published as A major), has a transient charm; the second, in E major, with its suave canonic imitations in the first movement and the gentle grace of the last, is disarmingly witty; but the more elaborate textures of the third (B flat minor) are less telling.

In Denmark, Carl Nielsen (1865–1931) perhaps had no more pianistic skill than Sibelius, but his piano works exercised a much bolder imagination. The gritty sonorities of the Chaconne, op. 32 are convincingly earnest and unsensuous, giving a far clearer image of the composer's personality. Nielsen's disciplines derived from Beethoven. In his Theme and Variations a characteristic tug-of-war between two alien tonalities (B minor and G minor) is played out with some genuinely pianistic inventiveness. His powers of single-minded inexorable musical argument reached their apex in the Suite, op. 45, which he wrote for Artur Schnabel. With Nielsen, as with Sibelius, the mark of nationality is to be found more in a sturdy relentless philosophical outlook than in any regional quirks of melodic line. They have both survived the twilight charm of Armas Järnefelt (1868–1958) and Selim Palmgren (1878–1951).

GREAT BRITAIN

The nineteenth century was a bleak one for British music, and the Germans complacently assumed that there was no such thing. Nevertheless, amongst the English composers who were drawn to Germany at least one achieved international fame. William Sterndale Bennett (1818–75) won Mendelssohn's admiration at a London concert with his op. 1, a piano concerto, when he was seventeen years old, and this close friendship determined the course of the young man's career and the style of his composition. Bennett's piano writing was at its best in the brilliantly decorative concertos, recalling Hummel as well as the inevitable Mendelssohn, but there are moments of touching beauty in the sonatas (some with programmatic connotations) and in numerous short pieces. They justify Schumann's high opinion of him, and the affectionate dedication of the *Études Symphoniques*. There was, however, little in Sterndale Bennett's music to betray the nationality of the composer.

The British musical revival that took place at the turn of the century was largely in the field of choral and orchestral music. The recently discovered *Concert Allegro* for piano by Elgar is little more than a historical curiosity, and does not alter the fact that the greatest composers to come out of the revival, like Elgar and Vaughan Williams, were least of all interested in the piano as a solo instrument.

Of the group of English composers who studied with Iwan Knorr at the Frankfurt Conservatoire, Percy Grainger, Balfour Gardiner, Roger Quilter, Norman O'Neill and Cyril Scott (1879–1920) only the last-named made any great impact with his solo piano works. His experimental and esoteric harmonies, a feature of his style which followed a deep absorption in Oriental philosophy and theosophy, were admired by Debussy. Percy Grainger's friendship with Grieg inspired him to energetic field work for the English Folk Song Society, and it is Grieg's harmonic idiom that permeates the delicate Three Preludes of Frederick Delius (1862–1934), an influence even more marked in his Piano

Concerto. Grieg is constantly recalled, too, in the volumin-
ous piano music of the American Edward Macdowell
(1861–1908). A similar nostalgic chromaticism flavours the
piano music of E. J. Moeran (1894–1950), a gently lyrical
composer of mixed Irish and East Anglian descent.

The Celtic Twilight fades over the piano works of Arnold
Bax (1883–1953) whose four piano sonatas substantiate his
description of himself as a 'brazen romantic . . . my music
is the expression of emotional states. I have no interest in
sound for its own sake or in any modernist "isms" or
factions.' The sound that he did produce reminds one
constantly of his reputation as an extraordinarily gifted
score-reader; all ten fingers are busily employed encompassing every possible space on the keyboard. Bax's First
Sonata bravely adopts Liszt's method of cyclic form, but
the themes lend themselves uneasily to metamorphosis.
There are signs of the powerful impression of his visit to
Russia in 1910 in the Second Sonata which, opening
impressively, builds up a sense of expectation frustrated with
a 'heroic' theme of crippling banality. Borodin is suggested
in the tenderly lyrical allegretto of the Fourth Sonata, parts
of which show a welcome paring-down. Nevertheless
lavishness of harmonic texture is the essence of Bax's
exuberant style, enjoyably deployed in his two-piano *Moy
Mell*. French Impressionism is another influence, but the
incidental arrival in an accompanying figure of Debussy's
Poissons d'Or adds little to *What the Minstrel Told Us*. His
best piano works have an individual, if self-indulgent
exuberance.

A similar romantic volubility, with an almost indiscrim-
inate pianistic ease, characterises the enormous output of
York Bowen (1884–1961), but a composer who transcends
his contemporaries both in quality and variety is John
Ireland (1879–1962). Although his *London Pieces* (*Chelsea
Reach, Ragamuffin* and *Soho Forenoons*) reveal an affection for
their subjects, it was the quiet isolation of the Channel
Islands and their magic associations with the remote past
that warmed his romantic imagination. This obsession

spanned two World Wars and more. Jersey inspired the popular Impressionistic *The Island Spell* of 1912 and Guernsey the three pieces of 1941 that take its ancient Roman name, *Sarnia*. (Ireland escaped from the island shortly before the Germans landed.) A strong preoccupation with the magical rites of the distant past was encouraged by his friendship with the writer Arthur Machen. A sure sense of structure marks the fine Rhapsody of 1915, in which a Brahmsian grittiness of argument and a pastoral melodic tenderness are combined in a spendidly spacious climax suffused with Ravelian pianism. The slow movement of his appealingly terse Sonatina has the disembodied aura of a Debussy prelude. Ireland's predilection for placing a jaunty tune in the middle of a chordal texture (in *Ragamuffin*, for example) stems from Debussy's *General Lavine–eccentric* but is translated into a totally English idiom. His harmonic language, always recognizable, is far more adventurous in his piano works than in his orchestral music. The starkness of the Ballade, surprisingly original for its time, and the impressive architecture of his Sonata will survive the swing of fashion that has swept aside so much of his contemporaries' work.

The purposeful energy of the Sonata of Arthur Bliss (born 1891) with its widely spaced textures, shows a sure sense of direction; and although the numerous piano works of William Alwyn (born 1905) are not compellingly individual, such works as *Movements*, the Twelve Preludes and the *Sonata alla Toccata* are pianistically inventive and rewarding.

CZECHOSLOVAKIA

Dr Burney, during his travels in 1772, made note of a curious anomaly: the Czechs, probably the most musical people in Europe, could not boast of a single great composer. The circumstances appeared propitious: every child in the most humble, remote village was taught music from a tender age and reared in the love of it. However, opportunities for a career were negligible; ideal ground for the seedling was death to the mature plant. The finest talents had the choice of going abroad – they usually chose Vienna – or withering at home. The country, then as now, was a victim of fortune, and poverty and foreign domination were the twin scourges. Not until the Italian victories over Austria in 1859 did things get easier for the patriots. Czech nationalism found its voice, and in music Frederick (Bedřich) Smetana (1824–84) was a leading figure. Largely self-taught, he made his début as a pianist when he was six. While still in his teens he became well known for his performances of Liszt, Thalberg and Henselt. His gifts as composer and pianist were turned to patriotic ends in his 'March for the Prague University Legion', celebrating the revolt of 1848, an act not forgotten or forgiven in the dark days of repression which followed. Five years, consequently, he spent abroad in Sweden, as conductor of the Harmoniska Sällskapet at Göteberg. Throughout this period he received warm encouragement from Liszt, and the Lisztian symphonic poem, not Czech folk-lore, was the main stimulus to his own creative development. But his return to Prague was also a return to the grass roots of Czech national folk-music. The national element in his style emerged spontaneously, though searches to identify actual folk-tunes are as fruitless in Smetana's music as in Chopin's. But the naïve, warm optimism that we associate with the *Good Soldier Schweik* springs out vividly from his many polkas for piano; they may lack the range and subtlety of Chopin mazurkas, but the neglect of them is surprising. Occasionally, too, Smetana turned Chopin's darker, melancholy harmonies to his own account, as at the opening of the A minor Polka, op. 12, no. 1.

Of the polkas, the best-known, and perhaps more characteristic, are the F major, the F sharp (from the *Three Salon Polkas*, op. 7) and the F minor, known as 'The Little Hen', in which the brilliant pianistic figuration of one of the Schubert–Liszt *Caprices Viennois* finds a delightful new context. Smetana's originality lies in content rather than in manner: the dances, which form the bulk of his piano works, are all in ternary or rondo form, and the more extended pieces, like the brilliant *Bohemian Country Festival* (*Slavnost Českých Sedláků*), adopt the shape – if such there be – of a Liszt rhapsody. His occasional programmatic excursions, such as *Macbeth and the Witches* and his concert study *On the Seashore*, are also furnished with weapons from the Liszt armoury.

When Smetana became conductor of the orchestra at the Czech Provisional Theatre, Antonín Dvořák (1841–1904) was one of the violists, and already an assiduous composer who modestly kept his works hidden from all but a few intimate friends. These works were closely modelled on the German classics and the liberating influence of Smetana had hardly matured in him when he wrote his only substantial work for solo piano, the Theme and Variations in A flat. Dvořák's theme, bearing a strong family resemblance to Beethoven's variation theme in his op. 26 Sonata, (also in A flat) is gently repetitious, but, for all its master-touches, the piano writing betrays an impatient hankering after the orchestra. His many salon miniatures are mottled in a similar way. Even the late *Poetic Tone-pictures*, op. 85, with often beautiful ideas, cry out for more effective realization. Of all his solo works only the G flat *Humoresque* has achieved universal popularity. Dvořák seemed happier writing for four hands than two, and only in the duets, the *Slavonic Dances* and the *Legends*, did he tap the vein of his finest orchestral and chamber music masterpieces, fusing German craftsmanship and Slavonic lyricism. (For the second book of *Slavonic Dances* he was able to demand ten times the fee received for the first.)

The river Morava divides not only land, but cultural sympathies. To the west is the industrialized part of Bohemia, its folk-song diatonic and European: to this school belonged Smetana and Dvořák. To the east, the predominantly agricultural Slovakia and East Moravia, we find modal folk-melody with irregular rhythmic divisions; from this region came one of the most original composers in musical history, Leoš Janáček (1854–1928). Janáček's earliest surviving piano work, Theme and Variations, was written in 1880 in Leipzig, and the suave, correct craftsmanship and elegant charm are basically Schumannesque with little sign of his gritty, aphoristic mature style. This only emerged when he was writing his opera *Jenufa*, and had become obsessed with the melodic contours of everyday speech. He brought the same thoroughness to the recording of vocal inflections as Messiaen, many years later, lavished on bird-song. (When Janáček came to London, Cockney speech was given the same attention.) 'When anyone speaks to me, I listen more to the tonal modulations in his voice than to what he is actually saying. From this I know at once what he is like, what he feels . . .' This discovery was the 'open sesame', enabling him to fuse all his early influences into a new creative language. From now on all his music grew from small melodic cells: modulations turned on modal inflections in the melody, and the rhythmic patterns became more and more asymmetric. The piano writing of *From an overgrown path* (1902–8) is pared down to the barest essentials, and sometimes the persistent *ostinato* accompaniments and austere textures would appear inhibiting were it not for the emotional force of the ideas themselves. A similar concentration invests the Sonata *Street Scene 1. X. 1905*, which was written in memory of a Czech working-man bayonetted to death while demonstrating in favour of the establishment of a Czech university in Brno. Originally in three movements, entitled 'Foreboding', 'Death' and 'Death March', Janáček burnt the last in a fit of self-criticism, and after the first performance of the other two he threw them into the river Vltava. Fortunately the performer, Professor Tuckova, retained a copy of these intensely poignant movements.

In his last piano work Janáček harked back to his early youth in his native village, Hukvaldy, on the border between Moravia and Silesia. The Suite *In the Mist* has a nostalgic inspiration, but in none of its four pieces is there a trace of sentimentality. Built again on tiny melodic fragments, the initial wistful remembrances either grow into a passionate enthusiastic glow or are dashed by angry and bitter regrets. In the last the suggestion of actual speech is inescapable.

Symptoms of a tired tradition are seen in Janáček's compatriots as with other nationalist schools that have narrowed their sights to limited objectives. The many individual felicities in the piano works of Vitzeslav Novak (1870–1949) compare very favourably with the insipid jottings of Zdenek Fibich (1850–1900) in his *Impressions*, which is an attempt to write a personal diary in musical terms.

RUSSIA

When Glinka was told by Siegfried Dehn, his teacher in Berlin, to 'go and write Russian music', he had a living storehouse of folk-song to draw upon; he became the father of the Russian nationalists. In 1855 he first met Balakirev (1837–1910) and found to his delight that the young man fully shared his ideals and hopes. Two years later, when Glinka died, Balakirev was already acknowledged as the most important member of the 'Mighty Handful' of Russian composers and became guide and mentor to the others: Mussorgsky, Borodin, Rimsky-Korsakov and Cui. He had an excellent grounding in piano from A. Dubuque, an old pupil of John Field, acquiring early familiarity with the most advanced territories of piano virtuosity. His Oriental fantasy, *Islamey*, was his first and most famous venture into the Lisztian field. It remains to this day one of the most daunting war-horses in the repertoire. Liszt himself played it frequently, no doubt gratified that the virtuoso writing of his own Tarantella had been extended still further with themes of true barbaric exoticism. The first one, a Kabardian dance tune, was noted down by Balakirev during a holiday in the Caucasus. It contains the characteristic augmented second, the hallmark of 'orientalism', later over-worked by Rimsky-Korsakov.

The increasingly difficult repetitions of two themes have a cumulative effect like that of a circle of folk-dancers, egging each other on to more and more extravagant acrobatics. Like Liszt's Tarantella, *Islamey* has a lyrical central episode, here based on a languorous melody which Balakirev had heard an Armenian actor singing at Tchaikovsky's home in Moscow. Without a hint of parody the same melody is speeded and whirled into the final frenzy.

After this exhilarating work, it is easier to carp at Balakirev's Piano Sonata. The fugal opening of the first movement, it might be said, is only fake-contrapuntal: the contrapuntal lines are merely a decorative outlining of the harmonies. There is no organic development of sonata form, merely repetition and juxtaposition of contrasted ideas, and not very contrasted at that: the mazurka second movement is a finely wrought piece, but as he saw fit to publish it separately, what place has it in the integral scheme of a sonata? The re-appearance of the following intermezzo in the midst of the wild dance of the finale, touchingly lyrical as it is, seems an artificially planted relief. Judged by German traditions it is unimpressive, yet these were the very traditions from which Balakirev was striving to break away. The character of Russian folk-melody, on which Balakirev based his own musical language, demanded such a break. (Balakirev's savage prejudice against Haydn was unfortunate, but inevitable.) If the work as a whole is more an elaborately unified 'dance suite' than a sonata, it still remains a sensitive and inspiring piece of music. Balakirev's personal sense of form and his superbly judged pianism (how effectively he varies his left-hand accompanying figure!) find their happiest meeting-place in his second Scherzo in B flat minor, a work of masterly panache and ingenuity; and in the delicately lyrical Berceuse.

If ever a work underlined the dangers that Balakirev was aiming to avoid, it is Tchaikovsky's G major Sonata. Opening in a stiff bombastic march-rhythm, it proceeds to fill out a pre-ordained plan with a resource that cannot disguise the seams. Nevertheless all four movements have characteristic flashes of genius, and a good performance can confound the expectations of those who only know it on paper, finding it only too easy to fill in, in their mind's ear, the orchestration, and, in their mind's eye, the *corps de ballet*.

Much of the piano music of Tchaikovsky (1840–93) was written at the behest of his publishers. He would ask his servant to remind him, at a fixed date each month, that a new piece for his collection *The Seasons* was due: he would complete it on the same day. Chore or not, he produced works of undeniable charm, even inspiration. The Theme and Variations, op. 19, no. 6, is ingenious and elegant (despite the thick-textured *alla Schumann* Variation). The Six Pieces on One Theme (a folkish one) are impressive in scope, particularly the elaborate fugue and the grandiose funeral march. But perhaps the most arresting is the *Dumka*, op. 59 (sub-titled *Russian Country Scene*) with its implied narrative, unmistakenly Russian in every detail.

A programmatic idea was the impetus for the one great piano work of Mussorgsky (1839–81): *Pictures from an Exhibition*. The paintings were by Mussorgsky's friend Hartmann, a famous architect as well as a painter, who had recently died at the age of thirty-nine. To judge from reproductions, the pictures themselves had little distinction; it is enough that they fired the imagination of the most original musical genius Russia had produced. The genre, that of a chain of varied pieces linked by programmatic ideas and by musical connotations, was probably suggested by Schumann's *Carnaval*. The work is introduced by the *Promenade*, which, according to Stassov, represented the composer himself, 'roving right and left, now desultorily, now briskly, in order to get near the pictures that had caught his attention'. As it reappears in different contexts, so the harmonies, rhythms and cadences are subtly altered. Not only do they reflect the progressive emotional states of the composer at the exhibition; they form the *ritornello* of the whole structure. The first picture, *Gnomus* (a gnome lurching on twisted limbs) is stark and violent. 'Life wherever it reveals itself; truth however pungent; point-blank speech – these are my leaven, these are what I want and am aiming at': Mussorgsky certainly achieved it in the dialogue between the two Jews, *Samuel Goldenberg and Schmuyle*, from the proud, ostentatious opening in bare octaves to those harmonies which, by some inscrutable alchemy, convey the cringing sycophancy of the humbler character.

Ex.13

The grandeur of the final *The Great Gate of Kiev* embodies choral splendours and carillons of bells recalling the coronation scene in *Boris Godunov*. Although Mussorgsky was a skilled pianist his unique *Pictures* are hardly 'pianistic' in the normal sense; of the many orchestrations Ravel's was the first – and the most effective.

Mussorgsky scorned the international vogue for Russian salon pieces, with their 'carefully measured drops of prettiness'. Arensky (1861 – 1906), once very popular, is now chiefly remembered for the second of his three suites for two pianos. Very little distinguishes his particular school of charm from that of Glière (1875–1956) whose domestic pieces, with their faintly folkish flavour, doubtless satisfy Soviet respectability. The long line is still unbroken. Liadov (1855–1914) deserves remembering for more than his *Musical Snuff-Box*. A pupil of Rimsky-Korsakov, he was commissioned with Balakirev and Liapunov to make researches into folk-song for the Imperial Geographical Society. His friends' accusations of laziness (chiefly because he confined himself mostly to writing piano music) make him appear as the Oblomov of the Nationalists, but his *Variations on a Theme of Glinka* have charms affectionately derivative from Chopin and Schumann. Glazunov (1865–1936) was the last to join the Balakirev circle. Though gifted from an early age with a superb memory and prodigious facility in composition he hardly turned out to be the hoped-for pioneering figure. His Theme and Variations in F sharp minor, op. 72, display a Mendelssohnian fluency and brilliance which cannot altogether hide a timid orthodoxy. Even the rather amateurish piano writing of Borodin (1833–87) – he was no pianist – has more to tell us in such pieces as *Au Couvent* from his *Petite Suite* and, still better, his fine Scherzo in A flat.

The free and experimental atmosphere in the Leningrad of the nineteen-twenties, the immense creative vitality in all the arts and the opportunities for acquaintance with the latest and most important Central European music, coloured the formative years of Shostakovich (born 1906), the one undisputed genius to have emerged since the 1917 Revolution. Sufficiently skilled as a pianist to represent his country in an international competition, his piano works, from the start, show a mature mastery of keyboard writing. The *Three Fantastic Dances*, op. 5, shed a wry glance at a genteel genre, but give little hint of the shock to come. His First Sonata (1926), adopting Liszt's principles of cyclic form, is in one continuous movement. Its three themes are highly chromatic, closely akin and eluding the pull of any key-centre. The intense emotional frenzy of Alban Berg, occasionally present in Shostakovich's First Symphony, but pervasive in this sonata, is wedded to the physical abandon of Prokofiev's most virtuoso pianism. The harmonic language, more advanced than in any of his other piano works, abounds in dissonance, sometimes designed to give percussive edge to the rhythm, at other times derived from the linear logic of the thematic intervals. The central lento section, based on an augmented inversion of one of the themes, inhabits the esoteric harmonic country of late Scriabin.

Ex. 14

The set of Twenty-four Preludes, op. 34, which followed six years later (in the same key sequences as Chopin's) is a storehouse of speculative ideas. The E minor, for instance, is a fugue in five–four time, solemn and contemplative, with a foretaste of the Piano Quintet and some of the fugues of op. 87; the E flat minor, in one page, traverses a symphonic range of emotion. In some he plays flippant games with tonality; wild excursions into foreign keys will take place in the middle of a soulful, sentimental phrase. The salon piece, the *chant sans paroles*, the nocturne, archly pretty ballet-music – all come in for malicious parody. Certainly the satirical and the melancholy (Chaplinesque?) are the ones that stay in the mind.

The influence of Mahler is more obvious in Shostakovich's symphonies than in his piano works. In his second piano sonata (1943), however, he adopts Mahler's dramatic method of placing a mundane tune in a profoundly serious context and, by emphasizing its irrelevancy, deepening the pathos. Though somewhat loose and discursive, this sonata has a unity of feeling and economy of texture consistent with the central idea.

Shostakovitch's major piano work, the Twenty-four Preludes and Fugues, op. 87, was written after attending a ceremony celebrating the bicentenary of Bach's death. In part pastiche, they constitute an affirmation of faith in the continued fertility of the diatonic system. The first fugue's subject (in C) derives from a bass solo in the composer's cantata, *Song of the Forest*, and its first notes re-appear in many of the other subjects.

This fugue is played entirely on the white notes, entries being made on all seven notes of the scale. Even the most chromatic of all the subjects, the D flat major, which embodies every note of the chromatic scale except one (this being reserved for the final entry) leaves no lingering doubt about its tonality, any more than do the humorous, parodic ones, with their occasional bi-tonal flurries (e.g. the A minor). It is in a sense of structure that the weaker ones fail most conspicuously: the feebler the material, the longer they last. The counterpoint is predominantly more decorative than mutually dependent. In this the most eclectic of Soviet composers is typically Russian. One of the most

moving of all is the F sharp minor, in which persistent
reiteration suits the gathering melancholy of the subject as
well as its counterpoint; and one of the most endearing, the
A major, follows a gentle parody of Bach with a fugue whose
subject is founded entirely on the common chord, a challenge triumphantly met. The B flat minor fugue hypnotizes
by remaining pianissimo throughout. The preludes range
widely in character, embracing eighteenth-century pastiche
(Bach, Haydn, Scarlatti), Slavonic choral music, Beethovenian scherzo, and so on. Perhaps the most finely integrated
prelude and fugue of all is the G sharp minor, whose prelude
is a passacaglia, with a genuine re-creation of Bachian
cantilena, leading to a vigorous five–four fugue subject
played at first forte and marcatissimo and later transformed into a quiet legato, ending with a subtle and
compelling cadence in the tonic major.

No evaluation of Soviet music can avoid examining the
effects of Party intervention. The vast difference in musical
language between Shostakovich's first and second piano
sonatas inspires a curiosity which cannot be completely
satisfied until the *personae dramatis* are granted free speech.
Meanwhile speculation is complicated by Russia's traditional view of the arts as educative and moral instruments.
The great literary resurgence of the nineteenth century,
with all its breadth and popular vigour, made a virtue of
universal comprehensibility. However the Party has
demanded more than simplicity of language, with an
emphasis on folk-song. An all-pervading 'optimism' is
expected. One gifted composer who seems able to fulfil the
prescribed conditions without the embarrassment of original
ideas is Kabalevsky (b. 1904). The Sonatinas, op. 13, have
a fragile, naïve charm, and several of the Twenty-four
Preludes, op. 38, show a gentle lyrical warmth and creative
energy. His strongest virtues find their most eloquent outlet
in his third piano sonata which has a disarmingly youthful
and jocular charm, transcending its two predecessors in
tautness of construction. For all its professional skill in a
language which has long since held no surprises, the impres-

sion that remains is one of parochial innocence. Perhaps his most valuable works will prove to be those he has written for educative purposes and for young people.

One composer who has had the good fortune to strike a genuinely popular vein is Khatchaturian (born 1903) whose Toccata exploits Armenian folk idiom in an adroitly pianistic fashion, and which sounds a great deal more difficult to play than, in fact, it is.

Political isolationism and artistic customs barriers have desiccated the lively popular Russian tradition, in a manner which, by the way, would have been anathema to the Karl Marx in whose name it has been done. Other national schools have withered even without the inescapable pressures of official intervention. In telling contrast, the continued vitality and self-renewal of the French tradition is as much due to their welcome absorption of ideas, musical and philosophical, from all quarters of the globe as it is to the happy confluence of ideas from the other arts.

7

The Twentieth Century

SUSAN BRADSHAW

*

THE advent of the age of specialization has led to the gradual disappearance of the virtuoso composer–pianist – who, in his dual capacity, contributed so much to the nineteenth-century repertoire of the instrument – and his decline has, in turn, contributed to a general decline in the amount of music written for the piano by any one composer. Similarly, the ousting of the instrument from its supreme position in domestic life by radio and record-player has meant that keyboard music is no longer a *sine qua non* of musical existence. Moreover, in his quest for new timbres, impelled by the need to escape the overwhelming weight of romantic tradition, the composer of today has tended to ignore standard solo instruments, just as he has rejected established chamber ensembles (such as the string quartet and the piano trio) in favour of more diverse and previously untried instrumental groups.

Even in the early years of this century, however, such composers as Debussy and Bartók were starting to redefine the possibilities of the piano as a solo instrument – a mission which has since been continued and extended by Messiaen, Boulez and Stockhausen and by the experiments of John Cage and others. The technical horizons of the instrument have been stretched to such limits in recent years that the word 'pianistic' no longer has any real meaning; new sound sources have been sought from above, below and within the piano, as well as from the keyboard – with the assistance of numerous distorting gadgets or merely with the fingers, fists, palms or arms. A new, multi-dimensional technique of piano-playing has evolved and will eventually have to be taught, along with the diatonic scales and arpeggios which hitherto have formed the basic educational diet. For a new dexterity is being demanded: an asymmetry of hand and finger movement which cannot be acquired solely through conquering the symmetries of the music of a previous age.

As a result, a new form of musical memory, unaided by the sophisticated rules of the diatonic era, is called for, as well as a much wider definition of the function of the performer in relation to the composer. At one extreme, the performer cannot afford to neglect the art of subordinating his own interpretative ideas to the dictates of the composer: he must discipline himself to react with machine-like precision to the splitting of musical hairs required by the notational accuracy of, say, Stockhausen – the art of 're-creation'. At the other extreme, an indispensable part of his equipment is the art of 're-composition', an ability to submit to the vagaries of chance in the Lotus-land dream world of some of the non-notated pieces of, say, John Cage. Here, it is the performer's instinctive aural imagination and sense of timing which alone can realize scores that, in themselves, consist only of loosely defined indications of procedure; here, he will discover how much discipline is needed in order to discard discipline – to accept the freedom of chance without consciously making a choice. Hence the growing demand for performers who think like composers.

But, even today, no performer can afford to specialize to the point of ignoring the existence of either of these extremes, lest he should deprive himself of full membership of contemporary musical society.

The aims of this chapter are twofold. First, to survey the many stylistic and technical trends of the present day (1968) with reference to piano music in particular and, incidentally, to compile a representative list of those composers who have added to the piano repertoire. Secondly, to discuss developments in piano technique with reference to particular works. Of course, such a survey cannot hope to be comprehensive. The recent emergence of a new generation of composers, vastly outnumbering their older contemporaries, precludes the possibility of a complete and up-to-date assessment; this review therefore confines itself to composers who had already arrived on the musical scene by the early nineteen-sixties.

More than those of any other composer of his generation – with the notable exception of Debussy – the piano works of Bela Bartók (1881–1945) survey the course of his musical development more completely and at greater length than do his works for any other medium, in spite of the restrictions imposed by his clearly defined view of the expressive limitations of the instrument. The pianist's debt to Bartók is incalculable; of his one hundred and ten works, thirty-five are for piano solo – though eight of them (including a sonata written at the age of sixteen) are unpublished juvenilia. Of the remaining twenty-seven, seven are direct re-compositions of Hungarian, Rumanian and Slovakian folk tunes (some, as in *For Children*, are transcribed as individual miniatures, others, like the Fifteen Hungarian Peasant Songs, are strung together to form a continuous whole). However, the Improvisations on Hungarian Folk Dances, for instance, are as far removed from the folk material from which they spring as is the Sonatina, based on Rumanian tunes; conversely, many of the shorter pieces have a strong 'folk' flavour, even when entirely based on original material.

Apart from the juvenilia mentioned above, there are only two works entirely uninfluenced by Bartók's folklore researches: the Four Pieces of 1903 and the Rhapsody of 1904 (later rewritten for piano and orchestra). Comparing these early pieces with the Seven Sketches, completed in 1910, one gets some idea of the liberating effect those researches were to have on the scope and direction of his work as a whole. The Four Pieces, all with key signatures, are diatonic in the late-romantic sense; although impressive in their technical efficiency, they show little of the original genius he was later to reveal: they are rather self-conscious in their management of fairly conventional forms and harmonic progressions. In the Seven Sketches, on the other hand, the anonymous musical handwriting of the promising student has been replaced by a recognizable, though still not completely formed, signature. The automatic harmonic gestures have vanished, giving way to an almost ascetic self-denial in a choice of sonorities that follows in the footsteps of Debussy and Ravel: modality has cleared the air of incipient chromaticism and freely changing time-signatures have removed the tyranny of the regularly spaced bar-line.

With the *Allegro Barbaro* (1911) Bartók finally came to terms both with his own personality and with his attitude to the piano as primarily a percussive instrument – able to produce and sustain a wide range of colouristic effects, certainly, but not thereafter to be used melodically. The magnetic rhythm of the *Allegro Barbaro* tends to obscure the harmonic subtleties of its mainly diatonic background, whose biting astringency is the result of bitonal spacing – as opposed to chromatic 'wrong-note' additions. The Suite, op. 14 (1916), is sparser in texture and even more economical in its use of material; the scherzo, for instance, is built almost entirely from fragments of the whole-tone scale (in the form of a series of augmented triads), alternating with a passage in semitones, thirds and sixths.

The first movement of the Sonata (1926) explores still further the climate of the *Allegro Barbaro*, but here the harmonic basis is more tenuous: when the key-destroying percussive motifs are not being hammered out in jabbing ostinatos, they are supported by widely spaced double-thirds which leave the music in an harmonic limbo. Yet the sonata as a whole is undeniably in the tonality of E, as the composer himself insisted. The middle movement is a study in sustained harmonic pedal-points; slow-moving and almost completely lacking in 'eventfulness', it builds up a grinding tension towards the final C minor/major cadence. Perhaps it is the Three Studies (1918) which most successfully combine all the best ingredients in Bartók's piano music. As studies, *per se*, they are all exercises in agility and freedom of hand movements, both in expanded positions (stretching across rotating tenths in no. 1, extended arpeggios in no. 3) and as regards the ability to move with speed and evenness over the whole keyboard (no. 2); but they – like the studies of Chopin and Debussy – are concert pieces, first and foremost.

Bartók has certainly incurred the gratitude of adult pianists of all abilities for the size and variety of his contribution to the general repertoire, but his contribution to the more meagre repertoire of children (as, indeed, of beginners of all ages) is unsurpassed. Apart from *Mikrokosmos*, a six-volume course in piano-playing, there are several sets of unproblematic pieces (notably *For Children*, seventy-nine arrangements of Hungarian and Slovakian folk tunes, in two volumes) which are 'childlike' but never 'childish'. *Mikrokosmos* is unique in being a musical as well as a technical survey of the fundamentals of twentieth-century pianism. Even the simplest pieces have an intrinsic musical value as well as an educational function, and the contents of the final volume are concert pieces in their own right. Considering the difficulties experienced by many children in grasping the sophisticated intricacies of the diatonic key system, Bartók's method of introducing a few notes at a time (in the form of five-note scales) is so logical as to seem retrospectively obvious. Extension beyond the five-note scale is deferred until a much later stage and the implications of an organized key structure are hinted at so gradually that most of the inherent problems are ironed out before they arise. Purely technical skills are acquired just as painlessly. Bartók's educational music is an outstanding example of the art of teaching without preaching – of writing for but not 'down to' children, without any sacrifice in musical standards.

The instrumental music of Zoltán Kodály (1882–1967) has become overshadowed by that of his compatriot, but his few piano works are well worth exploring, particularly the

Nine Pieces, op. 3, and the Seven Pieces, op. 11. Their special charm lies in a quasi-improvisatory 'wildness' which sets them apart from the more cosmopolitan style of Bartók. Kodály's music has stronger affinities with Hungarian culture in general than with folk music in particular, so that folk tunes, as such, are seldom identifiable as the basis of his inspiration. His Children's Dances (1946) are much to be recommended as simple exercises in transposition; written without key signatures, they are to be played entirely on the black keys of the piano.

Although only five years Bartók's senior, Ernest von Dohnányi (1877–1960) showed little interest in the new sound worlds emanating from all over Europe, nor even in the deeper implications of contemporary ethnological researches. Nevertheless, as a fine pianist who wrote fluently for his instrument in a romantic virtuoso style, the best of his keyboard works have a post-Brahmsian élan which ensures them a continuing place in the recital repertoire: the Rhapsody in C major (from the Four Rhapsodies, op. 11), for instance, is genuinely inspired within its ultra-traditional framework and relatively free from the ponderous musical verbosity which mars so much of his music. His belated efforts to achieve a degree of formal freedom had no lasting effect on his style, although the Six Concert Studies, op. 28, and particularly the Variations on a Hungarian Folksong, op. 29 (1921), undoubtedly benefited from these attempts: they hint at the creative fantasy of true composition, as opposed to mere formulation of musical ideas. Again, the seven pieces which make up the *Ruralia Hungarica*, op. 32a, have a genial charm, only intermittently plagued by repetitiveness and by the over-dressing of simple tunes, while the first of the Three Singular Pieces, op. 44 (1951), is surprisingly experimental in terms of rhythm (being based on the numerical sequence of 5, 4, 3 and 2 beats to the bar). Last, but not least, his finger exercises must be ranked among the classics of their kind.

Among the younger Hungarians, Attila Bozay (born

1939), Zsolt Durkó (born 1934) and László Kalmár (born 1931) have each written one piano piece. Bozay's Variations (1964) and Kalmár's Four Canons (1967) successfully adapt the post-Bartók idiom to current needs, while Durkó's *Psicogramma* (1964) applies avant-garde techniques to the abstracted 'Hungarianism' of repeated notes and ostinato rhythms.

Nevertheless, the younger composers in Eastern Europe do not, in general, seem to regard the piano as a solo instrument appropriate to their creative needs; relatively free, at last, to experiment with instrumental ensembles in styles previously frowned upon, they are currently concerned with discovering a wider range of sounds and colours than the piano alone can supply. There are, however, some interesting works being written by a few of the younger Soviet composers. The Variations of Edison Denisov (born 1928), written in 1961, are characteristically lucid, although they lack some of the compelling rhythmic vitality and imaginatively 'ventilated' textures of his more vividly conceived recent music. Alexander Karamanov (born 1934) has written two piano concertos and a quantity of music for children as well as three works for piano solo, all dating from 1962–3: *Music* No. 1 and No. 2, and a *Prologue, Idea and Epilogue*, which is a heady mixture of chromatic impressionism, improvisation on repeated chords and clusters, and clamorous ostinatos. The Variations on a Single Chord (1966) of Alfred Schnittke (born 1933) are stylistically more coordinated, as well as being economically imaginative. Nicholai Keretnikov (born 1930) wrote his Variations in 1961 and Arvo Paert's (born 1935) early Partita was followed in 1967 by a piece called *Diagrams*. Andrei Volkonsky (born 1933) wrote his only piano work, *Musica Stricta*, in 1957.

The Czech composer Bohuslav Martinů (1890–1959) was exceedingly prolific in all fields of composition (not least for the piano), in spite of the fact that he did not start composing seriously until his late thirties. His output is, however, noticeably uneven, both in quality and in characterization; the best of his music has an identifiable, if limited, flavour of its own, while the less good works (generally the larger, more loosely constructed) tend towards the nondescript. His natural feeling for quasi-folk-rhythmic syncopations and for repeated harmonic patterns gives a fascination to the smaller pieces – particularly the three books of Studies and Polkas for piano – which does not always survive transposition to a larger canvas.

The figure of Arnold Schoenberg (1874–1951), composer and teacher, bestrides the twentieth century like a musical Colossus, continuing to challenge the very foundations of contemporary musical thinking. His five works for piano are among the century's most significant contributions to the repertoire, remarkable for their keyboard 'orchestration', in spite of the fact that he himself was not a pianist. In time, they span nearly a quarter of a century, and thus embody the enormously wide range of artistic development which took place during this period: from the last echoes of the nineteenth century, heard in the Three Pieces, op.11 (1908), to the 'abstract', twentieth-century expressionism of the Two Piano Pieces, op. 33a and 33b (1928–31).

Already in the Three Pieces, op. 11, Schoenberg is starting to reject the classical principle of repetition in favour of a continuous organic growth, so that, at the end of the first piece, even the clear reprise of its opening is no more than a re-clarification of a theme which has been present, in one form or another, throughout the entire movement. The second, outwardly more conventional in its quasi-sonata guise, is just as closely knit within its more liberal thematic structure. The third piece steps out into the unknown, discarding the broad harmonic foundation and traditionally based thematic procedures of the earlier pieces and replacing them with an athematic melodic and harmonic structure which, based on recurring intervallic formulations, controls the inner logic of both the horizontal and the vertical aspects. Formally, it is completely unpredictable according to established laws: an inspired and

passionate progression of ideas, covering almost as many
varieties of mood as there are bars in the piece. And yet its
underlying unity of design is such as to forge these constituent phrases into a single elongated sentence, from
the hectic counterpoint of the opening, to the final stark
diminuendo.

The Six Little Piano Pieces, op. 19 (1911), are on quite
another scale and completely different in character from
the final piece of op. 11, although they too are free from any
feeling of tonality and without themes in the tonal, developmental sense. Nevertheless, they are essentially melodic.
Sometimes, as in the first piece, the most extended of the
six, there are as many as four lines of equal importance
woven into the harmony; sometimes, as in the second (with
its background of an ostinato major third) and the last
(based on two recurring three-note chords), the melody is
hardly more than a whispered suggestion. All are remarkably succinct within their structural brevity (the longest is
eighteen bars, the shortest only nine).

The Five Pieces, op. 23 (1920–23) are again short in
duration (about ten minutes in all) but not miniature in
construction, since they show considerable development in
the classical sense of a thorough 'working' of the material.
In the first piece, for instance, the opening three-part
counterpoint (a melody, supported and harmonized by
two subsidiary lines [see example below]) is present, in
various transformations, throughout – reappearing at the
end in its original form but with the parts transposed:

Similar procedures of melodic and harmonic interdependence are features of all five pieces; there is not a single note which cannot be musically accounted for. Yet such techniques are far from being restrictive; the variety-within-unity of each piece is evidence enough of their creative spontaneity. The fifth piece, Waltz, has been much discussed as one of the early examples of Schoenberg's twelve-note technique; but there is no stylistic divergence between this and the first four pieces: exactly the same structural methods are applied, with the sole difference that here the basic material contains all twelve notes of the chromatic scale as an ordered (and constant) 'shape'.

The Suite, op. 25 (1921–3), extends the line of twelve-note thought still further. Each of the five movements (Praeludium, Gavotte and Musette, Intermezzo, Menuet and Trio, and Gigue) is an exploration of one and the same 'basic set' of notes. The unique character of each and the many facets of each of these characters are thus drawn into an instinctively felt whole by their common thematic source. The Two Pieces, op. 33a and 33b, are freer applications of the same principle: freer, because the thematic relationships are less closely tied to the basic set. Op. 33a, for instance, develops out of three four-note chords which are only once unfolded as a complete melody towards the end of the piece. Both pieces fall into clearly defined sections: that is to say, first and second themes retain their separate identities as they are stated, restated and developed – more akin to the structure of op. 11, no. 2, than to the layered developments of groups of themes, as in op. 23.

As in all Schoenberg's piano music, the minutiae of expressive indications – at first a formidable barrier – are no more than signposts to the wealth of imaginative detail underlying the surface, an essential key to the pleasure of unending musical discovery which amply repays the effort involved.

Schoenberg's two most distinguished pupils, Anton Webern (1883–1945) and Alban Berg (1885–1935), each wrote one work for the piano of considerable importance in relation to their complete output. Webern's three-movement Variations, op. 27 (which he wrote in 1936 and also referred to as 'a sort of suite') is, in spite of its disarming simplicity, one of the most elusive works in the entire repertoire. It demands the utmost in subtlety of phrasing, control of dynamic levels and differentiation of touch – both in the interior balance of chords and the exterior balance of the overlapping melodic phrases. A rhythmic balance is even harder to achieve, since the rhythm of the strongly marked pulse (the bar-line accents) seldom coincides with the independent placing of the tiny two- or three-note phrase lengths.

The emotional range of the music is infinitely expressive within its strictly defined limits: the quality and degree of tension of each single interval – and its relationship both to other sounds and to the surrounding silences – is the central thesis of the entire work and the *raison d'être* for both the melody and the harmony. In form, these variations have the sculptured precision of cut glass, so perfect are their proportions. The first movement is built entirely from mirror phrases, symmetrical in themselves, but forming asymmetrical sentences by means of superposition and diminution. The brief scherzo-like central movement consists of a single melodic line (three times punctuated by overlapping notes, four times by chords) divided between the hands. This melody is formed by the canonic unfolding of two melodies, one being the mirror form of the other:

The unusual layout of the score (with each hand keeping
to its own form of the melody, regardless of whether the
left has then to play above the right, or *vice versa*) is a visual
illustration of the structure of the music, denying the
validity of any manual reorganisation for the sake of
pianistic convenience. The last movement is the most
extended of the three and also the only real 'variation'
movement, in that the canons and mirror-phrases are here
used to develop and expand the musical argument, in terms
of the kind of small-scale contrast more readily associated
with classical variation form.

Webern's rarefied textures and economical intervallic
sensibility are far removed from the more subjectively
'emotional' sound-world of Alban Berg. Nevertheless, the
harmonic richness and seeming melodic prolificity of Berg's
music is also the outcome of a singular economy of means.
The Sonata, op. 1(1906–8), his only work for piano, apart
from the unpublished Twelve Variations on an Original
Theme, written in 1908, is an outstanding example of this.
Wholeheartedly 'romantic' as it is, it yet shows an astonishing restraint and a high degree of technical control for a
composer of twenty-one. In a single movement, it follows the
outlines of traditional sonata form, even to the extent of
repeating the exposition and transposing the second subject
in the recapitulation. The shifting chromatic harmonies,

orientated towards the tritone and the augmented triad, are derived from the opening bars of the piece, which not only contain the germ of nearly all the subsequent material, but establish the warring undercurrents of chromatic versus diatonic harmony which permeate the entire work. These four opening bars (see example below) introduce first the tritone, then the augmented triad (with a falling chromatic accompaniment), finally closing with a perfect cadence in the home key of B minor. Not until the coda to the exposition does the all-pervading tritone become a perfect fifth in the melody, evoking the serenity of cadential repose and, when it reappears in the coda to the whole work, preparing the final diatonic close with logical inevitability.

Ex. 3

The complete list of Schoenberg's pupils during the early years of the century reads like a roll of honour. Among these, the Viennese composer Egon Wellesz (born 1885) and the Spaniard Roberto Gerhard (1896–1970), both later settled in this country (in Oxford and Cambridge respectively). Wellesz's piano music mirrors the wide range of his stylistic interests and therefore defies exact definition. Perhaps the strongest influences to which he responded during the twenty years which saw the composition of his six sets of piano pieces were those of Reger, Mahler, early Schoenberg and Debussy. The five *Epigrammes*, op. 17 (1913) are a set of miniatures couched in the elegant harmonic language of contemporary Vienna, although the third piece, *Vision*, approaches the aphoristic sound-world of Schoenberg's op. 19. The five *Idylls*, op. 21 (1917), on the other hand, are gently descriptive; the impressionism of Debussy is overlaid with a Straussian expressionism. The Five Dance Pieces, op. 42 (1927), show a significant rejection of the harmonic indulgences of the earlier pieces, in favour of two-part, mainly contrapuntal textures suggestive of Hindemith, while in *Tritychon*, op. 98 (1966), his lively mind is still at work absorbing yet more recent techniques.

Roberto Gerhard's singular originality and overpowering vitality are strikingly evident in every bar of his music and his inventive inspiration never dimmed, not even during the long years of isolation from public recognition. His two small sets of piano pieces – three, including his brilliant arrangement of some of the dances from his ballet *Don Quixote* – are tantalizing evidence of his ability to write effectively for the instrument. The *Dos Apunts* (1922) are miniatures (lasting under three minutes together) of extreme harmonic sensibility and, unlike the Three Impromptus (1950), devoid of overtly Spanish characteristics. The shifting, atonal harmonies of the Impromptus would seem to blend uneasily with the repetitive definition of their Spanish rhythmic devices, but Gerhard's skilled harmonic adjustments make the marriage of such unlikely elements as convincing as it could ever be – and are fascinating in themselves as early examples of the inspired technical manipulations used to such virtuoso effect in his recent large-scale orchestral works.

The talents and energies of Hanns Eisler (1898–1962) became to some extent shaped by, and diffused in the service of, his communist beliefs. Nevertheless, his musical gifts do not, on the whole, appear to have been dissipated, but rather strengthened in melodic endeavour by the wish to communicate on an inclusive level. Although the Sonata, op. 1, and the Piano Pieces, op. 3, were written under the spell of the teacher–pupil relationship, they already indicate a powerfully individual feeling for melody, and many of his songs and some of his best chamber music develop this melodic orientation into a simplified and more 'popular' style. The early post-war piano music, on the other hand (as, for instance, the Seven Piano Pieces, op. 32 and the Sonatina, op. 44), does seem somewhat debilitated by its stylistic concessions; it is not until the late works (the Variations of 1940 and Sonata No. 3, completed in 1944) that the more 'knotted' textures and endlessly flowering counterpoints of Eisler's earlier piano pieces find a place alongside the simpler melodic contours, rhythmic ostinatos and triadic relationships of the intervening years.

A pupil of Schoenberg who isolated himself from the main stream of Viennese influence in another way is the Greek composer Nikos Skalkottas (1904–49). He wrote an enormous amount of music (over a hundred and fifty works altogether) during a comparatively short career; but hardly any of it was published during his lifetime and not all of it has even now been traced and catalogued: for piano, he is known to have written a collection of Thirty-two Piano Pieces (only ten of which are published), four Suites, Fifteen Little Variations – and probably much more. Skalkottas's strength lies in the free-ranging simplicity of his melodic invention, inseparable from its rhythmic structure; his harmony is non-functional in its own right, serving rather to point and underline the controlling elements of melody and rhythm. The piano music (which gives little indication of the breadth of vision revealed in his larger works) is more grateful to play when the harmonic background is static (as in the early Fifteen Little Variations or the passacaglia from the Thirty-two Pieces), or when it is clarified by repetition (as in the *Thema con variazioni* from Suite No. 3), or when it is purely accompanimental (as in the Serenade from Suite No. 4). In other instances – such as the Minuet from Suite No. 3 and the Toccata and the Polka from Suite No. 4 – it is more difficult to prevent the fast-changing block chords from over-weighting the flow of the music.

The influence on European music of Paul Hindemith (1895–1963) – either directly, through his teaching, or indirectly, due to the readily acceptable logic of his musical thinking – has been as far-reaching as that of any other composer of this century. His direct, contrapuntal style, dependent on clear articulation of the rhythmic pulse, is well suited to the clarity and definition of attack traditionally associated with the mechanism of the piano. This is seen equally in the keyboard parts of his numerous instrumental sonatas and works for chamber ensemble, and in his works for solo piano. Apart from their vital musicality, however, the piano pieces written prior to 1925 reveal little of either the imagination or the mastery of technical invention evident in the later works. Both the *Tanzstücke* and the Suite (1922) are feeling their way towards a trenchant means of expression within a quasi-popular idiom, but are baulked by the self-destroying nature of their four-square rhythms, allied to intermittently chromatic harmonies. The relative failure of these pieces is perhaps due to the fact that they lack the single dominating feature – whether it be harmony, melody or rhythm – which is essential to good 'light' music, in whatever style.

The next piano pieces were the two books of *Klaviermusik* (1926–7). By this time, Hindemith was well on the way to discovering his personal ethos, as the result of a detailed rationalization of his hitherto instinctively applied principles of composition. His theoretical studies led him to a new tonality, based on the ordering of musical pitches according to their relative acoustical dominance within the basic harmonic series. This results in music which is non-diatonic, in the sense that it has forsaken the system of major and minor keys, but which has a strong tonal structure, in the sense of setting out from and arriving at clearly established tonal centres; moreover, like the diatonic scale, Hindemith's 'neo–tonality' is audibly orientated towards the octave and the fifth from the fundamental. In *Klaviermusik*, there is abundant evidence of the liberating results of a strict harmonic discipline which, because of its secure foundations, permits forays into remoter melodic territory than ever before, as well as removing the necessity to underline every division of the rhythmic beat. This also makes for more buoyant textures, free from the relentless octave-doubling of the earlier works.

The first of the three Sonatas (all dating from 1936) is the longest (five movements) and the weightiest. Some of the earlier block-chord procedures find a valid place in this more massive, basically harmonic context. In contrast, the jaunty rhythms and clear-cut melodic outlines of the Second Sonata are closer to the proportions of a classical sonatina, while the quieter romantic contours of the Third Sonata are less violently aggressive than those of the first, more elastic than the second.

Ludus Tonalis: Studies in Counterpoint, Tonal Organization and Piano Playing (1942) is, as its title suggests, a survey of half a lifetime's research into the theory and practice of composition. Consisting of twelve three-part fugues (based on the twelve degrees of the chromatic scale), preceded by a prelude, interspersed with modulatory interludes and concluded by a postlude (an exact repeat, backwards and upside down, of the opening prelude), it is Hindemith's last and also his greatest work for piano – in spite of the somewhat forbidding implications of its sub-title. Within the limits dictated by strictly imitative writing, the range and variety of 'fugable' material is remarkable and the free invention of the interludes provides the expansiveness of harmonic and textural contrast denied to the linear nature of the fugues.

Hindemith's craft of composition left a direct imprint on the styles of two English pupils: Arnold Cooke (born 1906) and Franz Reizenstein (1911–68). Although they developed along individual lines – Cooke, broadly speaking, being more interested in harmonic structures and Reizenstein in counterpoint – neither succeeded in breaking free from an almost obsessive regard for consistency within an already explored technique. Reizenstein's most substantial work for the piano is his Twelve Preludes and Fugues (1952–3), dedicated to Hindemith. They belong unmistakably to the already well-tapped mould of *Ludus Tonalis*, so that, in spite of their fluent musicianship, they seem to have little more than a half-life of their own. More successful, because less contrapuntally encumbered, are some of the shorter pieces, including the Scherzo in A (1948), *Scherzo Fantastique* (1952) and *Musical Box* (1956). Cooke's only published piano work, his Suite in C (1943) communicates a characteristically attractive gaiety which does not attempt to be profound.

Neither Boris Blacher (born 1903) nor Wolfgang Fortner (born 1907) are immune to the magnetic pull of the Hindemithian lodestone. Blacher's originality lies in his attempts to free the rhythmic outlines of music from their traditional dependence on melody and harmony. This is clearly seen in his handful of works for piano – notably the Seven Studies on Variable Metres, op. 37, and the Sonata, op. 39. Here, the formal structure of the music is dictated by a scale, or scales, of changing pulses: in other words, the barlengths change according to a pre-determined scale of rhythmic durations, which, in turn, effects an asymmetrical spacing on the main accents. Such rhythmic 'scales' or ratios may, for instance, be regularly repetitive, as in the last movement of the sonata (4, 5, 6, 7), or regularly accumulative, as in its first movement (2, 3; 2, 3, 4; 2, 3, 4, 5; 2, 3, 4 ... 8, 9).

Fortner is an alert observer of musical trends who has never been ashamed to graft alien techniques on to his own style. Basically, however, his music seems to have most in common with the more straightforward characteristics of Hindemith; for, although devoid of any great creative urgency, his works have a careful and immediately perceptible logic that makes them pleasing to both mind and ear. Whereas his early Sonatina (1935) might have been written by a latter-day Clementi, the mild harmonic asperities of *Chamber Music* (1944) are more adventurous: they reveal a tendency towards atonality which is explored further in the mainly two-part writing of the *Seven Elegies* (1950), while the *Epigrams* (1964) search for an escape from the relative rhythmic predictability of the earlier pieces.

The prolific German–American composer Ernst Krenek (born 1900) has written six piano sonatas as well as numerous miscellaneous works for the instrument. His fluent though impersonal academicism is combined with a chameleon-like reluctance to take any particular stand, giving most of his piano music a grey, faceless aspect. His Sonata No. 2 (1928), for instance, represents a particularly staid variety of neo-classicism, while, at the other extreme, the *Sechs Vermessene* (1958) adopt a selection of recent techniques, couched in a confusing, if novel, rhythmic notation; the G major *George Washington* Variations (1950) illustrate yet another facet of his sometimes inspiration-stifling talent for pastiche.

The music of the Norwegian composer Fartein Valen (1881–1952) and that of the Dutchman Willem Pijper (1894–1947) have always been overshadowed by the more significant impact of the second Viennese school; yet each, in his own way, has contributed to the development of contemporary musical thought and thus to the search for a technical basis for music divorced from a diatonic structure. Pijper's piano music (which includes three Sonatinas and a Sonata, none written later than 1930) is very characteristic of his polytonal, polyrhythmic and strangely unemphatic style, loosely hinged to tonality by the use of impressionistic ostinato chords. His controlled tempo relationships are often unnecessarily obscure; their interest lies mainly in the fact that they forecast the rhythmic developments of such composers as the American, Elliott Carter.

Valen's nine works for piano were written between 1907 and 1941, culminating in the Sonata *The Hound of Heaven*. Like Pijper – and like so many of their English contemporaries – Valen's development and consequent position might have been different had his musical and geographical environment been less isolated. As it is, his music seems to turn in upon itself through lack of outside stimulus. His original, almost entirely contrapuntal style is woven from melodic ideas which function almost like Schoenberg's note-rows. Unlike Schoenberg, however, Valen failed to overcome the incipient monotony of monothematicism – a failure mainly due to a lack of melodic characterization and to a basic rhythmic weakness. Although, like Schoenberg, Valen cast many of his works in classical forms, in his hands even the dance rhythms of waltz, gigue and gavotte do not escape the leaden chains of arbitrarily imposed rhythmic patterns, while the textural consistency of each of the Variations, op. 23, and the rhythmic amorphousness of the Prelude and Fugue, op. 28, turn even the most striking ideas into rather indigestible musical fare.

A fine pianist himself, the Swedish composer Niels Viggo Bentzon (born 1919) is alone among his immediate contemporaries in having written a number of large works for the instrument, including three Sonatas and three Concert Studies. His liking for full textures demands considerable virtuosity from the performer if they are not to emerge as merely opaque. Constant octave-doublings give body to a harmonic scheme based almost entirely on thirds and hammered into traditional formal shapes by the relentless energy of ostinato motor rhythms.

Among the younger Scandinavian composers, Bo Nilsson (born 1937) showed exceptional early promise. So far, however, his talents seem best suited to the colours of a large orchestral palette, so that his two piano pieces, *Schlagfiguren* and *Quantitäten*, both written during the nineteen-fifties, are hardly representative. Even so, it is clear from the second of these two miniatures that he has opted for an international rather than a national style – perhaps nearest in expression to the early, more flamboyant works of Boulez.

Contemporary with Valen, but at the other end of Europe a group of Italian composers (chief among whom were Malipiero, Casella, Pizzetti and Respighi) were deeply concerned with the need to free Italian instrumental music both from the national demands of opera and from the overpowering influence of German symphonic music. Their

common path towards the rediscovery of the glories of a
national instrumental heritage leads by way of a 'modal
impressionism' – the strongest antidote to the still prevalent
chromaticism of the late-romantic Austro-German composers. In the case of Gian Francesco Malipiero (born 1882),
this search for a national and personal identity of harmonic
language seemed to sap the strength of architectural
thought, leaving the music loose-limbed and rather inconsequential: it suffers from atmosphere at the expense of
memorability. His piano music, however, has the merit of
being exceptionally well laid out for the instrument, and
his collections of miscellaneous pieces are all unusually
pleasant to play – from the early *Poemetti Lunari* (1909–10)
to the *Cinque Studie per Domani* (1957). Even in the latter,
which are freely atonal, nothing is lost of the mellifluous
flow and smooth melodic outlines of the earlier pieces.

Alfredo Casella (1883–1947) was himself a fine pianist (as
well as an editor of most of the major classical piano works)
who wrote extensively for his instrument over a period of
more than thirty years. In the early works there is evidence
of a youthful ability to absorb divers conflicting influences,
including those of Debussy and Ravel, whose 'open'
harmonies based on fourths and fifths were later to form the
essence of Casella's own harmonic style. The Sonatina
(1916) offsets these harmonic preoccupations with an
awareness of the character of his Italian musical inheritance,
both instrumental (in his use of dance rhythms) and vocal.
In Sinfonia, Arioso and Toccata (1936), Casella returns to
a more diatonic environment and the French influence has
merged into the overtly neo-classical forms. If the outer
movements of this work have overtones of bravura harpsichord writing, the Six Studies (1944) are indebted to the
fluid piano writing of Chopin. Like all Casella's piano
music, these studies display a brilliance which is not dependent on a virtuoso technique.

Another fine pianist, Luigi Dallapiccola (born 1904), has
written only two works for solo piano, although he has used
the instrument extensively in chamber music. The early

Sonata Canonica sui 'Capricci' di Paganini is an uncharacter-istically dry 'realization' of the Caprices on which it is based, but *Quaderno Musicale di Annalibera* (1953) has the sensuous beauty and ultra-sensitive approach to the quality and relationships of sounds so typical of the composer's later music. The unobtrusively intellectual attitude to composition which pervades all his best works enables him to spin almost translucent webs of counterpoint: the eleven short movements of *Quaderno Musicale* are impressionistic studies, drawing light and shade solely from the use of canonic and other imitative procedures.

The Variations of Luciano Berio (born 1925) date from 1952 and are dedicated to Dallapiccola, a theme from whose *Canto di Prigioniero* is woven into the fifth and final variation. They are variations towards, rather than on, a theme; a set of loosely connected ideas, betraying the immaturity of the composer in the often incongruous stylistic juxtapositions. *Sequenza* (1967), the fourth in a recent series of works of the same title for various solo instruments and for solo voice, is a much more representative piece, a fine example of Berio's neo-baroque, highly decorative style. A series of chords, held by the centre pedal, creates harmonic 'areas' upon or around which other harmonies are superimposed, either in the form of short, staccato attacks or as ornamental arpeg-gios. At first rhythmically notated and interspersed with the chordal attacks, these arpeggios later become extended groups of grace-notes, eventually suffusing the texture, until the attacking chords break through the harmonic clouds to return full circle to the more disjointed style of the opening.

Like that of Bartók and Schoenberg, the piano music of Olivier Messiaen (born 1908) runs like a clear thread through his musical output, while his astonishingly fertile and original genius continues to blaze a straight trail across the musical field, undiverted by any ephemeral trends. An early interest in Eastern music led him to explore the possi-bilities of superimposing melody on intrinsic rhythmic development by repetition and variation of rhythmic cells.

The small-scale unit thus became, and has remained, one of the prime motivating factors behind the pulse of his music, such rhythmically 'mobile' sections contrasting with passages of quasi-static harmony and with melodic arabesques derived from birdsong. In other words, the characteristic sound of Messiaen's music results from his contrasting use of 'time' and 'colour' (rhythm and harmonic sonority), together with an indefinable quality reminiscent of – though not necessarily associated with – the 'timeless' rites of the Catholic Church. The fact that Messiaen is a primitive at heart, with a devout and instinctively emotional response to music, is countered by the civilizing influence of his intellect: his unique personality as a composer springs from this strange blend of naïvety and sophistication.

As early as the Preludes (1928), which inevitably lean heavily on those of Debussy, there were more embryonic characteristics of the mature Messiaen than any which could mistakenly be attributed to his predecessor; but the first truly idiomatic work for piano is the *Vingt regards sur l'enfant Jésus* (1944). Based on two motto themes and a series of four chords, it lasts two and a half hours; into it Messiaen poured the inspired totality of his invention, both musical (complex procedures of rhythmic variation and thus of melodic formation) and extra-musical (mystical/literary considerations, which control the formal outlines of the work as a whole). It is a remarkable *tour de force* of sustained inspiration, which seldom flags in intensity throughout its marathon proportions.

Mode de valeurs et d'intensité (1949) isolates the incipient rhythmic preoccupations of the *Vingt regards* and develops them into a system of control which can be applied equally to melody (pitch), touch (attack) and intensity (dynamics). This attempt to impose a rigid control over every element of composition was later explored at length by Boulez in his *Structures* for two pianos (1952) and has fascinated composers to varying extents ever since. Although most of them have been forced to temper their initial enthusiasm in the face of musical reality – not least because of the inhibiting effect of

such systems, both on themselves and on the performers –
others have continued to find such a self-imposed dictator-
ship an artistic necessity: the American Milton Babbitt, for
instance, is currently working along these lines, though from
a very different standpoint. Apart from its specialized
technique, *Mode de valeurs et d'intensité* is a linear study,
perfect in its way, of the contrapuntal crossing and re-
crossing of three separate melodic strands:

Ex. 4

Neumes rhythmiques (1949), *Île de Feu* I and II (1950) and
Canteyodjaya pursue the same train of thought, strengthened
by the experience of *Mode de valeurs* but, at the same time,
liberated from its strictures. *Canteyodjaya*, the longest and
most wide-ranging of the three, has affinities with both the
earlier and the later music, being tauter in form than *Vingt
regards* and much more generous in contrasts than the
monomorphic *Mode de valeurs*.

Two works for piano and orchestra, *Oiseaux exotiques* and
Réveil des oiseaux, were the precursors of the enormous and
comprehensive collection of thirteen pieces in seven volumes

entitled *Catalogue des oiseaux* (1956–8). Messiaen's lifelong concern with all aspects of rhythm has always been complemented by an intense interest in 'natural' sounds, a prolonged study of which has latterly led to the development of his extraordinarily original melodic idiom. The result of this research is comparable to the influence of folk music on the formation of Bartók's mature style, but the sounds of nature, like the folk music, are only a starting-point: the identifications of melodic sources printed in the scores are important only in so far as they are the equivalent of Schoenberg's 'principal part' (*Hauptstimme*), that is, for strictly musical reasons. This work is a catalogue of all the musical resources upon which Messiaen has drawn during a lifetime of composition, as much a panoramic view of his visionary symbolism as it is a synopsis of his characteristic attitude to the piano.

Messiaen's legacy to his pupils seems, above all, to be an awareness of the 'metaphysical' aspects of music and of the pliability of basic musical materials in the formation of new techniques. The first two of the three sonatas for piano by Pierre Boulez (born 1925), dating from 1946 and 1948 respectively, show traces of his teacher Messiaen (in the rhythmic devices), of Debussy (in the use of pianistic colour, *per se*) and of virtuoso keyboard writing in general. But they are extraordinarily forward-looking for the time at which they were written and virtually without models for their musical vision: their astonishing vitality, liberality of invention and technical confidence are of breathtaking impact, as is the virtuosity of the keyboard writing.

Like all his music (and that of many of his contemporaries), the piano sonatas proceed in a state of continuous development, so that conventional ideas of statement, contrast, development, and recapitulation are no longer valid; nevertheless, Boulez is a composer who is forcefully aware of shape, and there is nothing 'automatic' about either the form or the content of these works. Their kaleidoscopic and vividly complex aspect arises from a characteristic speed of musical thought, resulting in the telescoping of musical developments, as well as the compressing of a large number of notes or events into a small space of time. The two-movement Sonata No. 1 is sometimes rhapsodic and violent, as in the first movement, sometimes hair-raisingly brilliant, as in the toccata-like second movement, occasionally lyrical in interludes and always irregular in rhythm and asymmetrical in outline. In form, both movements follow the same pattern, developments of one type of material interrupting the progress of another. The whole work is sparse in texture (that is to say, it is mostly two-part counterpoint), deceptively simple on the printed page but exhilaratingly complex in performance.

Sonata No. 2 also pushes piano technique to its limits while remaining essentially 'pianistic' (in the generally accepted sense). On a considerably larger scale than its predecessor and more diffuse in texture, its four movements run to thirty-two minutes. In spite of its overwhelming impression of imaginative power and originality of language, Sonata No. 2 is less consistent stylistically than No. 1 and, in some ways, less mature; the composer seems trapped by his compositional virtuosity into producing a dangerously overblown pianistic virtuosity – very much in the grand manner. Nevertheless, its occasional stylistic incongruities form an integral, and even attractive constituent of its ethos.

As in Sonata No. 1, the opening movement is based on the interaction of two contrasting ideas. The first is a polyphonic structure which aims at a kind of confused ardour:

The second is monorhythmic and the pulse, while still irregular, is much more evident:

Ex.5b

The stark opening to the second movement gradually increases in decorative activity, until a return to the mood of the opening gives rise to still more frenzied ornamentation. This pattern continues throughout the movement, as the textures increase in density and rhythmic complexity, finally breaking into a scherzo-like section before the disjointed reminiscences of the coda. The third movement, unexpectedly, is a clearly defined scherzo and trio, whose principal section is based on a group of characteristic rhythmic ideas. In the last movement, it is as if the whole work were disintegrating in a final frenzied outburst, eventually burning itself out in a surprisingly meditative coda. The initially fragmented material settles into two sections of more protracted development: the first mainly loud and clear, with long lines drawn across the whole extent of the keyboard, the second pianissimo and swathed in pedal. A short interruption by the disjunct opening leads to another extended section of ever-increasing violence and harshness of attack, breaking off sharply before the coda.

Sonata No. 3 was not completed until 1958 and is still not

published in its entirety: of its five movements or 'formants', only two, *Trope* and *Constellation*, are at present available. *Constellation* is the pivot of the work, around which the other movements rotate in any order. After the almost grandiose formal indulgences of Sonata No. 2, Boulez seemed to feel that he had reached a stylistic dead end. He therefore spent some years reviewing and consolidating his position as a composer, during which time he wrote little which still remains, apart from the *Structures* for two pianos. This work is a musical manifesto, a statement of possibilities, which aroused tremendous interest when it first appeared – although it is now perhaps more important as a musical exemplar (an *Art of Fugue* of the technique of total serialization – a position filled by Schoenberg's Variations for Orchestra in relation to twelve-note technique) than for its intrinsic musical qualities. After the success of his chamber-musical masterpiece *Le Marteau sans maître* in 1954, Boulez was again approaching a crisis which in Sonata No. 3 led him to choose the opposite path of a limited – though, for him, revolutionary – freedom: that is to say, freedom to leave loose ends in the overall form of the work, together with the freedom to permit a calculated imprecision in the notation of certain figurations. These freedoms are, of course, only partial, because they do not deprive the composer of his ultimate responsibility, of his fundamental control over such integral ingredients of the music as tempo, modes of attack, pitch and dynamics – which therefore remain constant. A brief outline analysis of *Trope* and *Constellation* will show the nature of the choice open to both the composer and the performer.

Trope (originally the word for vocal embellishments of Gregorian chant) consists of four sections, in the ordering of which Boulez permits the performer to select from eight different possibilities. Two sections are simple and two more complex; in the complex sections the player has the additional choice of omitting certain of the variations or embellishments – those enclosed within brackets in the following extract:

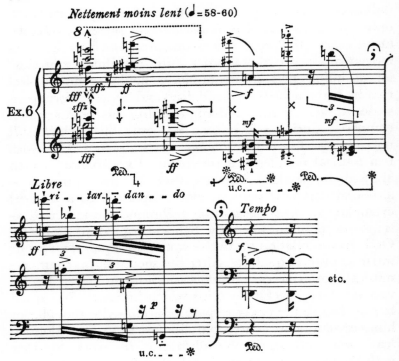

In *Constellation* (by far the longest and most complicated of the five formants) two distinctive developments of 'points' (patterns of individual notes) and 'blocks' (variously articulated chords) proceed side by side, printed, for convenience, in two different colours. The pianist has the choice of moving from one of these structures to the other, according to certain rules, and may also eliminate portions of each. This movement is a study in keyboard resonances: each 'attack' is calculated to contribute to the total resonance of widely contrasted dynamics and timbres.

Of the remaining movements, *Antiphonie*, *Strophe* and *Séquence*, only *Antiphonie* has reached its conclusive form, the others having been returned to the vast melting-pot of Boulez's 'work in progress', to await revision and even recomposition. *Antiphonie* is built from two antiphonal structures, each consisting of five sections: in other words, each of five 'simple' ideas corresponds antiphonally with one more complex. In performance the movement consists of five sections, which are drawn from these ten possibilities: the performer has the choice of which version to play at any given point, but must, in any case, proceed from section one to section five, having 'composed' his preferred version in advance.

It is not always realized that composers of today (as well as performers and audiences) have their difficulties in our fast-changing world, Boulez not least among them. Hence his reluctance to commit himself to the finality of print and his continuing search for a valid means of expression; his denial of the first-period techniques by the second and the second by the third; also his recent non-productivity as a composer. Whatever direction his future career may take, one thing is certain; he has already written some of the most stimulating – and important – music of our time.

The works of Jean Barraqué (born 1928 and, like Boulez, a pupil of Messiaen during the nineteen-forties) are as yet relatively little known. One of the few works so far published is his Piano Sonata, written between 1950 and 1952, but only available since 1965. This is undoubtedly an important as well as a substantial work; it lasts forty minutes and, although in one movement, divides naturally into two halves. The first part, preceded by an introduction, is based on a shifting tempo, varying between a moderate and a very fast speed; the second part ranges between a still more moderate and a very slow speed, closing with a recapitulatory coda which intersperses the two types of contrasting developments characterized by the two tempo areas. Superficially like Boulez, it has, on closer acquaintance, surprisingly little in common with either the early or the later piano music of his influential contemporary. While making less exhausting physical demands on the performer than either of Boulez's early sonatas (in its less continual use of the extreme ranges of the keyboard), it makes equal demands on his intellectual ability to grasp and to execute precise differentiations of dynamics and of rhythmic sub-divisions and superpositions. Barraqué's rhythmic cells, or motifs, retain their characteristic shapes as aural identities (unlike those of Boulez, which merge into the overall complex of a phrase or sound 'block'), and are often marked by repeated notes within their melodic contours; the recurring tempo changes paragraph the separate, sentence-length developments which give rise to the total design.

It is difficult, at this stage, to assess the importance of Barraqué's music in relation to that of his more prolific contemporaries; nevertheless, everything he has written so far communicates the tension of a genuinely creative conviction – sometimes derivative, but always intellectually questing and musically assertive – unlike Gilbert Amy (born 1937), whose *Epigrams* and Sonata are still too much over-awed by Boulez to reveal more than the considerable talents of a composer in the making.

The influence of Boulez on the Belgian composer Henri Pousseur (born 1929) can be detected in two early pieces, Improvisations and Variations, although even here his music is seen to have a 'gentler', more specifically harmony-conscious quality than that of any of his contemporaries. These qualities become more evident in the later keyboard works: *Caractères Ia* and *Ib*, a set of easy(ish) pieces entitled *Apostrophe et Six Réflexions* and a large, free-form work, *Miroir de votre Faust*, based on music from his opera *Votre Faust*. *Caractères Ia* and *Ib* have no pre-determined form or duration: both these aspects of the music are governed by rules which ensure the harmonic cohesion of any one of a number of structural decisions which the performer is obliged to make. This is harmonic music *par excellence*; there is no melodic *line*, as such, and no rhythm, in the sense of space being divided into pulsed units; rhythm exists only in relation to the number of notes present within a given space of time. The rhythmic aspect is thus an indication rather than a notation, and this allows the composer to dispense with specific durations as well as with accidentals in the notation of pitch: in these pieces, his adoption of black and

white notes for 'natural' and 'flattened' sounds is a welcome simplification of the more usual system of notational
symbols. *Apostrophe et Six Réflexions* are conventionally notated
studies: the *Six Réflexions* (six variations of the material set
out in *Apostrophe*) are exercises in the relationships of
changing tempi, in phrasing, dynamics, touch, sonority and
the playing of octaves. Pousseur's quest for the essence of his
harmonic thinking culminates pianistically in *Miroir de
votre Faust*. This, like the opera itself, is a large-scale exploration of the possibilities engendered by 'inter-stylistic'
harmonic relationships. At its most obvious (in the movement
called *La Chevauchée fantastique*), it gives a panoramic view of
harmony from Mozart to Wagner and beyond. At its most
subtle, it makes use of all these elements as independent
harmonic 'facts' – as separate items in an all-embracing
harmonic vocabulary, divorced from any stylistic implications.

Herma, by the Greek-born, French-domiciled composer
Yannis Xenakis (born 1922), is sub-titled '*musique symboli-
que*', because it is based, in the composer's own words, 'on
logical operations imposed upon classes of pitches. The elements of each class are presented stochastically, that is,
unrestrictedly, in order not to disturb the basic plan of
operations and of logical relationship between classes'. The
word 'stochastic' is new to the dictionary of musical defini-
tions and needs some explanation here. In the sense of 'goal'
or 'target' (from the Greek *stochos*), it was first used by
mathematicians in connexion with the law of large numbers;
in another sense, *stochos* means the concentration of one's
thought with a definite end in view. As a combination of the
two meanings, the music of Xenakis could be described as
being a vast number of complex possibilities, covering all
aspects of composition, leading (often with the aid of a
computer) towards the goal of the finished work. Again, he
himself has said that 'with music, it is necessary to find ways
of seeing, of feeling things ... first to establish an overall
view of the work, and *then* to choose the material and to work
with the elements ... until it becomes an organized and

living whole'. For Xenakis, the process of composition is thus one of fining down rather than building up, and the end result is a static view of a many-sided object – an exploration of different areas of sound – rather than a progressive musical form. There is, however, nothing 'static' about the tempo of *Herma*, which almost exceeds the bounds of imaginable speed:

From this point of view, *Herma* ('bond', 'foundation', 'embryo') deserves the label of the most difficult piano piece ever written.

Karlheinz Stockhausen (born 1928) is a major figure in post-war European music and, quite apart from their intrinsic merits, his eleven piano pieces have come to be regarded as text-book examples both of certain compositional techniques and of purely instrumental ones. They are also important in relation to his more overtly dramatic works, since they represent the 'purest' musical thought of his entire output, undisturbed as they are by external considerations and disdaining the temptation to explore the more peripheral possibilities of the instrument. Pieces I–IV (published in a single volume) are terse in utterance and ultra-precise in notation; but not even this almost academic insistence on complex rhythmic proportions can altogether subdue the fantasy latent in their restless violence. These pieces mark a stage in his career as vital as the 'totally serial' works in that of Boulez. It is as if Stockhausen was compelled to attempt the destruction of pulse (by the superposition of irregular rhythms) in order to discover the fallacy (for him) of its existence. In later works, rhythm becomes the filling of space, rather than the marking of points along a given line; each of the succeeding pieces has a time *scale* (of relative durations), as opposed to a *tempo* (of equally measured durations), and dependence on a time-dividing pulse has gone for good – even the barred pulsation of the reiterated chords in Piece IX can no longer be felt as 'tempo'.

In Piece V, the melodic connecting thread of long-held notes is intermittently crossed by arpeggiated harmonic eruptions, while a brief central episode allows for a burst of more regular rhythmic activity. Throughout, the occasional simultaneously sounded chords act as landmarks on an uncharted formal route. Apart from being one of the longest, Piece VI is perhaps the most complex – and certainly the most uncompromising. In a state of continual flux within the ratio of a specially notated time-scale, it hardly pauses to draw breath in the course of its frenzied enthusiasm. From roughly half-way through the piece, however, the musical shapes are allowed more time to 'speak', even to underline their articulation by repetition – so that the static speed and unadorned delivery of the cadential phrases are given a bleak sense of finality. Piece VII is concerned with the changing aspect of single pitches in different harmonic contexts. The C sharp which dominates the first section (see example below) is also the pivotal centre of the pitch-governed arch of the whole piece – an arch which is twice broken by harmonically 'splintered' episodes (so that the overall outline is as follows: 1. C sharp; 2. Episode; 3. A sharp–C sharp; 4. A; 5. A sharp–C sharp; 6. Episode; 7. C sharp, finally giving way to D sharp). The marking and sustaining of these pitch centres is achieved sometimes by hammered reiterations, often by sympathetic string vibrations touched off by staccato reminders, and by decorations which cover and uncover the foundation notes. Even the episodes are anchored to subsidiary pitch centres (G and C in the first, C and F sharp in the second).

Piece VIII consists of long, articulated melismas, which cross and re-cross each other in tangled counterpoints. This delicately woven texture is punctuated parenthetically by groups of staccato chords and paragraphed by isolated notes of longer duration, which overlap into the space between one melismatic sentence structure and the next. Piece IX opens with an extraordinary series of hypnotic diminuendos, the duration of which is dictated by the number of repetitions (at first continuous, later rhythmically spaced) of a single chord. This ostinato material is interspersed with, and at first clearly separated from, the very slow-moving chromatic harmonies of the interludes (initially unfolded as a rhythmicized chromatic scale). In the third slow section the two types of material start to merge, until they are developing simultaneously, the one surrounded by and entwined with the other. The final pages abandon the tight restrictions imposed upon the earlier sections and – leaving the obsessive single chord hanging swathed in pedal – plunge into a cadenza-like coda which circles around the top two octaves of the keyboard.

Piece X has an intensity of dramatic impact and an emotional breadth not foreshadowed by any of the preceding nine. In harmonic character, it begins where the coda to Piece IX left off, taking as its starting-point the free-flowing accompanimental textures which here weave around a legato melodic line. This figuration is again confined within the limits of two octaves or so, in contrast with the other types of material which range continually over the whole keyboard; fragments of chromatic scales occur repeatedly, both as the basis of the melodic embellishments and, later, in the form of both chordal and glissando note-clusters (a vertical version of the linear chromatic scale). The whole piece seems to be enacted as a battle between the opposing forces of selective harmony and non-selective chromatic totality: harmonic permutations emerge as a recognizable 'field' of sound, only to be roughly cancelled by battering cluster attacks or hidden by the smokescreen of multiple glissandi:

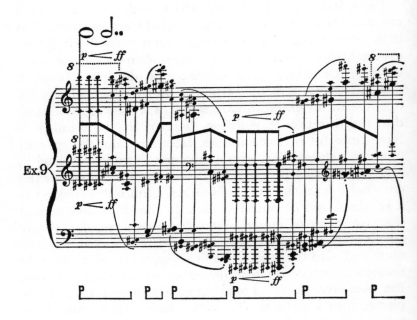

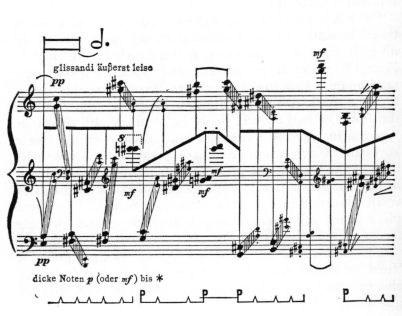

dicke Noten *p* (oder *mf*) bis ✳

The complex interaction of these two opposites takes place on a vast structural stage, where the many 'action-freezing' pauses heighten rather than relieve the tension – a tension which finally disintegrates without resolution.

The unpredictable form of Piece XI sets it apart from the other ten. Consisting of nineteen fragments, each of which can be joined to any other, entirely at random (and each of which must respond to a graded series of six tempi and six dynamic levels, as well as to six different touches or 'modes of attack'), its duration is dictated only by the proviso that no section be played more than twice. The structures of the individual fragments have, however, as much in common with Pieces I–IV (in their proportionately notated rhythms) as with Pieces V–X (in their freely rhythmicized grace-notes and use of clusters). Inevitably, because of its non-finite form, the overall character of the piece is ornamental and static, as opposed to dramatic and progressive – although, of course, it has as many different 'shapes' as there are possible permutations. This, in embryo, is the basis of 'moment-form', of a collage-like structural thinking which has influenced the formal designs of many of the present-day generation of composers as much as the more recent works of Stockhausen himself.

In spite of intercontinental exchange of ideas – and even of composers – American music has always cherished its national identity, regardless of internal divergences of stylistic emphasis and of the occasional surface gloss resulting from a variety of outside influences. Since the originator and definer of 'American-ness' in contemporary music was undoubtedly Charles Ives (1874–1954), it is somewhat ironic that he should have suffered long years of non-recognition and misunderstanding which caused him to give up composing altogether by the time he was fifty. Although he wrote most of his major works between 1906 and 1916, his sphere of influence has only been felt on a world-wide scale in the fifteen years since his death; in this sense, he was a composer half-a-century ahead of his time.

His concept of music as superimposed layers of sound, proceeding at various levels of conscious perception, was entirely original; such elements as the brass band passing the window (in his Symphony No. 4) were realities not to be rejected, but seized upon as contributory to his musical vision. This point of view reaches its ultimate conclusion of non-selectivity in Cage's *Radio Music* (1956) or his *4′ 33″* (1952), where the music only exists through the presence or absence of extraneous 'noises'.

Ives's music evolves from a heterogeneous conglomeration of ideas. His almost primitive innocence, strengthened, no doubt, by his eremetic artistic existence, allowed him to conceive music on a vast scale, while his sophisticated craftsmanship enabled him to control his impulsive flow of invention and to transfer his polymorphic vision to paper. His piano music – and, indeed, his entire output – conveys in every bar the generosity of his attitude to life: his eclecticism constantly affirms the value of everything in relation to everything else, so that, musically speaking, nothing is too naïve or too banal, too complex or too chaotic to be worthy of creative consideration. Fervent simplicity (as in *The Alcotts*, the third movement of the second or *Concord* Sonata) and rustic cheerfulness (as in the bar-parlour style 'choruses' in the second movement of Sonata No. 1) rub shoulders with percussive cacophony and rhythmic distortion (as in the fourth movement of the same work) and the exuberant harmonic counterpoints found everywhere (and clearly illustrated in the *Three-Page Sonata*):

Ives once compared the formal evolution of his music to the evolving situation of a man walking up a mountain: each time he stops to look down to the valley or up to the summit, he will see the same view, but from another angle, a different level – thus changing his own position in relation to the things around him, and, by implication, theirs in relation to him. Even the quasi-classical sonata mould (in which he chose to cast his larger piano works) cannot confine the fantasy of a perpetually evolving structure: in other words, the 'completeness' of the classical arch has been replaced by a multi-dimensional shape which is no more dependent for its validity on a beginning and an end than is, say, a cube. The walk up the mountain holds more in store for Ives than the prospect of merely reaching the top.

Today, fifty years later, Ives's fluid forms are seen to have been peculiarly prophetic: they are indirectly reflected in the changing outlines of Boulez's Sonata No. 3, the detailed but mobile form of Stockhausen's Piano Piece XI and in the formal amorphousness of many recent compositional formulae – even paving the way for arrival at the point where graphic design takes over from musical notation as a means of guiding and stimulating the performer, as in Cage's Piano Concerto or Stockhausen's *Zyklus* for percussion.

During the two decades either side of the turn of the century, American music saw the birth of an impressive crop of talented composers, each of whom has played an individual part in defining the post-Ives tradition. Among them, Henry Cowell (1897–1965) stands out by virtue of the prophetic eccentricities of his music. His collection of piano pieces must be among the 'happiest' and most exuberant (if also among the most bizarre) ever written, evoking smiles of pleasure from performer and listener alike. The aural titillations which he conjures from both the keyboard and the strings of the piano are sometimes allied to comparatively primitive musical invention, as in *The Tides of Manaunaun* and *The Harp of Life*. At other times, as in *Dynamic Motion* (see example below), *Antimony* and the more extended *Tiger*, the rippling sound-world of dense tone-clusters – a term coined by Cowell himself – is an integral part of the formal conception. *Banshee* and *Aeolian Harp* demonstrate the weirdly beautiful sonorities of the piano used as (but sounding quite unlike) a harp, and the massive chromatic arm-clusters of *Antimony* result in unprecedented clusters of sympathetic vibrations.

Ex. 11

Virgil Thomson (born 1896) is the Peter Pan among American composers: as debunker of artistic pomposity he is the transatlantic counterpart of. Satie (whose work, together with that of Gertrude Stein, he much admires), though without Satie's streak of very individual genius. His eclectic and quirkish diatonic style is exemplified in the series of *Portraits* – a collection of short pieces, written from 1927 onwards and scored for a variety of solo instruments, chamber ensembles and orchestras. There are well over fifty of these for piano alone, the best of which show a distinctive wit in the manipulation of simple material. His keyboard works also include four sonatas and ten studies – the latter dealing with conventional virtuoso problems but with the addition of exercises in double seconds, fifths and sevenths.

The music of Aaron Copland (born 1900) seems to draw strength from the pristine quality of its own limitations. His three major piano works span a period of almost thirty years; yet so seldom does he veer from the central stylistic path chosen early in life that it would be difficult to guess the order of their composition. The angular Variations (1930) have a skeleton-like, sculptured precision; the austerity of their musical background (based on various facets of the relationships of alternating major and minor thirds, sevenths and ninths) results in a rarified, though evocatively expressive, emotional atmosphere. The softer tonal outlines of the

Sonata (1939–41) again use major and minor thirds as the basis of the harmony, this time in conjunction with the more 'open' sounds of fourths and fifths. Here, however, the predominantly linear construction arises from the supporting chords. This is especially evident in the first and last movements, though even the contrary-motion phrase at the beginning of the second movement is retrospectively understood as a pervasive harmonic ostinato.

The Fantasy (1955–7) outstrips the preceding works in both length and expressive range. While the vast, continually developing cyclic form uses variation techniques on a monumental and intensely dramatic scale, its unifying contrasts can all be traced back to the bare bones of the opening declamation. Even the motivic propulsion of the central scherzi is imbued with the hypnotic spaciousness of long-drawn harmonic lines: single chords generate whole sentences, even paragraphs, however much disguised by the 'active' rhythm and the apparently independent melodic eventfulness. It is this deep-rooted harmonic serenity which is so characteristic of all Copland's work.

The international reputation of Roger Sessions (born 1896) has tended to become overshadowed by the towering figure of Copland. He is, however, a fine craftsman, with an impressive sense of musical design, even though a predilection for ornamental architecture – for perpetual motion, in the form of continually 'busy' textures – tends to blur the formal outlines. But his early one-movement Sonata (1930) is by no means lacking in light and shade, marked as it is by his insistence on tonal centres and by his evident appreciation of the functions of diatonic modulations. More exploratively chromatic are the four short sketches, *From My Diary* (1940). In Sonata No. ·2 (1945), Sessions has escaped from the apron-strings of diatonicism as a structural aid, replacing it with the self-discipline of a free tonality, which has since been characteristic of all his music – together with an attractive, natural-sounding logic in the use of variable-metre rhythm.

Elliott Carter (born 1908) has also been slow in finding a

means of harnessing his outstanding intellectual gifts to his manifest musical facility. The Piano Sonata (1945) was written at a relatively early stage of his career, but already shows signs (especially in the linked slow-fast tempi of the first movement) of the obsessive concern with metric ratios which are a hallmark of his later works. In spite of the preponderance of moving parts and octave doubling, the textures never become opaque; in the second movement, in particular, there is more than a suggestion of the harmonic 'wide-open spaces' – an atmospheric redolence common to so much American music.

Essentially a full-blooded romantic, Samuel Barber (born 1910) is a large-scale thinker even in his smaller works. His two works for piano were both written during the nineteen-forties. The first, a set of pieces entitled *Excursions*, is based, in the composer's words, 'on regional American idioms, couched in small classical forms'. His basically diatonic music is written in long harmonic sentences, much use being made of sustained pedal-points and harmonic ostinato patterns. This is especially true of his impressive Sonata in E flat minor, the outer movements of which also indicate his preference for full textures. In complete contrast, the light-fingered scherzo has a two-part texture, and the quasi-Stravinskian decorations of the slow movement show yet another side of his musical character.

Although almost contemporary with Barber, Milton Babbitt (born 1916) belongs to a new generation of composers. Babbitt's style has undergone a profound re-thinking during the last two decades, undoubtedly as a result of his experiments with computerized electronic music. The Three Compositions (1948), straightforward in a middle-of-the-road serial style, are strongly contrasted by *Partitions* and *Post-Partitions* (1966), whose virtuoso fragmentation, meticulously-notated rhythmic durations and scales of dynamics make them exceedingly difficult to perform.

The composer–philosopher John Cage (born 1912) has had a more tangible effect on the course of post-war music on both sides of the Atlantic than any other American composer – due as much to his musical philosophy as to the music itself. He has produced an enormous number of works, a large proportion of which are for piano or 'prepared' piano (a method of distorting both timbre and pitch by attaching various objects to the strings, originated by Cage in 1938), not to mention a group of works which can be played by 'any instrument or group of instruments'.

Cage was a pupil of both Cowell and Schoenberg, amongst others, and his earliest music (dating from the nineteen thirties) is simple, almost naïve and quasi-traditional. In 1947, however, he began his lifelong involvement with Oriental philosophy, which led him first to a static, objective and therefore entirely passive view of music and its functions: to the idea that a single 'sound-event' exists in its own right, unable to be manipulated into forming a relationship with any other sound or with a continuity of 'sound-events'. Ultimately, he has reached the point where there is no shape, no beginning, no ending and, above all, no sense of progress. He has recently said, 'I'm now involved in *dis*-organization and a state of mind which in Zen is called no-mindedness . . . in making processes, the nature of which I don't foresee.' But, like all Cage's (intentionally provocative?) statements, these are generalizations which are as false as they are true, which mislead as much as they inform. For Cage's undeniable dedication to music has led, not to abdication from involvement as an end in itself, but to involvement in the act of standing aside from creation – to a dedicated removal of personality and of intellectual choice from the act of composition. Instead, his intellect is applied to all considerations which are peripheral to the music itself, so that, having decided on the broad outlines of a course of action, he retreats to the sidelines to watch it take its course. The result of this consciously developed attitude is that many of his works are no more than suggestions – do-it-yourself performing kits – from which almost anything (literally 'nothing' in the case of the piece called *4' 33"*) may arise.

Before reaching this stage of 'nullity of composition', Cage explored various processes of 'composing' in the more or less accepted sense of calculating at least one of the musical elements. Amongst his piano music, *Music of Changes* (1951) represents an intermediate stage between 'composition' and 'non-composition', since it belongs to a group of works using (but not yet entirely dependent upon) chance operations. Lasting forty-three minutes in all, each of its four parts explores a rhythmic structure ($3:5:6\frac{3}{4}:6\frac{3}{4}:5:3$) expressed in changing tempi, the chance operations being derived from the *I Ching*, the Chinese *Book of Changes*. Although these 'chance-choices' are transcribed into precise indications of durations, as well as dynamics and even pedalling, Cage's notation does not include the placing of these durations in relation to a rhythmical pulse: the rhythmical aspect is measured by eye (in centimetres) within the overall metronome speed of each section:

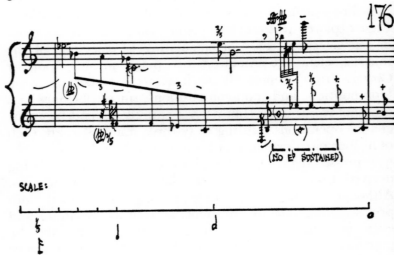

In this way, chance continues to operate on the performer, who becomes the medium for expressing the relationship between 'time' and 'space'. *Music of Changes* is a text-book application of selected rules of chance, representing the end of a period in Cage's career; from this point onwards, *time* becomes the most important element in his music, the sounding of events in 'time' being seen as the means of linking 'space' to 'space'.

It is easy to understand how attractive such ideas must have seemed to a trend in European music of the nineteen-fifties which, unable to extricate itself from doctrinaire entanglements of its own making, hopefully grasped at the means of escape offered by Cage's nihilist philosophy. Whatever direct bearing his temporal abstractions may or may not have on the future course of musical culture, the intrinsic quality of his metaphysical thought has already opened the minds and ears of two generations of musicians.

Earle Brown (born 1926), Morton Feldmann (born 1926) and Christian Wolff (born 1934) are three of the younger American composers often loosely linked together as an extension of the Cage tradition, but their music shows that each, while starting from similar premises, is branching out in an individual direction. Wolff's early pieces were conventional examples of a highly stylized serialism, but he is currently less concerned with the definitive roles of rhythm and form than with the essence of sound for its own sake. Feldmann's music, on the other hand, has, at its most characteristic, an a-rhythmic harmonic sensibility involving an element of choice far removed from the Cage extreme of 'no-mindedness': though one-sided in conception – a lot of it very slow, very soft and all evocatively timeless – its hypnotic qualities give it a true creative expressiveness:

Ex. 13   *From LAST PIECES*

Earle Brown uses more sophisticated techniques than Feldmann and is far less subjective; moreover, he is the only one of the three to consider rhythm and form, however freely organized, as necessary ingredients of music. But his two published piano works, *Three Pieces* (1951) and *Perspectives* (1952), give no hint of the structural and notational experiments of recent instrumental works, being tough and rather poker-faced examples of the total serial control which was fashionable at the time.

No survey of American music, however incomplete, could omit to mention George Gershwin (1898–1937). His

Preludes, written the year before his death, are perhaps less characteristic of his generally flamboyant piano style than either the works for piano and orchestra or the virtuoso arrangements of some of his own songs. But, in spite of their rather self-consciously 'careful' composition and preponderantly song-like structures, they are more than just song-substitutes: they rather transcribe the line of the song and the colour of the orchestra into composite keyboard terms, faintly tinted with shades of both Chopin and Debussy.

Even in a world which has so far extended the boundaries of musical influence as to approach the destruction of nationalism in music, the genius of Igor Stravinsky (1882–1971) occupies a unique position. For not only is he the supreme and all-embracing cosmopolitan (born in Russia, successively adopting Swiss, French and American citizenship) but he has never lost sight of the 'Russian-ness' in his character, nor, in spite of his 'magpie' tendencies, has he ever failed to stamp his personal identity on every bar of his music. His two major piano works, the Sonata (1924) and the Serenade in A (1925), both belong to his so-called neoclassical period, but are quite different in style and character. The Sonata takes its inspiration from Bach, both in the moto perpetuo style of the outer movements and in the continuously developing melody of the central adagietto, with its melismatic contours and ostinato accompaniments. The distant origins of the Serenade are harder to define: it is both archaic, almost medieval-sounding in its strange, unresolved dissonances, and at the same time oddly romantic in the richness of some of the chord distributions.

It would be hard to guess the composer of the youthful Four Studies (1908): these are brilliant, fluently constructed concert pieces, the latent genius of whose anonymously fluid style was to blossom so astonishingly in the first of Diaghilev's ballet commissions, *The Firebird* (1910). The *Piano Rag-Music* (1919) is a serious attempt to extend the horizons of the ragtime formula by means of more sophisticated techniques; the cadenza-like interludes – unbarred, in the manner of Satie – are composed in the improvisatory style of jazz 'breaks'. The *Tango* (1940) and the *Circus Polka* (1942) are, on the other hand, no more than musical jokes, albeit very good ones. *The Five Fingers* (1921), later transcribed by the composer himself for small orchestra, are eight short pieces for children, in each of which the melodic material is restricted to a range of five notes; the accompaniments, while not always so limited, are carefully constructed to lie within the grasp of a small hand. In spite of their apparent simplicity, the intriguing detail of the composition and the unexpected twists in both melody and phrasing make these miniatures typical and fully 'adult' examples of their composer's fascinating art.

The insular reluctance of the British to pioneer new developments in music – a reluctance which was perhaps an unconscious defence against the public glorification of continental musical products – left its mark on native music during most of the nineteenth and well into the twentieth century. Given a more stimulating musical environment, Frank Bridge (1879–1941) – who, like other English composers of his generation, seems to have been a victim of circumstances – might have made a far more substantial contribution to musical history. An early work of his, the Capriccio (1903), shows an adventurous use of tonality (and even an isolated use of piano harmonics, five years before the now famous example in the first of Schoenberg's Three Pieces, op. 11) which reveals just as many hints of possible future developments as do the earliest works of his near contemporaries, Bartók and Stravinsky. In his later works, especially in the Sonata (1922–5), the chromatic outlines of the melody and the economical use of thematic material transform the same melodic contours into different characters in different contexts, and show a distant but striking affinity with the early works of Berg: in particular, the forward sweep and overlapping developments of the first movement are closely related to Berg's one-movement Sonata, op. 1. But his slowness to appreciate the latent possibilities in his own style (and his consequent failure to organize them into a meaningful personal vocabulary) has meant that his works currently arouse little interest, apart from their period flavour. His smaller descriptive pieces mostly belong to the salons of a previous age, although some, such as the Three Improvisations for the Left Hand, have a more timeless, gossamer charm, while the wandering melody of *Midnight Tide* (from a set of three pieces called *The Hour Glass*) throws changing lights of more original thought on its static, bell-like harmonies.

A brilliantly versatile career as composer, conductor and writer on music, and a (self-defensively?) mocking attitude to most of the new paths being trodden by contemporary music (viz. *Music Ho!*, 1933), also prevented Constant Lambert (1905–51) from achieving more than a partial awareness of his own creative character. A lifelong interest in jazz pervades most of his music, giving a superficial identity to the best works, notably *The Rio Grande*, for piano, chorus and orchestra. The Sonata for piano, however, is a brittle work, whose cleverly constructed jazz rhythms cannot conceal its hollow harmonic gestures. Lambert's music is indicative of the rootlessness of British music between the wars: a whole generation of composers found themselves both lacking the support of a strong national tradition and devoid of sympathy for the main European trends. The most gifted of them, composers such as Berkeley, Bush, Rawsthorne and Tippett, were able to map out their own routes within the loosely-defined boundaries of 'English-ness', while there are others, like Edmund Rubbra (born 1901), whose Eight Preludes, op. 131 show him still, in 1967, devoted to an exhausted harmonic language.

Alan Bush (born 1900) has suffered from a neglect and consistent underestimation quite unconnected with the quality of his music. At the same time, it must be admitted that his determination to conform to the demands of communist ideology did lead him to make artistic judgements which were not always for the better. His piano music, although it forms a minor part of his output, is an indication of these stylistic alterations. The strongly reasoned one-movement Sonata in B minor, op. 2, reflects the bravura character of the first movement of Chopin's sonata in the same key; it is constructed within an entirely diatonic idiom, and has few surprises apart from the lilting asymmetry of its second subject. Likewise, the Prelude and Fugue op. 9, shows an analytical mind at work behind its ultra-conventional harmonic façade. *Relinquishment*, op. 11 (1938), is by far the most interesting of these pre-war piano works; while re-affirming its tonal loyalties, it moves into more distant harmonic realms, especially in the middle section, where the near-keylessness of the fragmentary figuration is held in check only by a characteristic tautness of rhythm. In some of the small post-war pieces, on the other hand, the intellectual substance seems to have been consciously withdrawn, leaving only a rather facile brilliance. Because of this, they fall between two stools: too difficult to be used as purposive teaching material, too insubstantial, by reason of their intentional 'straightforwardness', for regular inclusion in the concert repertoire.

Straightforward by nature, not by conscious design, the Six Preludes of Lennox Berkeley (born 1903), written in 1945, must be rated among the best of his smaller works; the gently flowing ostinato of the first, the undulating rhythmic unevenness of the fifth and the unobtrusive dissonances of the fourth and of the final piece are perfect examples of his undemonstrative style which, although expressed in a controlled 'mildness' of harmonic language, is nevertheless distinctly personal. Among his larger-scale instrumental works, the Piano Sonata (1941) is unusually successful in welding together its basically episodic ideas into a unified whole. Its genial virtuosity gives it a purposeful urgency, to which sideways glances at both the Stravinsky Serenade (in the first and last movements) and the Impromptus of Fauré (in the second movement) add the charm of a neo-classical flavour. The clear musical character and technical accessibility of the Five Short Pieces (1936) make them an attractive – and instructive – introduction to the larger works.

The two piano sonatas of Michael Tippett (born 1905) are as different in character as the twenty-five years separating them would presuppose. The first, written in 1938 (originally called *Fantasy Sonata*) and later revised, overflows with the unselfconsciously exuberant harmonic polyphony which characterises all Tippett's music. In this he is the English counterpart of the German Hans Werner Henze (born 1926), the only other contemporary composer not afraid to use traditionally 'romantic' harmony (with all its suggestive overtones) as a means of expressing his very individual musical personality – although neither of Henze's two works for piano are representative of his generally more mellifluous style. The Variations (1948) are somewhat academically 'contrived', and the structural corners are not always smoothly turned, while the more skilful Sonata (1959) adopts an angular style, whose complex and rather unmanagable counterpoints are not found in such superabundance elsewhere in his music. Tippett's harmony is, however, less diffuse than Henze's; the Sonata No. 1 is firmly anchored to key-centres over long stretches, giving it a spaciousness only partially contradicted by the busy-ness of its internal movement. This is, above all, bright, optimistic music, in which sinuous two-part writing contrasts with opulent harmonies, and in which the clear cut, episodic form of the opening variations is set against the headlong rush of the through-composed last movement; thematic and figurative cross-references strengthen the formal unity of the work as a whole. In Sonata No. 2 (1962), overall unity is cemented both by the single movement form and by an intriguing formal device of 'juggling' with various motifs and tempi – a Stravinskian juxtaposition of ideas which creates the illusion of a simultaneous and continuous development of contrasting elements. But neither the comparatively untypical objectivity, nor the tough, mainly linear outlines can wholly disguise the urgency of its intensely personal élan.

Alan Rawsthorne (1905–71) has produced one sub-stantial piano work in each decade since the nineteen-thirties. The Bagatelles (1938) show his predilection for melodic lines dominated by thirds and fourths, which in turn give rise to the triadic references of his ambiguous tonalities. Tenuous brilliance (the first and third Bagatelles and the outer movements of the Sonatina, 1949), and passive melancholy (the second and last Bagatelles and the slow movement of the Sonatina) are the counteracting constituents of his musical expression. His clear textures are the result of sinewy passage-work and implied counterpoints; only in the last of the Four Romantic Pieces (1953) does he exploit harmony for its own sake. The Ballade (1967) is a direct descendant of the Ballades of Chopin, both in its fervent virtuosity and its flowing structure: basically a stormy allegro, it starts from, periodically returns to, and finishes with a hesitant andante centred on middle C.

Alone among English composers of her generation, Elisabeth Lutyens (born 1906) was aware that a musical era had ended and she stands apart from her contemporaries by her refusal to accept the inevitability of a national stylistic convention anchored to a loosely based tonality. Her persistent search for a valid and personal means of expression led her to a theory of composition with twelve notes parallel to, though discovered independently of, that of Schoenberg. In the years since the end of the last war, her music has acquired an unmistakable stylistic homogeneity, and a profusion of works of remarkable consistency and quality mark the progress of a continually developing and expanding originality. Her most important piano works are *Piano e Forte*, op. 43 (1958), and the Five Bagatelles, op. 48 (1962). *Piano e Forte* is a musical examination of two opposite characters of the instrument: the direct and dramatic *forte* and the contemplative, colouristic *piano*. These two elements are both contrasted and integrated throughout seven sections which are strikingly differentiated in mood, tempo and texture and which are marked by the harmonic richness which is a feature of all her best works. The seven sections form a continuous whole, lasting about twelve minutes, but the piece can also be played in six alternative and shorter versions. The Bagatelles are tiny, but concisely developed within their brief span; the first and last, especially, show something of the 'disembodied' character of her most recent music, seeming to float in space, divorced from the rhythmic background which gives them shape.

The South African composer Priaulx Rainier (born 1903) also belongs firmly to the present. Her astonishing technical developments over the last ten years have released a flow of works of – for her – an unprecedented freedom of expression. However, her only work for piano, *Barbaric Dances* (1949), is characterized by the terseness of an earlier style, tensely expressive, even then within the tightly-tied knots of its motivic technique.

The 'classical' twelve-note technique of the Hungarian expatriate Matyas Seiber (1905–60) is characteristically shown in his tiny *Scherzando Capriccioso* (1944) for piano. Eminently successful in miniature forms, a didactic insistence on motivic relationships seems to have limited his development on a larger scale. That Seiber's Australian pupil, Don Banks (born 1924), has profited from a similarly analytical approach is clear from his single piano piece, *Pezzo Dramatico*.

Benjamin Britten (born 1913) has reserved his best piano music for the piano parts (much more than just accompaniments) of his songs; for solo piano he has written only the early suite, *Holiday Diary* (1934), and the short *Night-Piece*, commissioned as a test-piece for the 1963 Leeds International Piano Competition. Certainly not all test-pieces are as musically distinguished as this one; nevertheless, it lacks, perhaps inevitably, some of the magic of his best music. *Holiday Diary* is not, as its title might suggest, a suite to be played by any but the most gifted children, although its uninhibited virtuosity makes for immediately attractive listening; the second and fourth pieces, in particular, show early signs of Britten's unique genius for investing simple harmonies with the significance of rediscovery.

Near-contemporary with Britten, but belonging to another school of musical thought, are Humphrey Searle, Peter Racine Fricker and Iain Hamilton. Humphrey Searle (born 1915) closely modelled his one-movement Sonata (1951) on that of Liszt (for whose 140th anniversary it was composed) – not only in form, but also in the bravura style of the keyboard writing and in dramatic utterence. Nevertheless, it is no mere serial pastiche, since it contains some passages of original pianistic inspiration and has a real sense of total cohesion, in spite of the near-incongruity of the Lisztian accompaniments to the main themes. The harmonic idiom of Peter Racine Fricker (born 1920) is more difficult to pin down. It seems to arise naturally from his fluent musicality, which in turn leads to a natural facility in writing for the keyboard. The easily flowing arabesques of some of the early pieces, notably the Four Impromptus, op, 17, are reminiscent of Fauré, while the Fourteen Bagatelles and the Four Sonnets have the miniature charm of sketches (on the free use of diatonic keys and on a twelve-note series, respectively). The Variations, op. 31 and the Twelve Studies, op. 38 are on quite a different scale. The six linked Variations of op. 31 are sparked off by the six ideas stated in the introduction; they thus form a continuous development of a sextuple statement, quite unlike the sectional explorations of a single theme traditionally associated with variation form. The Twelve Studies are the culmination of all the foregoing piano works. In these, it is as if the concern with piano technique, as such, had freed him from subjective concern with the technique of composition, as such: the result is a series of brilliant character studies, deriving musical inspiration from the challenge of their outwardly conventional technical demands. The highly charged Sonata (1951) of Iain Hamilton (born 1922) sounds most effectively laid out for the keyboard, in spite of certain passages which fit awkwardly under the hand. In style, it is unusually free of obvious influences; the bitonal elements in its clearly established harmony add splashes of atonal colour to an otherwise tonal structure and allow freedom of movement to the surrounding figurations. The lighter-textured Three Pieces, op. 30 (1955), have outwardly relinquished their hold on tonality but, because of their motivic repetitions and harmonic pedal-points, they cannot escape references to tonal areas.

The impulse which gave rise to a second-wave English musical renaissance was generated from two main sources in the early nineteen-fifties; from the Royal Academy of Music in London, where Richard Rodney Bennett, Cornelius Cardew and Nicholas Maw were contemporary pupils, and from the Royal Manchester College of Music, whose students included Harrison Birtwistle, Peter Maxwell Davies, Alexander Goehr and John Ogdon. Their contemporaries, Alun Hoddinott, Thea Musgrave, Malcolm Williamson and Hugh Wood, had no direct connexion with either of these 'groups'.

Thea Musgrave (born 1928) is a composer–pianist who, like Britten and Dallapiccola, has written more for chamber music with piano than for piano alone, but the Sonata (1956) and *Monologue* (1960) are characteristic respectively of the attractive 'dryness' of her early style and of the more dramatic gestures of her recent works. In the Sonata, the rhythmic impetus of the mainly two-part writing is constantly underlined in thirds, thus providing a harmonic strengthening rather than a harmonization. *Monologue* is an instrumental *scena* in seven short sections, proceeding from the nocturnal colours of the opening recitative (which is insistently tied to the note B flat), through the ostinato rhythms of the ensuing allegro and the stuttering asymmetries of a brief fugato, to a tumultuous cadenza and a final reference to the recitative (with the B flat as a resonant bass to the harmony).

The large output of Alun Hoddinott (born 1929) is the result of his musical facility and exceptionally fluent technique. His piano works include five sonatas (the first of which dates from 1959, the fifth from 1968) and a considerable number of smaller pieces, all of which are enviably free of the stylistic pressures to which many composers today feel themselves oppressively subjected; but this insulation is both a strength and a weakness. Although the formal reasoning is always lucid, the characteristic toccata-like brilliance of his fast movements and the menacing colours of his more contemplative pieces are not always well enough digested to emerge as essential to the formal designs.

The Australian composer Malcolm Williamson (b. 1932) has overtones of Copland and Stravinsky in his concise and light-textured Sonata (1956), both in its asymmetrical rhythmic accents and in the wide spacing of some of the chords and contrapuntal lines. While the outer movements are centred on the key of F, the ternary slow movement is just as strongly magnetized by the tonality of F sharp. Throughout, clear part-writing, as in the four-part chorale of the second movement, contrasts with more open, linear sections, where the melody is sometimes accompanied by a single line, sometimes, as in the last movement, freely harmonized. The Five Preludes (1966) are more relaxed structurally and the mainly contrapuntal textures of the Sonata are replaced by the long-held harmonies and by the static, impressionistic effect of triadic chords in close position. Williamson's contribution to the educational repertoire in the field of opera' is well known, and for the young or inexperienced pianist he has written five books of graded miniatures, entitled *Travel Diaries*. Not all the pieces are as easy as they look; nevertheless, there is plenty of attractive material, and some intriguing combinations of musical and technical problems.

Hugh Wood's (born 1932) Three Pieces, op. 5, are sonata-like, in that they have an overall formal arch as well as a detailed internal structure. The first piece is as clearly anticipatory as the third is quietly conclusive to the central argument of the second. They are typical of the composer in their blend of harmonic sensibility and sinewy elasticity of rhythm. While Wood's attitude to composition shows certain obvious affinities with the second Viennese School, his music is unselfconsciously original.

The recent works of Birtwistle, Maxwell Davies and Goehr strengthen the tenuous identity of the Manchester Group by their individual progress towards a simplification of means. The early one-movement Sonata, op. 2, of Alexander Goehr (born 1932) however, is curiously lacking in signs of identity with his later music; more 'verbose' musically than anything he has written since, and untypical in its reliance on quasi-traditional keyboard gestures, it is also – perhaps for this reason – more gratefully pianistic than either the Capriccio, op. 6 or the recent Three Pieces, op. 18. An overriding concern with the contrapuntal development of complex rhythmic figures makes the miniature Capriccio an interim work, whose characteristics are much more successfully deployed in the comparative formal freedom of the Three Pieces. The last of these especially, a passacaglia, shows Goehr's taut counterpoints given more breathing-space within the imaginatively varied textures and clearly defined harmonies common to all three.

The two works for piano by Peter Maxwell Davies (born 1934) show the stylistic simplification which his music has undergone since the mid fifties. The ebullient and often aggressive counterpoints of the Five Pieces, op. 2 (1955–6), are in complete contrast with the pithy and explicit statements of the Five Little Pieces (1960–64). In terms of keyboard writing, the earlier pieces are contradictory; the large-scale gestures of their harmonic outlines are immediate and often brilliant in effect but, at the same time, much of the inner detail tends to be lost in performance, since the contrapuntal involvements of their widely-spaced melodic lines preclude ideal realization on what is essentially a non-legato instrument:

The Five Little Pieces, on the other hand, present no such problems; while linear considerations are still paramount, the textures are uncluttered and each piece is a perfect example of the telescoping of profound musical thought into a miniature form. In this respect, they are true descendants of Schoenberg's op. 19 – although occupying a less exploratory place in Davies' career. In all his music, the formal logic is 'disguised' as a result of his acute awareness of the developmental properties of each tiny phrase – a characteristic which is illustrated by the continual variation processes of op. 2 and even, at its simplest, in the tenuous, a-rhythmic lines and straightforward ternary forms of the Five Little Pieces.

Harrison Birtwistle (born 1934), a later developer than the other members of the group, is not well represented by his one piano piece, Précis. This is a small-scale example of the fragmentary form made fashionable by Stockhausen's Piano Piece XI, though characterized, even here, by Birtwistle's preference for recognizable motifs. Another composer to make a late entry on to the musical scene is Antony Gilbert (born 1934). The neat proportions of his Piano Sonata show less evidence of his current concern with musical architecture than does the impressive design of his more recent Sonata for Four Hands.

Like Cornelius Cardew, Richard Rodney Bennett (born 1936) studied first with Howard Ferguson (born 1908, and himself the composer of a tempestuous, neo-Brahmsian Sonata in F minor and of Five Bagatelles), before going to Paris as a pupil of Pierre Boulez. The early Sonata is an outstanding example of his precocious stylistic maturity: written at the age of eighteen, it already shows many of the characteristics of his later music as well as an exceptional technical virtuosity. Although formal clarity is paramount, even at this stage, the logical extension of phrases into sentences and sentences into paragraphs is quite free from academic 'stiffness', just as the harmony evolves naturally out of the predominantly contrapuntal and figurative textures. In fact, Bennett's ability to balance the musical elements of melody, harmony and rhythm into a homogeneity of internal contrasts is perhaps the most remarkable aspect of his all-round technical skill. The Fantasy of 1962, is, because of its three movement structure and straightforward ternary forms, really a simplified sonata: the 'fantasy' occurs in the overlapping evolution of its phrases. While musically demanding, the Fantasy makes only moderate technical demands on the performer: like Bartók, Bennett is a supreme exponent of the art of writing relatively simple music without over-simplifying the musical thought behind it – as further exemplified by his pieces for children (*A Week of Birthdays*, *Seven Days a Week* and *Diversions*). The Five Studies explore a rather different level of pianism from any of the previous works. The first is concerned with the rhythmic flexibility of slow-moving harmonies, the second with occasional interruptions to a single florid line (for the right hand alone), the third with the harmonic and rhythmic 'clouding' which results from the superposition and alternation of ten and twelve units of the pulse (see example below), the fourth with dramatic decorations of a cadenza-like melody (for the left hand alone) and the fifth with contrasts between sustained and brilliant arpeggiated harmonies. In these studies, Bennett has produced some display pieces of the highest quality which also represent a virtuoso expansion of his own musical language through the medium of the keyboard.

Ex.15

Cornelius Cardew (born 1936) has felt the need to escape from the neo-academicism of his own compositional technique in order to give free rein to the possibilities of a fantasy based on chance. His works for solo piano, however, are 'composed' down to the smallest detail as well as up to the more or less precise formal outlines. The early (unpublished) sonatas are relentlessly insistent on an accurate presentation of both rhythm and dynamics, on which they depend for their structural validity. The tiny *February Pieces* (1959) cast aside the confines of a rigid pulse – which, in any case, was always based on durational rather than rhythmic necessity – in favour of extended lines of melody, encased in spasmodic figurations. This musical standpoint is established and its possibilities more imaginatively explored in *Three Winter Potatoes* (1961–5), a substantial work, lasting fifteen minutes. Apart from the simple and intermittent 'preparation' of the piano strings, the pieces are relatively conventional in keyboard lay-out. They do, however, suggest the possibilities inherent in the cross-fertilization of old and new techniques – 'old' both in the musical sense (repeated motifs, octave-doublings and overt references to diatonic harmony) and the pianistic repeated notes and trills).

The breadth of this survey has naturally been dictated by the space available (precluding mention of the many important works for four hands, two, and even three pianos), and it ends as abruptly as it began. It hopes to have succeeded in suggesting some of the confusion, excitement and endless variety of the contemporary musical scene in which we are all – composers, performers and listeners – inextricably involved. Whatever happens next (and the future of our art – or perhaps its several futures? – is anybody's guess), music will continue to stimulate and to bore, to delight and to sadden, to arouse and to calm, to speak to the deeper reaches of the soul or merely to the soles of the feet . . . as it has always done.

Index of Names

Abel, cellist, 110
Abert, 132
Albéniz, Isaac, 283–4, 290–94, 296
Alberti, Domenico (and Alberti figurations), 111, 116–19, 136, 139, 158, 182, 242
Alkan, C. H. V., 237, 239, 254–5
Alwyn, William, 303
Ammerbach, Elias Nicolas, 51
Amy, Gilbert, 346
Antico, Andrea, 31
Arcadelt, Jacob, 247
Arensky, Antony, 310
Arne, Thomas Augustine, 28
Artaria, publisher, 113, 128, 139
Aston, Hugh, 19
Attaingnant, Pierre, 41
Auber, D. F. E., 246
Auric, Georges, 286, 287

Babbitt, Milton, 339, 359
Bach, Carl Philipp Emanuel, 59, 80, 81, 96n., 105–7, 110, 112, 115, 116, 123, 125, 126, 131, 143, 146, 163, 261
Bach, Johann Christian, 105, 110, 112, 117, 118, 141–4, 163
Bach, Johann Sebastian, 8, 36, 38, 47, 55–60, 68–105, 107, 110, 125, 141, 148, 149, 158, 162, 167, 168, 179, 183, 185, 199, 200, 202–4, 214, 218, 219, 230, 242, 246, 247, 253, 255, 256, 258, 261, 264, 278, 283, 286, 287, 313, 314, 364

Bach, Wilhelm Friedemann, 59, 81, 105
Badura-Skoda, Paul, 173n., 186, 191
Balakirev, Mily, 239, 255, 284, 307–8, 311
Banchieri, Adriano, 35
Banks, Don, 370
Barber, Samuel, 257, 359
Barraqué, Jean, 345–6
Bartók, Bela, 235, 240, 244, 253, 258, 260, 299, 316, 318–22, 337, 340, 365, 376
Bartolino da Padova, 31
Bartolozzi, Mrs, see Jansen, Teresa
Bax, Arnold, 302
Bedyngham, John, 18
Beethoven, Ludwig van, 7, 9, 72, 78, 102, 110, 113, 120, 121, 136, 139, 140, 148, 152, 155, 156, 166–87, 189, 190, 192, 193, 195–9, 201, 209, 212, 213, 219, 221, 223, 224, 227, 236, 237, 241, 244–8, 252, 258, 262, 264, 269, 300, 305, 314
Belgiojoso, Princess, 247
Bell'haver, 35
Bellini, Vincenzo, 214
Bennett, Richard Rodney, 372, 376–7
Bentzon, Niels Viggo, 335
Berg, Alban, 311, 326–8, 365
Berio, Luciano, 337
Berkeley, Lennox, 366–8
Berlioz, Hector, 190, 200, 223, 243–5, 260, 264